Praise for *Web Services Platform Architecture*

"Other books claim to present the complete Web services platform architecture, but this is the first one I've seen that really does. The authors have been intimately involved in the creation of the architecture. Who better to write this book?"

—*Anne Thomas Manes, vice president and research director, Burton Group*

"This is a very important book, providing a lot of technical detail and background that very few (if any) other books will be able to provide. The list of authors includes some of the top experts in the various specifications covered, and they have done an excellent job explaining the background motivation for and pertinent details of each specification. The benefit of their perspectives and collective expertise alone make the book worth reading."

—*Eric Newcomer, CTO, IONA Technologies*

"Most Web services books barely cover the basics, but this book informs practitioners of the 'real-world' Web services aspects that they need to know to build real applications. The authors are well-known technical leaders in the Web services community and they helped write the Web services specifications covered in this book. Anyone who wants to do serious Web services development should read this book."

—*Steve Vinoski, chief engineer, Product Innovation, IONA Technologies*

"There aren't many books that are as ambitious as this one is. The most notable distinguishing factor of this book is that the authors have tried to pare down the specifications for the user and rather than focusing on competing specifications, they focus on complementary ones. Nearly every chapter provides a business justification and need for each feature discussed in the Web services stack. I would recommend this book to developers, integrators, and architects."

—*Daniel Edgar, systems architect, Portland General Electric*

Web Services Platform Architecture

Web Services Platform Architecture

SOAP, WSDL, WS-Policy, WS-Addressing, WS-BPEL, WS-Reliable Messaging, and More

Sanjiva Weerawarana
Francisco Curbera
Frank Leymann
Tony Storey
Donald F. Ferguson

PRENTICE
HALL
PTR

Upper Saddle River, NJ ■ *Boston* ■ *Indianapolis*
San Francisco ■ *New York* ■ *Toronto* ■ *Montreal*
London ■ *Munich* ■ *Paris* ■ *Madrid* ■ *Capetown*
Sydney ■ *Tokyo* ■ *Singapore* ■ *Mexico City*

The publisher offers excellent discounts on this book when ordered in quantity for bulk purchases or special sales, which may include electronic versions and/or custom covers and content particular to your business, training goals, marketing focus, and branding interests. For more information, please contact:

U. S. Corporate and Government Sales
(800) 382-3419
corpsales@pearsontechgroup.com

For sales outside the U. S., please contact:

International Sales
international@pearsoned.com

Visit us on the Web: www.phptr.com

Library of Congress Catalog Number: 2004116713

ISBN 0131488740

Text printed in the United States on recyled paper at Courier Stoughton in Stoughton, Massachusetts.

4th Printing   September 2006

To my parents, Kamal and Ruby Fernando, for their trust and support to send me to a university in the U.S., which enabled me to do all of this.
And to my wife, Shahani, and children, Rukmal, Sashi, and Rukshi, for their tolerance of my crazy life.

—Sanjiva Weerawarana

To my wife and my daughters.

—Francisco Curbera

To Susanne and Lukas: Thanks for your patience and love.

—Frank Leymann

To my wife, Jacky, and my two sons, Peter and David, for their patience and understanding of the things that motivate and drive my life.

—Tony Storey

To Kaitlin and Kristen.

—Donald F. Ferguson

Contents

PART 6 SECURITY 261

PART 7 SERVICE COMPOSITION   311

14 *Modeling Business Processes: BPEL*   313

Foreword by Steve Mills

Web services are about enabling complete business-level interoperability across vendor middleware platforms. Starting with the first baby steps—in the form of SOAP—more than five years ago, I have seen the industry moving steadily toward this integration platform with the introduction of one key component after another. While we are not completely there yet, I am confident that a solid technical foundation has been laid and that now the community building process is under way.

This book is about that technical foundation. Starting with an explanation of some of the motivating factors driving customers toward full, in-depth integration of middleware platforms, the authors take you through the entire Web services platform and give you an understanding of why this platform effectively solves the integration problem. Two case studies, one in a business-to-business setting and the other in an enterprise application integration setting, illustrate how the Web services platform can be effectively applied to meet all the integration requirements. Finally, the authors provide an outlook of what is still coming down the pipe, in terms of both the short-term and long-term evolution of the integration space.

While there are dozens of books out there about Web services, this book is unique for two critical reasons: it is the first book to provide comprehensive coverage of the entire Web services platform; and, rather than providing an unguided explanation of a plethora of "WS-*" specifications, the authors make subjective judgment calls on which specifications are core to the platform and which are not. Their bold assertions of what is core to the platform makes it clear that the Web services platform has a clear underlying architecture and that it is not just a collection of specifications, as is commonly held.

The second reason above hints at a key reason for why this book is extremely unique: the authors are in fact the very same people who have been involved with defining *all* of the specifications that comprise the Web services platform. This is as "from the horse's mouth" as it can ever get!

Given the importance of true interoperability across vendor platforms, no one can afford to not fully understand Web services. I suspect this book will be a key milestone in your travels down the Web services roads.

Steve Mills
Senior VP and Group Executive
IBM Software Group
December 2004

Foreword by Ronald Schmelzer

One of the constant struggles for enterprises of all types, sizes, and industries is the ability for their Information Technology (IT) systems to meet their evolving business needs. Because most enterprises' IT systems are a hodgepodge of systems of different types, ages, architectures, and technologies, companies must continue to invest in their increasingly complex IT infrastructure while seeing gradually diminishing benefits. At times, it seems that the more that companies spend on IT, the less business benefit they receive, because more time is spent on making existing systems talk to each other rather than on making them accomplish new, productive tasks for the enterprise.

Part of the reason for the ongoing IT problem is that companies don't make technology and architecture decisions all at once. Rather, most companies have to make IT decisions as they go using the best information and reasoning they have at the time. At times, these decisions are made due to expediency, and at other times, the decisions are made for strategic reasons that are lost when the company goes through significant change, such as a merger or acquisition, or during a period of significant economic downturn. As a result, many of these IT decisions result in significant expense for the company.

Furthermore, as a company accumulates IT assets, new technologies emerge that seem to make older ones implemented in the enterprise obsolete. However, companies are loathe to throw out their previous IT investments (legacy systems) and replace them with new systems, and as a result, these companies are faced with trying to make their old systems work in new environments. So, rather than simplifying their IT ecosystems over time, the problem only grows more complicated, more expensive, and more inflexible as new systems are introduced. This problem of heterogeneity is at the core of why integration challenges continue to plague so many organizations.

To solve these problems, companies need two sorts of solutions: technology solutions that aim to simplify integration problems through a combination of standards-based interoperability and enable reuse of legacy environments, and architectural solutions that aim to change the way in which companies build, deploy, manage, secure, and scale their IT systems. While the latter solution requires changes in IT management, structure, and governance, the former solution requires a standards-based, comprehensive technology platform for working in a heterogeneous IT environment. Web services-based Service-Oriented Architectures (SOA) hope to provide both of the above sorts of solutions to the enduring problem of IT inflexibility.

Smart enterprises are increasingly realizing that the real value in Web services is in using loosely coupled, standards-based technologies to build SOAs. Many enterprises have achieved success implementing Web services to solve point-to-point integration problems and are now looking to leverage the power and flexibility of Web services strategically across the enterprise, which means building loosely coupled, standards-based SOAs.

The power and flexibility that SOAs can offer the enterprise are substantial. If an organization abstracts its IT infrastructure so that it presents its functionality in the form of coarse-grained services that offer clear business value, then the consumers of those services (whether they are with the same company or one of that company's business partners) can access those services independent of the underlying technology that supports them. Furthermore, if service consumers can dynamically discover and bind to available services in an agile manner—building applications out of composed services—then the IT infrastructure behind those services can offer extraordinary flexibility to the businesses that invoke them.

The difference between the practice of SOA and other approaches to enterprise architecture is in the business agility that SOA offers. Companies have become used to the fact that IT decision making and implementations impede their organization and that technology and its limitations often drive business decisions. Service orientation, however, has the potential to change this equation and enable business decisions to finally drive their technology decisions. Business agility is the ability of a company to respond quickly and efficiently to change and to leverage change for competitive advantage. For the architect, building an architecture that provides business agility means creating an IT infrastructure that meets as-yet unknown business requirements—a situation that throws traditional IT planning and design out the window.

Today's distributed computing transition, while every bit as significant as the ones that came before, has an entirely different economic model. Instead of massive IT investment, today's IT executive is concerned with thrift. Thrift depends on one of the holy grails of software development: code reuse. In an SOA, developers should construct the services to be as simple as possible, where they continually refactor them so that they are as broadly applicable as is practical. The resulting services are then reusable at runtime—both fine- and coarse-grained nuggets of software functionality that can be used in a variety of situations, as contrasted to typical code reuse, which is a design time principle.

Once the SOA is in place, new business requirements will continue to generate the need for new and updated services. The IT staff can then make the required changes on an ongoing basis. In addition, taking an ad hoc upgrade approach to services, which are composed into business applications, reduces the need to "rip and replace" large portions of the IT infrastructure. Companies thus only consider a rip and replace strategy as a last resort, and then only within a service orientation context.

There is an additional, related concept to broad applicability that goes even further: the concept of consumability. It's not enough for a service to have the potential to be used in a variety of situations; it must actually be usable. Not only must the service's functionality be technically applicable to various situations, but people must know about the service, understand its use, and be able to find it when they need it. As such, technologies such as repositories and metadata management tools are rapidly becoming as important as the runtime and design-time infrastructure for the services themselves.

While the concepts of SOAs sound compelling to most enterprises, building service-oriented infrastructures is not easy. That is why this book, *Web Services Platform Architecture: SOAP, WSDL, WS-Policy, WS-Addressing, WS-BPEL, WS-Reliable Messaging and More*, is such an important and critical reading. In this book, Sanjiva Weerawarana, Francisco Curbera, Frank Leymann, Tony Storey, and Donald Ferguson make the effective argument that Web services and SOA are required technologies that help businesses meet their continually evolving requirements.

The book offers not only implementation-level coverage of the technologies and specs as required by technical developers, it also provides the right technical context for business readers. An emerging audience of "enterprise architects," which are more business focused than developers, yet tasked with more specific technical requirements than purely line-of-business users, will find significant value in the book. This book gives these users the ammunition to discuss the topics with their more technical developers, and the nuts-and-bolts to implement higher-level concepts decided by their more business-level superiors.

In the first chapter, the authors make the correct observation that SOA is a new paradigm shift that requires not only a change of technology, but also a cultural mind shift in how to create, manage, secure, and deploy service assets in the network. The concepts are on target—correctly mapping the business driver of agility, or flexibility, to the technical capabilities of an SOA to enable rapid change with low economic penalty. The book then continues to discuss business flexibility in the abstract while tying the concepts to specific notions of the business process.

As the book progresses, the reader will learn incrementally more about the basic, core Web services specifications—SOAP, WSDL, and UDDI, as well as the XML-based underpinnings of those formats. What makes this book stand out are its detailed discussion on emerging specifications, including WS-Policy, WS-Addressing, WS-ReliableMessaging, WS-AtomicTransaction, WS-BusinessActivity, as well as the BPEL specification, which—while still emerging specifications as of the time of writing this foreword—will surely be the formative specifications for SOA in the future.

In addition, the authors spend a considerable amount of time discussing the practical implementations of SOA, especially in a messaging-centric context. Their discussions can immediately be applied to a wide range of message-oriented middleware approaches as well as emerging Enterprise Service Bus implementations.

In fact, what makes this book credible is the experience of the authors. The authors, hailing from the pioneering software group at IBM, have not only rich experience with Web services and SOA, but have also been involved in the creation of the specs themselves. As such, the authors not only bring their experience in implementing Web services and SOA at IBM, but also their experience in crafting the very specifications they outline in the book—this book is an "insider's" guide to Web services and SOA, if you will.

In conclusion, service orientation represents the next major trend in enterprise computing, and as a result, requires a new perspective, new techniques, and new tools for implementing technology solutions that meet the needs of business. At this point in time, the IT industry stands at a cusp—a tipping point where sporadic applications of Web services become a movement toward agile, thrifty computing based on SOAs. When people stand at such a threshold, they often have a difficult time planning for the future because many of the business patterns that have applied in the past may no longer apply. It is our hope that through learning the basic precepts of SOA and Web services and the detail required to implement them in your most important applications, you can become informed and educated enough to participate and lead the revolution that SOA means to the enterprise.

Ronald Schmelzer
Senior Analyst
ZapThink, LLC
December 2004

Preface

"Web services are a mess!"

"There are more than 150 Web services (WS-*) specs!"

"Simple? This stuff is more complicated than CORBA!"

"There is no architecture; just a bunch of competing specs!"

"These specs are denser than plutonium!"

Those are some of the statements we've heard from people—including our own colleagues—about Web services. That's why we wrote this book: to show that the WS-* platform is not a random walk through a space of WS-* specifications but rather an organized, structured architecture with well-defined design and architectural objectives. We apply these objectives when working on WS-* specifications and when deciding whether or not we need a new specification in a certain area.

The objective of this book is to present the cohesive, structured architecture of the Web services platform that we have been helping to define. The architecture is designed to enable loosely coupled interaction between services with business-quality reliability, security, and transactional capabilities. We start by presenting some of the business world–driving forces that are motivating the creation of the service-oriented computing platform (Chapter 1, "Service-Oriented Architectures"). Then we focus on Web services as a realization of this service-oriented computing platform and indicate which specifications contribute to the platform (Chapter 3, "Web Services"). After that, we consider each major part of the platform and offer the insight that went into defining the specifications that govern that component. We cover the messaging framework, describing metadata, reliable interaction, security, and service composition in different parts of the book. Before concluding, we consider two case studies to illustrate how the Web services platform can address both intranet and extranet integration scenarios. In the concluding part, we summarize the platform and give our perspectives on why the integrated architecture we present makes sense and will "win" the standards battle. Finally, we present our thoughts on the future of the Web services platform.

At the end of this book, you should no longer feel that Web services has no architecture or that the architecture is hidden somewhere between 150+ WS-* specifications. You might not agree with our choice of components that comprise the architecture, but we chose the set based on the fact that those were designed from the ground up to work together to solve a single problem: that of being a ubiquitous platform for integrating heterogeneous systems to enable rich business communication.

Who Should Read This Book?

We wrote this book for technical professionals and students. Although Chapter 2, "Background," briefly introduces the requisite background material about major XML technologies, we assume that you have a fair grasp of those technologies coming into this book. Developers who want to understand the overall Web services platform will appreciate this book. However, this is not a "developer book" in the sense of providing detailed, code-level understanding. That was not our objective. Architects, consultants, and technically oriented management should find this book useful. Students who have already attended introductory courses in distributed systems or database systems will be able to understand the Web services platform.

Acknowledgments

This book is the result of the contributions of numerous people. We would especially like to acknowledge and pay tribute to our many colleagues in IBM, too numerous to mention individually, who work alongside us in this fascinating area on a daily basis and whose innovation and stimulus have been a significant factor in making Web services a reality. Within that group of people, we would particularly like to thank Bob Sutor, Karla Norsworthy, Diane Jordan, Dan House, and Greg Clarke, who worked tirelessly in helping to bring this work to the world at large in the form of specifications and standards.

We would like to thank Eric Newcomer of IONA Technologies, Daniel Edgar of Portland General Electric, Ronald Schmelzer of ZapThink LLC, and Max Loukianov of Netprise Corp, for their insightful reviews and comments of earlier drafts of this book. Also thanks to Mark Little of Arjuna Technologies, with whom we had extensive helpful dialogue on wide-ranging Web services–related topics. Their input and comments brought about significant improvements and additions to the published version. We're also grateful to the many people in the IT industry—in particular our customers who've listened to what we had to say about this subject over the years and provided feedback that has helped to fashion our views about SOA and Web services. This book is also the result of collaboration with colleagues at Microsoft. We would like to acknowledge their contributions to the specifications that helped realize the vision outlined in this book.

We would also like to thank everyone on the publishing team for their excellent guidance on the focus of the book, for their help in realizing this project, and particularly for their patience in an endeavor that was more difficult than we had anticipated.

About the Authors

This book was a team effort by the folks at IBM who have been working on designing and building the Web services platform. The lead authors of this book—Sanjiva, Francisco (Paco), Frank, Tony, and Don—wrote parts of the book and coordinated contributions from the others. We'll start with descriptions of the five lead authors and then talk about the others who contributed.

Sanjiva Weerawarana received a Ph.D. in computer science from Purdue University in 1994. After a few years at Purdue as visiting faculty, he joined IBM Research in 1997, where he is a research staff member in the Component Systems Group and a member of the IBM Academy of Technology. Sanjiva's research interests are in component-oriented programming in general and specifically about component-oriented distributed computing architectures. He got involved with the Web services stack early by contributing to SOAP 1.1 and then by building the first implementation of it, which was later released to the Apache Software Foundation to start the Apache SOAP open source project. After that, Sanjiva cocreated WSDL (with Paco) and coauthored many Web services specifications, including WS-Addressing, WS-MetadataExchange, BPEL4WS, and WS-Resource Framework. In addition to developing specifications, Sanjiva has implemented many of them, in addition to technologies that are related to Web services, including Apache WSIF and the Web Services Gateway. He has been an active contributor to IBM's technical strategy for Web services and has helped coordinate IBM's Web services activities for the past five years. After Web services, Sanjiva's second love is open source, where he's a member of the Apache Software Foundation and the cofounder of the Lanka Software Foundation, an open source foundation in Sri Lanka. In his leisure time, he teaches at the University of Moratuwa, Sri Lanka, where he lives and telecommutes to his job in New York. You can e-mail Sanjiva at sanjiva@watson.ibm.com or sanjiva@opensource.lk.

Francisco Curbera is a research staff member and manager of the Component Systems Group at the IBM T.J. Watson Research Center in Hawthorne, New York, where he has worked since 1993. He holds a Ph.D. in computer science from Columbia University. His current research interests are in the use of component-oriented software in distributed computing system. In the past, he has worked in the design of algorithms and tools for processing XML documents, and in the use of markup languages for automatic UI generation. He has worked in different Web services specifications since the initial Web services concept surfaced in late 1999, first as one of the original authors of the Apache SOAP implementation of SOAP 1.1, and then as coauthor of WSDL 1.1, BPEL4WS, WS-Policy, and WS-PolicyAttachments, WS-Addressing, WS-MetadataExchange, and other Web services specifications. He currently represents IBM in the Web Services Addressing working group, standardizing WS-Addressing at the W3C, and in the Web Services Business Process technical committee standardizing BPEL4WS at OASIS. You can reach Paco at curbera@us.ibm.com.

Frank Leymann is a professor of computer science and the director of the Institute of Architecture of Application Systems at the University of Stuttgart, Germany. His research interests include service-oriented computing, workflow and business process management, transaction processing, and architecture patterns. Before taking over as a professor, Frank worked for two decades at IBM Software Group in the development of database and middleware products. During that time, he built tools that support conceptual and physical database design for DB2, as well as performance prediction and monitoring, co-architected a repository system, built both a universal relation system and a complex object database system on top of DB2, and was coarchitect of the MQSeries family. In parallel to that, Frank has worked continuously since the late 1980s on workflow technology and has become the father of IBM's workflow product set. As an IBM Distinguished Engineer and elected member of the

IBM Academy of Technology, he has contributed to the architecture and strategy of IBM's middleware stack and IBM's on-demand computing strategy. From 2000 on, Frank worked as coarchitect of the Web service stack. He is coauthor of many Web service specifications, including WSFL, WS-Addressing, WS-Metadata Exchange, WS-Business Activity, and the WS-Resource Framework set of specifications. Together with Satish Thatte, he was the driving force behind BPEL4WS. Frank has published many papers in journals and proceedings, co-authored two other text books, and holds numerous patents. You can reach Frank at Frank.Leymann@informatik.uni-stuttgart.de or LEY1@de.ibm.com.

Tony Storey is an IBM Fellow, Fellow of the Royal Academy of Engineering, and Fellow of the Institute of Electrical Engineering. He graduated from the Royal Institute of Chemistry and received his doctorate from the University of Durham. Tony joined IBM at the UK Scientific Centre and spent some years there in pioneering work on relational database technology. Subsequently, he has worked for more than two decades in the IBM development laboratory at Hursley, engaged in the development of distributed computing and middleware. He has played a leading role in the creation and development of many of IBM's world-leading middleware products, such as Customer Information Control System (CICS) and MQSeries. He was a key contributor to the development of Java specifications and technology for use in enterprise computing environments for which he earned a corporate award. Tony has most recently helped develop Web services and Grid computing within IBM and more broadly across the industry. He is a coauthor of many Web services specifications, in particular the transaction and messaging specifications. He is actively involved in providing guidance to the UK e-Science strategy that leverages a significant portion of the Web services infrastructure covered in this book. Prior to joining IBM, he worked in the development of Real Time computing systems for military applications. You can e-mail Tony at tony_storey@uk.ibm.com.

Donald F. Ferguson is one of approximately 55 IBM Fellows, the company's highest technical position, in its engineering community of 190,000 technical professionals. He is the chief architect and technical lead for IBM's Software Group family of products, and he chairs the SWG Architecture Board. Don's most recent efforts have focused on Web services, business process management, Grid services, and application development. He earned a Ph.D. in computer science from Columbia University in 1989. His thesis studied the application of economic models to the management of system resources in distributed systems. Don joined IBM Research in 1987 and initially led research and advanced development efforts in several areas of system performance and management. Starting in 1993, Don started focusing his efforts in the area of distributed, Object-Oriented systems. This work focused on CORBA-based SM solutions and frameworks and evolved into an effort to define frameworks and system structure for CORBA-based object transaction monitors. The early design and prototype of these systems produced the IBM Component Broker and WebSphere family of products. Don has earned two corporate awards (EJB Specification, WebSphere), four outstanding technical awards, and several division awards at IBM. He was the coprogram committee chairman for the First International Conference on Information and Computation Economies. He received a best paper award for his work on database buffer pools, has written more than 24 technical publications, and has nine granted or pending patents. In addition, he has given approximately 15 invited keynote speeches at technical conferences. Don was elected to the IBM Academy of Technology in 1997 and was named a Distinguished Engineer on April Fool's Day, 1998. No one is sure if the joke was on IBM or Don. Don was named an IBM Fellow on May 30, 2001. You can reach him at dff@us.ibm.com.

A team of 10 other writers coauthored specific chapters whose underlying technology they helped create. We provide their bios in alphabetical order here.

John Colgrave is a senior software engineer based in IBM's Hursley Laboratory in the United Kingdom. He has a B.S. degree in electrical and electronic engineering and an M.S. degree in computer science. Both degrees are from Manchester University. John has 20 years of experience in the architecture, design, and development of distributed systems and middleware. He is an active member of the OASIS UDDI Specification Technical Committee. He has authored several technical notes and contributed to the main UDDI specification. He is the architect of the IBM implementation of UDDI Version 3. You can contact John at colgrave@uk.ibm.com.

Christopher Ferris is a senior technical staff member in IBM's Standards Strategy group. He has been involved in the architecture, design, and engineering of distributed systems for most of his 25-year career in IT and has been actively engaged in open standards development for XML and Web services since

1999. Chris currently chairs the WS-I Basic Profile Working Group, which is responsible for the development of the WS-I Basic Profile, and is an elected member of the OASIS Technical Advisory Board. He is a coauthor and editor of the WS-Reliable Messaging specification. Prior to joining IBM, Chris served as chair of the W3C Web Services Architecture Working Group and as a member of the W3C XML Protocols Working Group. You can e-mail him at chrisfer@us.ibm.com.

Thomas Freund, coauthor of Chapter 11, "Transactions," is a senior technical staff member in the Emerging Technology group at IBM. He has worked extensively in the areas of transaction systems and Web services and has participated in the development of standards for OMG, Java, and Web Services. These specifications include the OMG/Object Transaction Service, the J2EE/Java Transaction Service, and Web Service's WS-Coordination, WS-AtomicTransaction, and WS-BusinessActivity. You can contact Tom at tjfreund@us.ibm.com.

Maryann Hondo, co-author of Chapter 7, "Web Services Policy," is a senior technical staff member at IBM, having joined IBM/Lotus in 1996. Her previous background includes work for HP on DCE- and PKI-based Single SignOn, for Digital on a B1/CMW operating system, and for AT&T Bell Labs on B2 UNIX. Currently, she is the security architect for emerging technology at IBM, concentrating on XML security. Maryann is one of the coauthors of the WS-Security, Policy, Trust, and Secure Conversation specifications announced by IBM and other business partners. Before joining the emerging technology group, she managed the IBM Tivoli Jonah team (IETF PKIX reference implementation) and was security architect for Lotus e-Suite, participating in the development of Java Security (JAAS). Send e-mails to Maryann at mhondo@us.ibm.com.

John Ibbotson is a member of the Emerging Technology Services group based at the Hursley Development Laboratory near Winchester in the UK. He is the IBM prime representative on the World Wide Web Consortium (W3C) XML Protocol Working Group that is standardizing SOAP, a key component of the Web services architecture. He is also a coauthor of the WS-ReliableMessaging specification. Earlier in his career, John developed scientific image-processing systems and digital libraries. John is a Chartered Engineer and Fellow of the Institution of Electrical Engineers (IEEE). You can contact him at john_ibbotson@uk.ibm.com.

Rania Khalaf is a software engineer in the Component Systems group at the IBM T.J. Watson Research Center. She received her bachelor's and master's degrees in computer science and electrical engineering from MIT in 2000 and 2001. Rania is a codeveloper and coarchitect of the IBM BPEL4WS prototype implementation (BPWS4J). She is an active member of the OASIS WS-BPEL Technical Committee standardizing BPEL. She has published numerous papers in the field and has served on the program committees of conferences and workshops. Rania is currently pursuing her Ph.D. studies under Professor Dr. Frank Leymann with the University of Stuttgart. Rania can be contacted at rkhalaf@us.ibm.com.

Dieter König is a software architect for workflow systems at the IBM Germany Development Laboratory. He joined the laboratory in 1988 and has worked at the Resource Measurement Facility for z/OS, MQSeries Workflow, and WebSphere Process Choreographer. Dieter is a member of the OASIS WS-BPEL Technical Committee, which is working toward an industry standard for Web Services Business Process Execution Language (WS-BPEL). He holds a master's degree (Diploma in Informatics) in computer science from the University of Bonn, Germany. You can contact him at dieterkoenig@de.ibm.com.

Hiroshi Maruyama is a Distinguished Engineer at the IBM Tokyo Research Laboratory, Japan. In 1997, his team developed XML Parser for Java, one of the first fully compliant XML processors. Since then, he has worked on XML and Web Services. In particular, he has focused on the security aspects of these technologies, such as XML Signature, XML Encryption, and "WS-Security standards." He wrote *XML and Java: Developing Web Applications*, published by Addison-Wesley. He is one of the coauthors of WS-Security standards. He has a master's degree from Tokyo Institute of Technology and a Ph. D. in computer science from Kyoto University. Contact Hiroshi at maruyama@jp.ibm.com.

Anthony Nadalin is a Distinguished Engineer and the chief security architect who is responsible for security infrastructure design and development across IBM SWG and Tivoli. Anthony serves as the primary security liaison to Sun Microsystems' JavaSoft division for Java security design and development collaboration. In his 23-year career with IBM, he has held the following positions: lead security architect for VM/SP, security architect for AS/400, and security architect for OS/2. Anthony has also authored and coauthored more than 30 technical journal and conference articles and two books. Anthony has been on the technical committee of three major scientific journals and one conference, and has reviewed extensively work that peers in the field have published. E-mail Anthony at drsecure@us.ibm.com.

Chris Sharp is a senior technical staff member working on Web services specifications and standards in IBM's Software Group, based in the IBM Hursley Laboratory in the United Kingdom. Chris is also a member of the IBM Academy of Technology. He joined IBM in 1990 as a graduate of computer science and has worked in the field of integration and Internet standards since 1994. He worked extensively on the development of IBM's integration middleware and exploitation of Internet standards. Chris is the editor of the WS-PolicyAttachment specification, coauthor of the WS-Policy specification, and contributor to WS-Addressing, WS-MetadataExchange, and the WS-ResourceFramework specifications. Chris is a Fellow of the British Computer Society. You can reach him at sharpc@uk.ibm.com.

Part 1

Introduction

The first part of this book introduces you to Service-Oriented Architectures (SOAs) and Web services. The three chapters of this part cover service orientation, background, and Web services.

Chapter 1, "SOA," starts by motivating the current trend toward service orientation and then explains what it is and how it differs from other technologies. The chapter wraps up by articulating the structure of a framework for service orientation.

Chapter 2, "Background," presents a brief review of some key background concepts that are used throughout the book.

Chapter 3, "Web Services," goes back to the service-oriented framework and introduces Web services as a realization of that platform. It briefly covers each of the specifications, which are discussed in detail in the rest of the book.

Chapter 1

Service-Oriented Architectures

This chapter introduces the concept of *Services* and the associated architectural paradigm, *Service-Oriented Architecture* (SOA). SOA has emerged as a direct consequence of specific business and technology drivers that have materialized over the past decade. From the business side, major trends such as the outsourcing of noncore operations and the importance of business process reengineering have been key influences driving the surfacing of SOA as an important architectural approach to business information technology (IT) today. From the technology side, the past 15 years have resulted in a realization of the importance of middleware standards and architectures, learning in particular from the successes and failures of distributed object systems and message-oriented middleware.

As an architectural concept, SOA permits multiple approaches for the realization and deployment of an IT system that has been designed and built around its principles. This book focuses on a specific technology that, arguably, has the most significant commercial visibility and traction, and that is *Web services*. Web services technology is a standards-based, XML-centric realization of an SOA. This chapter examines the motivation behind Web services and some of the main architectural concepts of SOA. Chapter 3, "Web Services," presents an overview of a Web services platform that provides the foundation to accomplish an SOA stack. Chapter 2, "Background," offers some required background so that you can understand the rest of this book.

1.1 Virtual Enterprises

Most companies produce and sell products to their customers to achieve defined business goals, such as specific financial targets. Their *business processes* prescribe how products are designed, manufactured, marketed, distributed, and sold. From a certain level of abstraction, a company's business processes are a direct reflection of the products it offers. Therefore, the speed of changing the existing infrastructure or creating new business processes corresponds to the speed of changing or creating products.

To survive in highly dynamic markets and constantly changing environments, companies must be flexible. Flexibility here means the ability to react quickly (preferably faster than the competition) to new customer requirements, new product offerings by existing and new competitors, technology advances, and so on. The flexibility of an enterprise is a refection of its ability to adapt its business processes quickly.

The constituents of the definition of a business process (see [Ley 2000]) translate directly into actions that are necessary to alter business processes: changing the flow of activities of a business process, changing the actors who are performing these activities, changing the tools that support these activities, and so on. These might result in moving the execution of (a subset of) the activities of the business processes to partners. The result could be multiple business partners having to cooperate to perform the business processes of a given company. The company in fact becomes a *virtual company* (or *virtual enterprise*). This term indicates that externally, the company looks like a real company—performing all of its business processes itself—but in practice, that is not what is actually happening. Others are partially running the company's business processes, making the company virtual in this sense.

1.1.1 Business Process Optimization

The model of a business process prescribes the order in which a business must execute the activities that constitute it and under which conditions it must perform each of the activities. Collectively, this kind of prescription is called *control flow.* The control flow massively influences business-relevant properties of a business process—such as its total cost and its overall duration—and thus the competitiveness of a company:

- The execution of each step or activity within a business process is associated with certain costs, such as people costs that are associated with the activity if human intervention is required, or the cost of computer resources that are required to execute activities within the IT environment. Based on this information, a company can derive the overall cost for performing a business process. For example, if policy associated with a credit allocation process determines that someone must check credits with an amount greater than $1,000, and more customers are asking for credits above this limit, a business could change the policy to set manual intervention at a higher value to reduce the overall costs for running the process.

- Activities have temporal characteristics, such as the average duration for executing an activity or the average time elapsed until an activity is picked up and performed. Based on this information, you can derive the average interval for executing a business process. For example, when you are booking a business trip, you can reserve hotel and flight reservations in parallel, resulting in a shorter execution time for the overall business process relative to its sequential execution.

There are other business-relevant properties of business processes and the activities they encompass. Changing the control flow of a business process might alter the corresponding properties of the business process in an unexpected manner. For example, introducing parallelism between activities might result in a longer duration of the overall process in those cases in which the parallel activities compete for the same resources (such as staff members who have rare skills).

Therefore, modeling a business process is a non-trivial endeavor, supported by specialized design and analysis tools. After having modeled and optimized a business process, it must be executed in exactly the way it was specified to ensure the business properties that the process is optimized for. Special middle-ware is available that enforces the correct and model-compliant execution—so-called *workflow systems* [Ley 2000]. Workflow systems allow monitoring of the business properties of individual business processes or aggregations of business processes at runtime. They also support the analysis of corresponding execution histories. Based on monitoring and analysis of results, you can change the model of a business process, if required, to further optimize it, especially when benchmarking shows that the execution of a business process is not competitive in terms of its key business parameters, such as cost or duration.

Sometimes, modifying the control flow of a business process is insufficient to hit the target values for certain business properties. For example, the cost structure within a company or wages for certain required staff might be too high to meet business expense targets. In such situations, a company's business process cannot gain competitiveness without significant re-engineering. The company (or a certain branch or location within a company) should probably determine its core competencies, focus on executing only the activities that correspond to these core competencies, and outsource the noncore competencies. Of course, the constraint is that outsourcing must result in hitting the target objectives of the subject business properties. SOA and Web service technology facilitates this kind of outsourcing in a secure, reliable manner.

1.1.2 Collaborations, Mergers, and Acquisitions

Figure 1-1 demonstrates an original process (denoted by "P") that a company runs. The company determines that it is no longer competitive in performing activities A, B, and E. It finds two partners that can run these activities and meet the business goals. Partner 1 runs activities A and B, and Partner 2 runs activity E. The company re-engineered the original process into a new process (P'). In the new process, activity AB kicks off the execution at the first partner (Partner 1), and E' starts the execution at the second partner (Partner 2). The company now has a new process P', which results in increased competitiveness.

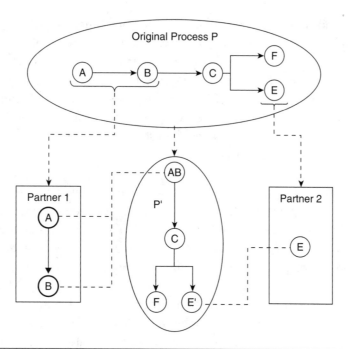

Figure 1-1   Outsourcing activities to partners.

In general, a company can work in several ways with partners that run the out-sourced activities. One way is for a business to acquire a partner that can effec-tively run some of the activities that it could not run in a competitive manner before. A company might take this approach if the activities that it has trouble performing competitively are core to its business. A company might also choose this acquisition if it is cheaper to acquire the partner than pay the partner to perform the activities. A company might also choose to merge with a partner, essentially combining its own business with that of the partner in a peer man-ner. This could exploit synergies between the two companies, further reducing costs and enhancing the competitiveness of the aggregate. Usually, mergers and acquisitions result in business processes that are run in a distributed manner, across partners or virtual enterprise as described here.

Mergers or acquisitions can have a deep impact on companies, and they, thus, generally take a less radical approach. They determine appropriate partners and negotiate long-term contracts for performing specific activities on behalf of the outsourcing company. These contracts especially include *service level-agreements*, which are specifications of service objectives such as availability of the outsourced activities, penalties applied when objectives are not met, bonuses paid if the objectives are overachieved, and so on [Dan 2004]. The result is a network of collaborating partners.

Situations might be highly dynamic. Multiple partners might provide the same services, and a company should choose on a case-by-case basis one of these to perform specific activities. For example, the cost of performing activities on behalf of a company might change depending on the actual load at each partner side. The company can then determine the partner on a best-price basis.

Collaboration might not only result from process optimization endeavors, but from supply chains that are typical within an industry. In this situation, a company and its partners are not distinguished. All partners are peers, collaborating to realize an overall business process that is spread over the partners. Some industries even have standards to define the various kinds of partners, the activities each of them runs, and how they relate. For example, RosettaNet [RN] defines such a standard and is currently moving toward Web service technology [RNWS].

1.1.3 Resource Sharing

In addition to business process optimization, businesses outsource activities or complete business processes for total cost of ownership considerations. Perhaps a business process is competitive overall, but the overall cost for running parts of it on IT equipment that the company owns is too high. In this situation, a company looks for a partner to run the corresponding activities or the whole business process on behalf of the company. This partner, also called *application service provider (ASP)*, not only runs parts of the business process on its IT equipment, but it also runs the corresponding software, covering the whole spectrum from managing prerequisite software to monitoring the software and performing periodic backups.

Web service technology, technology from the area of Grid computing that is based on Web services, and autonomic computing facilitate the ASP model and extend it toward a model called *utility computing* (see [Ley 2004], [Rappa 2004]). Within this utility computing model, computer resources and other IT related resources are offered in a similar manner to traditional utilities such as electricity or telephone. The usage of the utility IT resources to run parts of a business process is metered and charged on this basis. You will read more about this topic later.

1.2 The Need for Loose Coupling

Enabling communication with services, possibly dynamically discovered, requires *loose coupling* between a requester and the service to be used. The notion of loose coupling precludes any knowledge or assumptions about the specific platforms that the requester or the service provider run on, specifics about the implementation that either of the partners uses, or the formats and protocols used to interoperate between them. Making such assumptions significantly limits the usefulness of a service or the choice of services that might be available. The notion of loose coupling is a fundamental underpinning of SOA. The following section sheds more light on it.

1.2.1 Issues with Current Distributed System Technologies

Distributed system technology that has been developed in the past allows building applications, the elements of which can run on different machines in a network. However, dealing with the business scenarios outlined earlier has some other issues.

Fragility of Object Systems

Typically, current distributed system technology is centered on object technology. In this case, a service is offered as a method of a class implemented by an object. A requester who wants to use a service must tie the whole object into his application. In other words, a person who needs a single function has to use the whole class or—even worse—the whole class hierarchy within his program. When the class used or the class above it in the class hierarchy changes, he must also change the application that uses that class. The requester and the service are tightly coupled, which means that the requester's application is fragile because of its association with and dependence on this detail.

Lack of Interoperability

Today, different distributed system technologies such as Common Object Request Broker Architecture (CORBA), Java 2 Platform, Enterprise Edition (J2EE), and Component Object Model (COM) are based on quite different and incompatible object models [Emm 2000]. As a result, interoperability between these platforms is difficult. Communication between a requester on one platform and a service on another is at best cumbersome, if it's possible at all. Not only are the object models different, but higher-level frameworks (middleware) that support them (such as transactions, security, management, and messaging) are also incompatible. This significantly compounds the interoperability problem because you have to deal with quality of service differences. These differences can include running a transaction with participants on different platforms that operate incompatible transaction services, which is not an easy task!

1.2.2 Advantages of Message-Oriented Middleware

A significant consequence of these interoperability problems is that islands of middleware and corresponding applications that are based on this middleware have been created. In parallel, the ability to easily integrate applications, especially from different islands, has become a strong requirement (Enterprise Application Integration – EAI). In tandem, products that provide special integration middleware have been created. A key aspect of such integration middleware is message orientation.

Adapters and Channels

Message orientation refers to messages being exchanged between the applications that are to be integrated. For this purpose, adapters wrap existing applications that need to be integrated. One kind of adapter signals the occurrence of an event that needs to be passed to other applications (*source adapter*), and another kind of adapter receives such events and passes them to the application that they are wrapping (*target adapter*). Events are represented by messages that are transported via a so-called "channel" from the source adapter to a target adapter. The channel ensures a certain quality of services, such as "exactly once delivery". Also, the channel can have other side effects, such as transforming the message into a format that the recipient understands. Figure 1-2 shows a source adapter A that wraps application A. Adapter A passes a message of format M to the channel, which transforms the message into format M' and delivers it reliably to target adapter B. Adapter B in turn understands how to pass the data from M' to B. See [Hohpe 2004] for additional perspectives in this space.

Figure 1-2   Message-based integration.

Based on this message-based architecture, applications A and B are loosely coupled. For example, the owner of application A can change the format of message M, generally without affecting his ability to integrate application B. The message M that A produces can be appropriately transformed by the channel into the format M' that B expects. A message-based approach like this fosters loose coupling.

Interaction Patterns

Often, interaction and communication styles, other than the synchronous request/response approach that is predominant in distributed object systems, are necessary for loosely coupled interactions. For example, the asynchronous send and receive pattern that was mentioned in the previous section can increase a requester's perspective of the overall availability of the requested service. Operating in a "send-and-forget" mode, the requester doesn't have to synchronously wait for a response from the service. The requester doesn't have to deal with potential connection problems between the requester's side and the service's side because the channel can operate in a store-and-forward manner, finally delivering the message to the target destination.

Other patterns are also desirable. For example, a message might be delivered to multiple recipients, only a subset of which responds to the originator of the message. This pattern is useful in auction-type scenarios in which a request for bids is sent and bids are returned. This also contributes to loose coupling because the requester is unaware of who the recipients are. The underlying integration middleware deals with these aspects. To overcome rigidity in distributed object systems, you must support the ability to define message exchange patterns (MEP), which provide advanced interaction patterns. MEP is discussed in Chapter 6 in more details.

Web service technology is built on the concept of messaging. As a result, requesters and services can run on different platforms with channels connecting them. Wrappers hide the implementation specifics of the wrapped application function. In other words, requesters and services that are built according to different programming models can interact with each other. Protocols that are underlying a channel are hidden from the communication partners, and different formats can be transformed within a channel. The messaging architecture underlying Web services—SOAP—also foresees exchange of information required by higher-level functionality, such as transaction context or security context. Therefore, a messaging-based approach supports many of the requisite features at the beginning of this section.

1.2.3 Future Proofing

The concept of a wrapper allows switching implementations of application functions without impact to the other communication partner. This in turn facilitates loose coupling between a requester and a service (their corresponding wrappers). That is fine, but a universally agreed or standard approach to specifying the wrappers is required to describe, in a machine-readable way, the interface that a service provides to its potential users. The Web Services Description Language (WSDL) provides precisely this capability.

Technology Abstraction

WSDL provides a standard way of describing the interfaces of the wrappers that hide the specific implementation details of a service. Such an interface describes, in abstract terms, the functions that services provide. A requester can use any service that implements a particular interface to satisfy his requirement. This contributes to loose coupling between a requester and the service and provides some element of *future-proofing*. It gives the requester the freedom to select a different service implementation of the same interface at any time. In particular, the requester can benefit from any future advancements in implementation technology for services by being based on WSDL interfaces.

Provider Abstraction

Services are described not only by their WSDL interfaces, but also in terms of the quality of service they provide. For example, a service might assert that it can participate in a transaction, thereby ensuring overall integrity of a series of service invocations. It might also assert that it can cope with encrypted messages, ensuring that in the course of an interaction between a requester and the service, no confidential data will be revealed to unauthorized parties. The ability to annotate quality of service descriptions is important, and incorporated into

Web service technology by means of the Web service policy specifications discussed later in this book (Chapter 7, "Web Services Policy").

Also, you can associate services with business-relevant data. The directory features of the Universal Description, Discovery, and Integration (UDDI) technology (discussed later) offer and support such a capability and allow information about the company that is providing the service, including contact information, additional documentation, and geographic details. This allows discovery of suitable services based on detailed business criteria. For example, as a requester, a restaurant might want an online service that supplies ordering, settlement, and delivery of vegetables, meat, and so on within a distance of less than 50 miles.

As a consequence, the boundary for describing and discovering services is moved from specialized IT personnel toward business professionals. Again, this contributes to loose coupling by supporting discovery of providers that offer identical services and allowing switching between them dynamically with little or no change to the application.

1.3 What Is a Service?

In everyday life, you can point to many metaphors with which you can associate the concept of a service. These might include utilities such as water, gas, telephone, or electric, in addition to credit card services, transportation, travel agents, instant messaging, Internet service providers, search engines on the Web, and so on. These services represent some sort of publicized package of functionality. They are *composeable*. For example, a travel agent makes use of transportation (airline and rental car) and credit card services. Services are *discoverable* based on their descriptions, terms and conditions for use, and so on, based on *metadata* that fully describes the service. Actual use of a service is often based on an agreed-upon contract with the provider, including what in detail is provided and what the associated quality of services are, such as availability, cost, and other specified conditions that govern its use. Generally speaking, the user of the service requires little or no knowledge as to the specifics of how the service is implemented or how it is provided. The following sections relate these characteristics and apply them to software services.

1.3.1 Evolution of Major Software Granules

The idea of *packaging* software into artifacts that have a wider context, use, and applicability than a single application has been given a lot of attention since the early days of computing. This objective also relates to more flexible units of deployable software. Additional benefits are derived through separation of concerns, which leads to a significantly better understanding of the overall anatomy of complex software systems. This in turn enables improved software development methodologies necessary for tackling today's complex problems, in addition to improvements in software maintainability. Over the past decades, the ideas that have been applied to this problem have evolved quite significantly.

Functions and Packages

One of the first attempts to decompose software was centered on functional decomposition that resulted in functions or subroutines as individual software units. Such a unit offers coherent functionality that you can easily understand and build. This decomposition into functions enables modularization of software systems. However, this approach frequently brings about partial simplification that can only address simple problems. Added value comes with aggregations of related functions that help solve more complex tasks that are associated with a particular problem domain. Such approaches have, for example, been pioneered by Ada in the form of packages.

Objects and Classes

A package is a mere syntactic unit. To improve on and extend this concept further, the notion of a *class* evolved. A class describes the behavior of objects from a problem domain; therefore, it carries certain semantics in addition to being a syntactic unit combining functions and data. Classes, together with the concept of *polymorphism* and *inheritance,* have turned out to be a powerful concept for building software. Polymorphism allows the resulting software to become more flexible, whereas through inheritance, class lattices can be built that stimulate reuse and ease communication among developers within a given community.

Although classes represent objects and carry some semantics, a class lattice mostly captures syntax—namely, the signature of the functions aggregated. The semantics that a class lattice captures are typically understood only within a limited community, such as a development team. Few class lattices are known, the semantics of which are shared across larger communities.

In contrast to this, services are described not only via their interfaces, but also via business terms. Thus, the semantics that a service description provides go beyond that of a class and a class lattice. As such, services support comprehension by much broader communities.

Components

Besides being coarser than objects and classes, components go further by dealing with *deployment.* Addressing the issue of deployment allows a component provider to focus specifically on application logic, while qualities of services are folded in by the runtime environment that is hosting the component. For that purpose, quality of service requirements are factored and parameterized by *deployment descriptors* [J2EE]. By setting appropriate values in the deployment descriptors, you specify the behavior of a component with respect to such things as transactions, security checking, state management, and so on. In addition, you can resolve dependencies on other components and resources (such as databases and queues) via deployment descriptors. Finally, you can set up values governing application-specific context (such as local tax rates) via deployment descriptors.

Dealing with these aspects of deployment eases customization. You can tailor a piece of application logic to a company's specific use by setting values in deployment descriptors accordingly. The container that is hosting the application logic interprets the deployment descriptors and ensures the specified behavior. For a customized context that the application logic requires, the deployment descriptor provides the standardized contract. Deployment descriptors enable components to become *tradeable* artifacts.

1.3.2 The Software Version of a Service

Services represent another step forward in the evolution of software packages. Services can provide an abstraction of specific component models, allowing users of these components to think only in terms of Web services and ignore specific details of the component model and how it its implemented. For example, services can hide the details about whether the component is a J2EE-based component or a .NET based component. This provides significantly enhanced interoperability between computing platforms that have programming models based on these differing component models, such as WebSphere and .NET.

Characteristics of a Service

A service is available at a particular endpoint in the network, and it receives and sends messages and exhibits behavior according to its specification. The service has specific functionality and is deployed with appropriate quality of service at the endpoint. (For example, the service is set up with certain transactional or security or reliable messaging behavior.) The functional aspects of a service are specified using WSDL, and the constraints and conditions that are associated with the use of the service are specified via policies that you can attach to various parts of the WSDL (see chapter 7). Interfaces and policies describe the terms and conditions that govern the use of the service. These are published so that potential users of the service can discover and be given all the information they need to bind (perhaps dynamically) to that service.

The information that is published about a service provides details of what the service is and does (its semantics). It further provides all the information that allows the environment hosting a potential user to access the service and successfully interact with it. This can include information about the transport protocols that can be supported and used to send a messages to the service, the wire format of this message expected by the service, whether and how the message has to be encrypted or signed.

Although the environment that is hosting needs this information, the requester doesn't need this kind of access information, and it certainly doesn't need to understand details about the implementation of the service. You can implement this service as an EJB, a database stored procedure, or a CICS or IMS transaction made available via a wrapper. The environment that is hosting the service and receiving the request message, often referred to as a *container,* must deal with that detail necessary to interact with a particular implementation. The requester can think in terms of using a Web service. In that sense, Web service technology is virtualization technology for making use of services, but an implementer of a service can use the technology he is acquainted with to build the service implementation.

Solutions—Composition of Services

One valuable aspect of the services model is that you can create new services from existing ones without leaving the service paradigm. A technology called *choreography* facilitates the composition and orchestration of the execution of existing services to create more powerful ones (see Chapter 14, "Modeling Business Processes: BPEL"). Choreographies support the idea of *programming in the large* (see [Ley 2004], [Ley 1997], [Wied 1992]), which fosters the creation of new functionality, in particular by non-IT personnel.

Using the terminology introduced earlier, a business process corresponds to the choreography of services designed to address a high-level business problem. The choreography specifies which services to use, in which order, and under which conditions. Services within the choreography correspond to an activity, some kind of well-identified step in the process. You can define the choreography as a service and incorporate it as an activity within another choreography, again, providing functions from the business domain of a company. Because the collection of services and the choreography that uses them solve a business problem, this collection is sometimes called a *solution* [BaS04]. Without examining the detail, note that a solution typically contains additional artifacts, such as user interfaces or more complex rules that the choreography uses (see Figure 1-3).

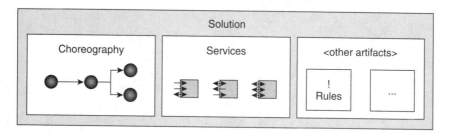

Figure 1-3   The concept of a solution.

Choreographies use services and render the results as services again. Therefore, one choreography can serve as a base for other choreographies, together with services that have been implemented based on other technologies. Thus, choreography provides a powerful technology for recursive composition of services.

1.4 Service-Oriented Architecture

SOA is a specific architectural style that is concerned with loose coupling and dynamic binding between services. Some critically important factors at the heart of SOA are necessary to make it work effectively.

1.4.1 Bind/Publish/Find

The basic principles that underpin SOA are illustrated in Figure 1-4. First, it is necessary to provide an abstract definition of the service, including the details that allow anyone who wants to use the service to *bind* to it in the appropriate way. Second, those people who are the providers of services need to *publish* details of their services so that those who want to use them can understand more precisely what they do and can obtain the information necessary to connect to use them. Third, those who require services need to have some way to *find* what services are available that meet their needs. Also, to make this bind/publish/find approach work well, standards must be defined to govern what and how to publish, how to find information, and the specific details about how to bind to the service. Web services technology is at the heart of addressing these questions and is the subject of this book. It also forms a basis for the notion of a *service bus* (infrastructure) that supports SOA.

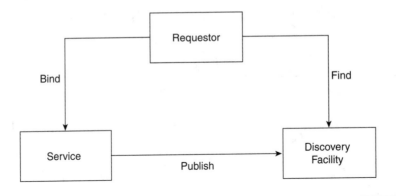

Figure 1-4   The SOA Triangle.

The provider of a service describes its semantics, that is, the functions it supports in addition to its operational characteristics and required details about how to access the service. This descriptive information (or *metadata*) about the service is published to a directory or registry. A requester uses a discovery facility that is associated with the registry to find services that he is interested in and selects the one that is required. Based on the access information published about the service, the requester can bind to the selected service.

Descriptive information about a service, as indicated earlier and described in detail later, is based on WSDL and policy. At one end of the spectrum of service publishing and discovery is a separate registry or directory, such as UDDI, which holds WSDL and policy information about registered service and additional information such as business data about the service provider. This information is queried for services that match the requester's criteria. At the other end of the spectrum, more rudimentary mechanisms can provide access to and retrieval of metadata about a service, the existence of which is known to the requester perhaps by private means. However, after a service has been chosen, the information regarding how to access the service is used next to actually bind to it and send requests to it.

Figure 1-5 illustrates the various steps and artifacts that dynamically discover and bind a service. First, the requester describes the service needed via functions required and nonfunctional properties. Based on this input, the discovery facility produces a list of candidate services that satisfy those needs. From this candidate list, the requester chooses a service. The selection facility shown for that purpose can be as simple as performing a random selection or as sophisticated as considering additional criteria such as cost of use. After the requester has chosen the service, he determines its address and binding details, such as which protocol to use and which message format is required. This information is either already returned within the candidate list details or is retrieved in a separate step.

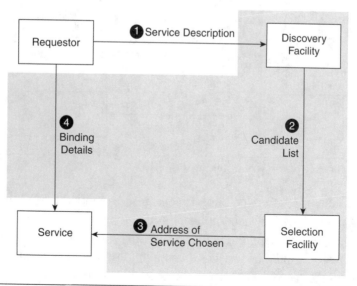

Figure 1-5   Selecting and binding services.

This processing looks cumbersome. However, middleware called a *service bus* (see [Voll 2004], for example) can simplify the process and make it more transparent. As illustrated in Figure 1-6, the requester simply passes to the service bus the description of the service and the data that the request message expects to be sent. Next, the requester gets the response to his declarative request. Based on this request, all services that qualify under the service description are undistinguishable for the requester, and the bus can unilaterally select from all candidates. The bus virtualizes these candidate services from the requester's perspective. For this purpose, the bus implements the shaded area in Figure 1-6. In other words, the bus takes the service description and uses a discovery facility to find the list of qualifying services, selects one of them, retrieves the necessary binding information, binds the service accordingly, transforms the input data from the requester properly, sends the corresponding request message to the service, receives the response, and passes this response in the proper format to the requester. A service bus provides a significantly improved ease-of-use experience for a Web service–based implementation of SOA.

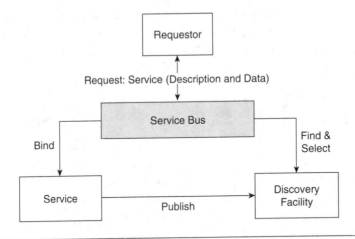

Figure 1-6   The role of the service bus in SOA.

The functionality that a service bus provides goes beyond virtualizing application functionality. Not only can application functions be described via WSDL, but also the usage of resources such as processing power (CPUs) or storage (disks) can be considered as services thus being described via WSDL. Thus, a requester might describe his need for processing power and storage to the bus, and the bus will make this available. Of course, this requires much more sophistication, including scheduling features and extensions of the Web service model. Nevertheless, the service bus is a major enabling technology for a distributed computing environment called Grid (see [Fost 2004], [Czaj 2004]). You can think of it as service-oriented middleware.

Note that CORBA already had some aspects of the SOA in it based on its Trader services. However, from an overall SOA perspective, these trader services were incomplete. Often, they were not implemented, and they certainly weren't universal in the sense of being platform neutral.

1.4.2 Framework for SOA

Web service technology is a base for implementing SOA, and the service bus is the centerpiece of this implementation. Thus, we want to sketch the high-level architecture of a service bus.

Figure 1-7 depicts the high-level architecture of the service bus as a stack of SOA capabilities. The bottom layer presents its capabilities to cope with various transport protocols to communicate between a service and a requester. The messaging layer on top of the transport layer enables the bus to deal with messages, both XML and non-XML. The latter is important, for example, if a requester and the service needed reside in the same J2EE application server and the bus can simply transport the data in its Java rendering, avoiding unnecessary transformations. The next layer of the bus facilitates and deals with the description of services in terms of functions supported, quality of services of these functions, and supported binding mechanisms. The actual quality of services that the bus enforces based on appropriate parameterization via polices resides in the layer that follows. This layer copes with security aspects such as message integrity, confidentiality, and nonrepudiation, but also with reliable transport of messages and various kinds of transactions. The top layer represents the various kinds of virtual components that Web services represent. This layer has atomic services that are not composed as far as a requester's experience with the service is concerned. Composed services that the service bus inherently supports are choreographies and societies of services that cooperate following an agreement protocol to decide on the success of the cooperation at the end of the cooperation. Finally, another layer provides features for discovery of services and their descriptions and to agree on a mode of interaction between a requester and a service.

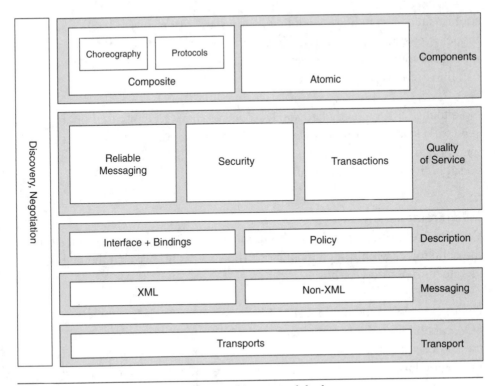

Figure 1-7   The SOA stack: High-level architecture of the bus.

Chapter 3 revisits this topic and describes how various specifications fit into this SOA stack, with special focus on Web service specifications.

1.5 Summary

This chapter covered two major drivers that foster SOAs: an ever-increasing number of collaborations between enterprises that result from focusing on core competencies and enhancing agility, and the pressing need to solve the integration problem by loosening the coupling between functional components. This chapter explored the concept of a service as an evolution of software component technology and discussed the impact of services on application structures. It also presented the principles of SOA and introduced a framework of an environment that supports SOA applications.

Chapter 2

Background

This chapter discusses some background information that is crucial to understanding the rest of the book. This material is not intended to be a thorough introduction but rather a quick refresher. If you are already familiar with these topics, feel free to move on to the next chapter. The topics reviewed in this chapter are XML concepts (including basics, schemas, Infoset and XPath) and Web concepts (URIs, HTTP and MIME).

2.1 XML

This section briefly reviews the core concepts of XML. Basic reviews of eXtensible Markup Language (XML), Document Type Definitions (DTDs), XML Schema, RelaxNG (pronounced *relaxing*), XML Namespaces, XML Infoset, and XPath are provided to ensure that you are familiar with these technologies.

2.1.1 XML Basics

The world of Web services builds heavily on the core set of XML [XML] specifications. XML is actually not a language, but a metalanguage for defining new languages. The definition of XML is platform independent and is defined using Unicode, which allows it to represent content from many natural languages.

Because of these factors and because of the wide support of XML by basically every software vendor, XML has rapidly become the de facto format for data interchange between disparate entities.

XML provides a small set of core concepts for defining new languages:

- **Elements**—An XML element is a named construct that has a set of attributes and some children. The children of an element can be other elements, literal text, comments, and a few other types. Elements are written using angle brackets:
  start element foo "<foo>" and end element foo "</foo>"

- **Attributes**—Attributes are name-value pairs that are associated with an element. An element can have any number of attributes and is written as follows:
  <foo name1="value1" name2="value2" ...>

- **Comments**—Comments are enclosed within "<!--" and "-->" character sequences and are meant for the processor to ignore.

- **Literal text**—Elements can contain character sequences consisting of Unicode characters. A key quality of XML is that all characters contained within XML documents are represented in Unicode. By using Unicode, XML can store characters from almost any language. Therefore, XML is internationalized by definition.

- **Document**—An XML document is a unit of XML packaging that consists of exactly one element (called the *document element*) and might contain comments and a few other items.

Using these concepts, you can define new languages simply by deciding on a set of element names, their valid content, and the kinds of literal text that are permissible as attribute values and element content. A key improvement of XML over SGML (its precursor) was the notion of well-formed, but not necessarily valid, documents. A document is said to be well formed if it adheres to all the XML syntax rules. A well-formed document is also valid if it conforms to some DTD or XML Schema or some other document structure definition language. By creating the concept of *well formed*, the creators of XML enabled its rapid adoption because that allowed applications to use XML as a syntax without having to have a DTD or an XML Schema and having to validate the XML structure.

The elements that define the SOAP message format is an example of an XML vocabulary. WSDL is another example. Thus, most of the Web service specifications define one or more XML languages.

2.1.2 DTDs, XML Schema, and RelaxNG

As indicated earlier, it is simple to define a new XML language. How do you declare the structure of an XML language? That is, how do you indicate what the document element of an XML document must be, what elements it can have as children, what attributes the elements have, and so on? That is the role of DTDs, XML Schema [XML Schema], and RelaxNG [RelaxNG].

DTDs

DTDs were created for SGML (the precursor to XML) to declare the structure of SGML documents. When XML was designed, the DTD mechanism was the de facto mechanism for defining the structure of XML documents. Using a non-XML syntax, the DTD language allows you to define the names of elements, the number of times an element occurs within another, and so on.

People used DTDs widely during the early days of XML because that was the only standard structure definition language. However, with the advent of XML Schema, the use of DTDs has declined rapidly and is primarily of historical interest at this point.

XML Schema

XML Schema is a document structuring and type definition specification that the World Wide Web Consortium (W3C) developed. Using an XML syntax, XML Schema allows you to specify XML structures similar to DTDs but in a much more powerful manner. In addition to structure, XML Schema also allows you to specify data types. It defines a set of primitive data types that you can use to define attribute and element values and recursive type constructors for defining arbitrarily complex type structures. XML Schema is powerful and sometimes daunting, but it has wide industry support. Today, it includes tools that make it quite simple to define schemas.

All of the Web services specifications that this book discusses have associated schemas written using XML Schema.

RelaxNG

RelaxNG is a merger of two schema languages: TREX by James Clark and Relax by Mukato Murato. TREX (Tree Regular Expressions for XML) is a regular expression way to define only the structure of XML. Relax is a tree-automata-based regular expression language. Thus, RelaxNG focuses only on defining the structure of XML documents, not their types. The premise is that XML Schema has become complex partly because of mixing structure and typing declaration capabilities.

Although RelaxNG is indeed technically solid, its adoption in the industry has been weak due to the proliferation of XML Schema.

2.1.3 XML Namespaces

Because you can easily define XML languages by choosing a set of element and attribute names and defining how they relate to each other, many XML vocabularies are available. If you want to combine two such vocabularies, however, you might run into trouble with name conflicts. Two or more languages might have chosen the same element names.

Enter XML Namespaces [XML Namespaces], which is a way to scope element and attribute names to a *namespace* so that their usage is always unique, regardless of their context.

Thus, XML Namespaces introduces the concept of *qualified names* (QNames). A QName is a combination of a namespace name and a local name. The namespace name scopes the local name.

XML Infoset

Although common understanding of XML is in its "angle bracket" form, the XML Infoset defines the fundamentals of XML [XML Infoset]. The XML Infoset defines the underlying information model of XML. In other words, it abstracts from the angle bracket syntax and defines what information is contained in an element, an attribute, and so on.

The XML Infoset defines a set of information items that correspond to the syntactic constructs of XML. The important information items are as follows:

- **Element information item (EII)**—An EII is the abstraction of an element. EII properties include a list of children (which might be other EIIs, character information items, and so on), a list of attributes, the name and namespace name, and so on.

- **Attribute information item (AII)**—An AII is an abstraction of an attribute. Thus, an AII has as properties its name and namespace name, its value, and so on.

- **Character information item (CII)**—A CII represents literal text found as element content.

If an XML Schema has been used to validate a document, the Infoset might be augmented to form the Post Schema Validation Infoset (PSVI). The PSVI basically has additional properties containing the type information and the validation status of each element.

Although many people think of the angle bracket form when they think of XML, the real action of XML lies at the Infoset level. The familiar angle brackets are simply a serialization of the Infoset. Two such serializations are already defined: XML 1.0 and XML 1.1, both of which use the familiar angle bracket form.

Going into the future, serializations of the XML Infoset likely will not use Unicode text characters as XML 1.0 and XML 1.1 do. Rather, binary serializations—which are extremely space efficient and fast to parse—are beginning to appear. See, for example, [W3C Binary XML]. The emergence of such serializations allows you to address some of the biggest criticisms of XML: that it is bloated and slow to process.

Many of the Web service specifications have taken this abstract concept one step further. SOAP 1.2 and WSDL 2.0, for example, are now defined at an abstract level, and their XML representation is simply a serialization of the abstraction. Therefore, you can use SOAP 1.2 and WSDL 2.0 and never serialize them using XML!

DOM, SAX, And So On

Document Object Model (DOM), Streaming API for XML (SAX), and so on, are programming APIs for accessing the Infoset. Because this book does not cover programming aspects of Web services, this topic is not discussed further.

XPath

The XML Path Language (XPath) [XPath] was designed as part of XSL [XSL] as an addressing mechanism to identify elements, attributes, and other information items within XML documents. Using XPath, you can use a familiar file path notation to identify locations within XML documents. You can use XPath as a query language to select and extract a set of items or as an addressing mechanism to identify a specific location.

XPath has been hugely successful and has been used in numerous settings, including in BPEL4WS, as you will see later. XPath is also the basis of XQuery [XQuery], a full query language for XML.

2.2 World Wide Web

The Web is built on a few core standards that are universally adopted. This section briefly reviews uniform resource identifiers (URIs), HyperText Transfer Protocol (HTTP), and Multipurpose Internet Mail Exchange (MIME).

2.2.1 URIs

A URI [URI] is a format for identifying an abstract or concrete resource, which can be basically anything with an identity. Uniform Resource Locators (URLs) are a popular form of URIs—basically those URIs that can be de-referenced to obtain a representation of the resource identified by the URI. Although recent revisions of the URI specification do away with the URL concept and treat all URIs the same, the basic idea of some URIs being de-referenceable and others not still exists.

It is important to note, however, that even URIs that look de-referenceable (for example, http://this-is-a-fake-name.com/foo) might not be. Thus, the only assertion you can make about a URI is that it identifies some resource and might be de-referenceable to obtain a representation of that resource.

Many Web service specifications use URIs to identify components defined by those specifications. Some specifications, however, use QNames, and the question of whether URIs or QNames identify things is a frequent debate among the Web community. The use of QNames to identify components received a boost by the XML Schema specification because it uses QNames to identify types and elements that a given schema defines. QNames allow you to formalize the fact that a set of definitions are related because they have a shared namespace name. If you were to use URIs to name a group of related items, you would need to understand the structure of the URI so that you could recover the relationship. Significant parts of URIs (depending on the URI scheme) are supposed to be opaque except to their creator.

The debate of URIs versus QNames continues. Unfortunately, some of the Web service specifications use URIs for naming (WS-Policy in particular), although many others use only QNames, bringing this debate to the world of Web services as well.

2.2.2 HTTP

HTTP [HTTP] is the communication protocol that transfers representations of resources on the Web. The use of HTTP and URIs on the Web has been modeled by an architectural style called Representational State Transfer (REST) [F00].

Web services (SOAP in particular) uses HTTP as a transport (rather than transfer) protocol to carry SOAP messages from one endpoint to another. The use of HTTP in this manner has been quite controversial at times because SOAP can be carried on many transport protocols and does not really adhere to the HTTP semantics. However, the widespread deployment of HTTP means that SOAP will continue to use HTTP as a transport protocol for the foreseeable future, despite its "breaking of the religion" of HTTP as an application level transfer protocol rather than a transport protocol.

2.2.3 MIME

MIME [MIME] is a standard that was originally developed to address the problem of sending nontext content as e-mail attachments. MIME's generality and power were so attractive that HTTP also adopted it as the mechanism to type HTTP messages, thereby gaining MIME's advantages for transmitting multipart content.

MIME defines a set of media types that you can use to tag the type of some media being sent or received as a binary sequence of bytes. The SOAP with Attachments specification (see Chapter 4, "SOAP") uses HTTP's MIME transport capability to define a packaging model for how to transmit messages that involve SOAP messages and attachments of various binary forms conforming to MIME media types.

2.3 Summary

This chapter has given you a brief review of some of the key technologies that the Web services platform builds on. If you need more information about any of these topics, there are many excellent books available.

Chapter 3

Web Services: A Realization of SOA

People often think of Web services and Service-Oriented Architecture (SOA) in combination, but they are distinct in an important way. As discussed in Chapter 1, "Service-Oriented Architectures," SOA represents an abstract architectural concept. It's an approach to building software systems that is based on loosely coupled components (services) that have been described in a uniform way and that can be discovered and composed. Web services represents one important approach to realizing an SOA.

The World Wide Web Consortium (W3C), which has managed the evolution of the SOAP and WSDL specifications, defines Web services as follows:

> *A software system designed to support interoperable machine-to-machine interaction over a network. It has an interface described in a machine-processable format (specifically WSDL). Other systems interact with the Web service in a manner prescribed by its description using SOAP messages, typically conveyed using HTTP with XML serialization in conjunction with other Web-related standards.*

Although Web services technology is not the only approach to realizing an SOA, it is one that the IT industry as a whole has enthusiastically embraced. With Web services, the industry is addressing yet again the fundamental challenge that distributed computing has provided for some considerable time: to provide a uniform way of describing components or services within a network, locating them, and accessing them. The difference between the Web services approach and traditional approaches (for example, distributed object technologies such as the Object Management Group – Common Object Request Broker Architecture (OMG CORBA), or Microsoft Distributed Component Object Model (DCOM)) lies in the loose coupling aspects of the architecture. Instead of building applications that result in tightly integrated collections of objects or components, which are well known and understood at development time, the whole approach is much more dynamic and adaptable to change. Another key difference is that through Web services, the IT industry is tackling the problems using technology and specifications that are being developed in an open way, utilizing industry partnerships and broad consortia such as W3C and the Organization for the Advancement of Structured Information Standards (OASIS), and based on standards and technology that are the foundation of the Internet.

This open, standards-based approach in which every Web services specification is eventually standardized by an industry-wide organization (such as W3C or OASIS) introduces the possibility that the specifications described in this book might undergo significant changes before becoming formal standards. This is a natural consequence of the standardization process in which both technology vendors and consumers provide input and push their requirements into the final standard. However, the basic concepts and the design supporting each of the specifications are unlikely to change in fundamental ways, even if the syntax is modified or the supported set of use cases is significantly expanded. At the time of publication, several of the specifications covered in this book have already been submitted to standards, and significant changes may ensue in some of them (for example, in the case of WS-Addressing, now being discussed at W3C). Readers interested in the details of the specifications should be aware of this fact and carefully follow the results of the standardization process. Please refer to the Web site, www.phptr.com, "Updates and Corrections," where you will find the latest updates to the specifications covered in this book.

3.1 Scope of the Architecture

The high-level schematic introduced in Chapter 1 (Figure 1-7) illustrates a lay-ered view of the important foundational capabilities that are required of SOA. This chapter introduces a specific rendering of this conceptual framework with a particular collection of Web services specifications that are based on and extend basic Internet standards that were described in Chapter 2, "Background." Note that specifications used in this rendering are those that IBM has developed in a collaborative effort with other industry partners, most no-tably Microsoft. The description in this chapter is intended to give a high-level "fly by" only, with the express purpose of providing an overall summary per-spective. The following chapters of this book discuss these Web services specifi-cations in much greater detail.

Web services had its beginnings in mid to late 2000 with the introduction of the first version of XML messaging—SOAP, WSDL 1.1, and an initial version of UDDI as a service registry. This basic set of standards has begun to provide an accepted industry-wide basis for interoperability among software components (Web services) that is independent of network location, in addition to specific implementation details of both the services and their supporting deployment infrastructure. Several key software vendors have provided these implementa-tions, which have already been widely used to address some important business problems.

Although the value of Web services technology has been demonstrated in prac-tice, there is a desire to use the approach to address more difficult problems. Developers are looking for enhancements that raise the level and scope of inter-operability beyond the basic message exchange, requiring support for interopera-tion of higher-level infrastructure services. Most commercial applications today are built assuming a specific programming model. They are deployed on plat-forms (operating systems and middleware) that provide infrastructure services in support of that programming model, hiding complexity, and simplifying the problems that the solution developer has to deal with. For example, middleware typically provides support for transactions, security, or reliable exchange of mes-sages (such as guaranteed, once-only delivery). On the other hand, there is no universally agreed standard middleware, which makes it difficult to construct applications from components that are built using different programming models

(such as Microsoft COM, OMG CORBA, or Java 2 Platform, Enterprise Edition
(J2EE) Enterprise Java Beans). They bring with them different assumptions about
infrastructure services that are required, such as transactions and security. As a
consequence, interoperability across distributed heterogeneous platforms (such
as .NET and J2EE) presents a difficult problem.

The Web services community has done significant work to address this interoperability issue, and since the introduction of the first Web services, various organizations have introduced other Web services–related specifications. Figure 3-1
illustrates a population of the overall SOA stack shown in Figure 1-7 with current standards and emerging Web services specifications that IBM, Microsoft,
and other significant IT companies have developed. The remainder of this chapter provides a high-level introduction to these Web services specifications that
realize more concretely the capabilities that are described in the SOA framework
in Chapter 1 and that extend the earlier Web services technology of XML, SOAP,
and WSDL to provide secure, reliable, and transacted interoperability. The specifications define formats and protocols that allow services to interoperate across
those vendor platforms that provide conformant implementations, either natively
or by mapping them onto existing proprietary middleware offerings.

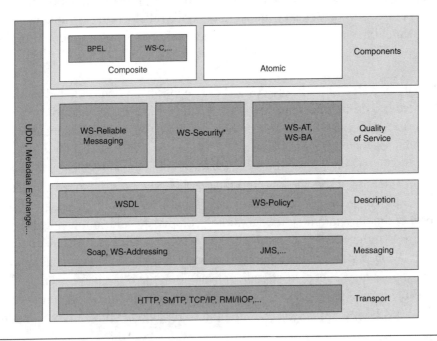

Figure 3-1   Web services architecture.

```
<definitions targetNamespace="...">
      <!-- WSDL definitions in this document -->
      <!-- referenced using "tns" prefix -->

      <types>
            <!-- XSD definitions for this service -->
            <!-- referenced using "xsd1" prefix -->
            <xsd:schema>
                 <xsd:import
namespace="http://www.purchase.com/xsd/svp-svc">
            </xsd:schema>
      </types>

      <message name="purchaseResponse">
            <part name="purchaseResponse"
element="xsd1:PurchaseStatus"/>
      </message>
      <message name="purchaseRequest">
            <part name="purchaseRequest"
element="xsd1:PurchaseRequest"/>
      </message>
      <message name="ServicePacValidationInput">
            <part name="spvDataInput"
                  element="xsd1:ServicePacValidationData"/>
      </message>
      <message name="ServicePacValidationOutput">
            <part name="spvDataOutput"
                  element="xsd1:ServicePacValidationData"/>
      </message>

      <portType name="spvPortType">
            <operation name="purchaseServicePacs">
                 <input name="purchaseInput"
message="tns:purchaseRequest"/>
                 <output name="purchaseOutput"
                       message="tns:purchaseResponse"/>
            </operation>
            <operation name="validateServicePac">
                 <input name="Input"
                       message="tns:ServicePacValidationInput"/>
                 <output name="Output"
                       message="tns:ServicePacValidationOutput"/>
            </operation>
      </portType>

      <binding name="spvBinding" type="tns:spvPortType">
            <wsp:PolicyReference
                 URI="http://www.purchase.com/policies/DSig">
            <soap:binding style="document"
transport="http://schemas.xmlsoap.org/soap/http"/>
            <operation name="purchaseServicePacs">
```

```
        <wsp:PolicyReference URI=
            "http://www.purchase.com/policies/Encrypt">
        <soap:operation soapAction=

"http://www.purchase.com/spvPortType/purchaseServicePacsRequest"/>
        </operation>
        <operation name="validateServicePac">
            <soap:operation soapAction=

"http://www.purchase.com/spvPortType/validateServicePacRequest"/>
        </operation>
    </binding>

    <service name="spv-svc">
        <port name="spv-svc-port" binding="tns:spvBinding">
            <soap:address
location="http://www.purchase.com/spv"/>
        </port>
    </service>
</definitions>
```

3.2 Transport Services

Web services is basically an interoperable messaging architecture, and message transport technologies form the foundation of this architecture. Web services is inherently transport neutral. Although you can transport Web services messages by using the ubiquitous Web protocols such as HyperText Transport Protocol (HTTP) or Secure HTTP (HTTPS) to give the widest possible coverage in terms of support for the protocols (see Chapter 2), you can also transport them over any communications protocol, using proprietary ones if appropriate. Although transport protocols are fundamental to Web services and clearly are a defining factor in the scope of interoperability, the details are generally hidden from the design of Web services. A detailed discussion of these is not included in the scope of this book.

3.3 Messaging Services

The messaging services component of the framework contains the most fundamental Web services specifications and technologies, including eXtensible Markup Language (XML), SOAP, and WS-Addressing. Collectively, these specifications form the basis of interoperable messaging between Web services. XML (discussed in Chapter 2) provides the interoperable format to describe message content between Web services and is the basic language in which the Web services specifications are defined.

3.3.1 SOAP

SOAP, one of the significant underpinnings of Web services, provides a simple and relatively lightweight mechanism for exchanging structured and typed information between services. SOAP is designed to reduce the cost and complexity of integrating applications that are built on different platforms. SOAP has undergone revisions since its introduction, and the W3C has standardized the most recent version, SOAP 1.2.

SOAP defines an extensible enveloping mechanism that scopes and structures the message exchange between Web services. A SOAP message is an XML document that contains three distinct elements: an *envelope*, a *header*, and a *body*. The envelope is the root element of the SOAP message. It contains an optional header element and a mandatory body element. The header element is a generic mechanism for adding extensible features to SOAP. Each child element of header is called a *header block*. SOAP defines several well-known attributes that you can use to indicate who should deal with a header block and whether processing of it is optional or mandatory. The body element is always the last child element of the envelope, and it is the container for the *payload*—the actual message content that is intended for the ultimate recipient who will process it. SOAP defines no built-in header blocks and only one payload, which is the Fault element used for reporting errors.

SOAP is defined independently of the underlying messaging transport mechanism in use. It allows the use of many alternative transports for message exchange. You can defer selection of the appropriate mechanism until runtime, which gives Web service applications or support infrastructure the flexibility to determine the appropriate transport as the message is sent. In addition, the underlying transport might change as the message is routed between nodes. Again, the mechanism that is selected for each hop can vary as required. Despite this general transport independence, most first-generation Web services communicate using HTTP, because it is one of the primary bindings included within the SOAP specification.

SOAP messages are transmitted one way from sender to receiver. However, multiple one-way messages can be combined into more sophisticated message exchange patterns. For instance, a popular pattern is a synchronous request/response pair of messages. The messaging flexibility that SOAP provides allows services to communicate using a variety of message exchange patterns, to satisfy the wide range of distributed applications. Several patterns have proven particularly helpful in distributed systems. The use of remote procedure calls, for example, popularized the synchronous request/response message exchange pattern. When message delivery latencies are uncontrolled, asynchronous messaging is needed. When the asynchronous request/response pattern is used, explicit message correlation becomes mandatory.

Messages can be routed based on the content of the headers and the data inside the message body. You can use tools developed for the XML data model to inspect and construct complete messages. Note that such benefits were not available in architectures such as DCOM, CORBA, and Java Remote Method Invocation (RMI), where protocol headers were infrastructural details that were opaque to the application. Any software agent that sends or receives messages is called a *SOAP node*. The node that performs the initial transmission of a message is called the *original sender*. The final node that consumes and processes the message is called the *ultimate receiver*. Any node that processes the message between the original sender and the ultimate receiver is called an *intermediary*. Intermediaries model the distributed processing of an individual message. The collection of intermediary nodes traversed by the message and the ultimate receiver are collectively referred to as the *message path*.

To allow parts of the message path to be identified, each node participates in one or more *roles*. The base SOAP specification defines two built-in roles: *Next* and *UltimateReceiver*. Next is a universal role in that every SOAP node, other than the sender, belongs to the Next role. UltimateReceiver is the role that the terminal node in a message path plays, which is typically the application, or in some cases, infrastructure that is performing work on behalf of the application. The body of a SOAP envelope is always targeted at the UltimateReceiver. In contrast, SOAP headers might be targeted at intermediaries or the UltimateReceiver

SOAP is discussed in detail in Chapter 4, "SOAP."

3.3.2 WS-Addressing

WS-Addressing provides an interoperable, transport-independent way of identifying message senders and receivers that are associated with message exchange. WS-Addressing decouples address information from the specific transport used by providing a mechanism to place the target, source, and other important address information directly within the Web service message. This specification defines XML elements to identify Web services endpoints and to secure end-to-end endpoint identification in messages. This specification enables messaging systems to support message transmission through networks that include processing nodes such as endpoint managers, firewalls, and gateways in a transport-neutral manner.

WS-Addressing defines two interoperable constructs that convey information that transport protocols and messaging systems typically provide. These constructs normalize this underlying information into a uniform format that can be processed independently of transport or application. These two constructs are *endpoint references* and *message information headers*.

 A Web services endpoint is a *referenceable* entity, processor, or resource in which Web services messages can be targeted. Endpoint references convey the information needed to identify/reference a Web services endpoint, and you can use them in several different ways. Endpoint references are suitable for conveying the information needed to access a Web services endpoint, but they also provide addresses for individual messages that are sent to and from Web services. To deal with this previous usage case, the WS-Addressing specification defines a family of message information headers that allows uniform addressing of messages independent of underlying transport. These message information headers convey end-to-end message characteristics, including addressing for *source* and *destination* endpoints and message *identity*.

Both of these constructs are designed to be extensible and reusable so that other specifications can build on and leverage endpoint references and message information headers. WS-Addressing is covered in detail in Chapter 5, "WS-Addressing."

3.4 Service Description

Service description defines *metadata* that fully describes the characteristics of services that are deployed on a network. This metadata is important, and it is fundamental to achieving the loose coupling that is associated with an SOA. It provides an abstract definition of the information that is necessary to deploy and interact with a service.

3.4.1 WSDL

Web Services Description Language (WSDL) is perhaps the most mature of metadata describing Web services. It allows developers to describe the "functional" characteristics of a Web service—what actions or functions the service performs in terms of the messages it receives and sends. WSDL offers a standard, language-agnostic view of services it offers to clients. It also provides noninvasive future-proofing for existing applications and services and allows interoperability across the various programming paradigms, including CORBA, J2EE, and .NET.

WSDL is an XML format for describing (network) services as a set of endpoints that operate on messages containing either document-oriented or procedure-oriented information. The operations and messages are described abstractly and then bound to a concrete network protocol and message format to define an end-point. Related concrete endpoints are combined into abstract endpoints (services). WSDL is extensible to allow description of endpoints and their messages regardless of what message formats or network protocols are used to communicate.

A WSDL document has two parts: *abstract definitions* and *concrete descriptions*. The abstract section defines SOAP messages in a language- and platform-independent manner. In contrast, the concrete descriptions define site-specific matters such as serialization.

WSDL provides support for a range of message interaction patterns. It supports one-way input messages that have no response, request/response, and one-way sends with or without a response. The last two patterns enable a service to specify other services that it needs. WSDL is discussed in detail in Chapter 6, "Web Services Description Language."

3.4.2 Policy

Although WSDL and XML Schema describe *what* a service can do by providing a definition of the business interface (including business operations such as open/close account, debit/credit/transfer, and so on), they do not provide information about how the service delivers its interface or what the service expects of the caller when it uses the service. *How* the service implements the business interface, the sort of permissions or constraints it expects of or provides to requesters, and what is expected or provided in a hosting environment is incredibly important in ensuring the correct interaction with and execution of the service. For example, does the service require security, and if so, what specific scope and type? Does it support transactions? What outcome protocols are supported? To achieve the promise of an SOA, it is important to extend the current Web service interface and message definitions to include the expression of the constraints and conditions that are associated with the use of a Web service.

Although you can use inherent extensibility of XML and WSDL to achieve some of these requirements, a much better approach is to define a common framework for Web services constraints and conditions that allows a clear and uniform articulation of the available options. Such a framework must enable those constraints and conditions associated with various domains (such as security, transactions, and reliable messaging) to be composeable, so that Web service providers and consumers are not burdened with multiple domain-specific mechanisms. Also, such a framework can provide support for determining valid intersections of constraints and conditions, where multiple choices are possible. Although the programming that is implementing the business logic of the Web service can deal explicitly with the conditions and constraints, providing a declarative model for this factors such issues out of business logic, thereby providing an important separation of concerns. This allows for more automated implementation by middleware and operating systems, resulting in significantly better reuse of application code by the organizations that provide, deploy, and support Web services. The *WS-Policy* family of Web services specifications provides an extensible framework that is intended to specifically deal with the definition of these constraints and conditions.

The *WS-PolicyAttachments* specification offers a flexible way to associate policy expressions with Web services. The *WS-Policy specification* defines a common framework for services to annotate their interface definitions to describe their service assurance qualities and requirements in the form of a machine-readable expression containing combinations of individual assertions. The WS-Policy framework also allows the use of algorithms to determine which concrete policies to apply when the requester, provider, and container support multiple options. WS-Policy is critical to achieving interoperability at the higher-level functional operation of the service. Security, transactions, reliable messaging, and other specifications require concrete WS-Policy schema. This allows services to describe the functional assurance that they expect from and provide to callers.

The WS-Policy specifications are discussed in detail in Chapter 7, "Web Services Policy."

3.5 Discovery Services

The transport, description, and messaging layer are fundamental to allowing Web services to communicate in an interoperable way using messages. However, to facilitate this, it is necessary to collect and store the important metadata that describes these services. The metadata must be in a form that is discoverable and searchable by users who are looking for appropriate services they require to solve some particular business problem. Also, such metadata aggregation and discovery services are a useful repository/registry in which many different organizations might want to publish the services that they host, describe the interfaces to their services, and enable domain-specific taxonomies of services.

3.5.1 UDDI

The *Universal Description and Discovery Interface* (UDDI) is a widely acknowledged specification of a Web service registry. It defines a metadata aggregation service and specifies protocols for querying and updating a common repository of Web services information. Solutions developers can query UDDI repositories at well-known locations at design time to ascertain those services that might be compatible with their requirements. After they locate a directory, they can send a series of query requests against the registry to acquire detailed information about Web services (such as who provides them and where they are hosted) and bindings to the implementation. They can then feed this information into an assortment of development time tools to generate the appropriate runtime software and messages required to invoke the required service. Solutions can also query UDDI repositories dynamically at runtime. In this scenario, the software that needs to use a service is told at execution time the type of service or interface it requires. Then it searches a UDDI repository for a service that meets its functional requirements, or a well-known partner provides it. The software then uses this information to dynamically access the service.

UDDI repositories can be provided in one of three ways:

- **Public UDDI**—These are UDDI repositories that can serve as a resource for Internet-based Web services. An example of this is the UDDI Business Registry [UBR]—hosted by a group of vendors led by IBM, Microsoft, and SAP—that is replicated across multiple hosting organizations.

- **Intra Enterprise UDDI**—An enterprise has a private internal UDDI repository that provides much more control over which service descriptions are allowed to be placed there and used by application developers within that specific enterprise.

- **Inter Enterprise UDDI**—This basically scopes the content of the UDDI to services that are shareable between specific business partners.

As discussed in Chapter 1, service discovery (publish/find) plays an important role in an SOA. You can achieve this in other ways, but within a Web services world, UDDI provides a highly functional and flexible standard approach to Web services discovery.

UDDI is covered in detail in Chapter 8, "UDDI."

3.5.2 MetaData Exchange

WS-Policy proposes a framework that extends the service description features that WSDL provides. Having more refined service descriptions, qualified by specific WS-policies, supports much more accurate discovery of services that are compatible with the business application that is to be deployed. In a service registry (such as a UDDI registry), queries of WS-Policy-decorated services enable the retrieval of services that support appropriate policies in addition to the required business interface. For example, a query might request all services that support the creditAuthorization WSDL interface (port type), use Kerberos for authentication, and have an explicitly stated privacy policy. This allows a service requester to select a service provider based on the quality of the interaction that delivers its business contracts.

Although service registries are important components of some Web services environments, it is often necessary to address the request of service information directly to the service itself. The *WS-MetaDataExchange* specification defines protocols that support the dynamic exchange of WS-Policy and other metadata that is relevant to the service interaction (such as XML Schema and WSDL descriptions) between interacting Web services endpoints. WS-MetadataExchange allows a service requester to ask a service provider directly for all or part of its metadata, without the involvement of a third-party registry. Using the WS-MetadataExchange protocol service, endpoints can exchange policies at runtime and use them to bootstrap their interaction from information about the settings and protocols to be applied. This is especially useful when not all policy information is in a repository or when a requester receives a reference to a service through some mechanism other than a direct query on a registry. This direct dynamic exchange of policies also supports the customization of each interaction based, for example, on the identity of the other endpoint or any other aspect of the context under which the interaction takes place. This flexibility allows Web services to be designed to offer different qualities of service for different targeted audiences.

WS-MetadataExchange is discussed in detail in Chapter 9, "Web Services Metadata Exchange."

3.6 Quality of Service

Specifications in this domain are related to the quality of the experience associated with interaction with a Web service. The services in this layer specify the requirements that are associated with the overall reliability of Web services. The specific issues involving this layer include security, reliability of message delivery, and support for transactions (guaranteeing and agreeing on the outcome of a business application).

3.6.1 WS-Security

Security is of fundamental concern in enterprise computing. *WS-Security* is the basic building block for secure Web services. Today, most distributed Web services rely on transport-level support for security functions (for example, HTTPS and BASIC-Auth authentication). These approaches to security provide a basic minimum for secure communication, and the level of function they provide is significantly less than that provided by existing middleware and distributed environments. WS-Security uses existing security models (such as Kerberos and X509). The specifications concretely define how to use the existing models in an interoperable way. Multihop, multiparty Web service computations cannot be secure without WS-Security.

Security relies on predefined trust relationships. Kerberos works because participants trust the Kerberos Key Distribution Center. Public Key Infrastructure (PKI) works because participants trust the root certificate authorities. *WS-Trust* defines an extensible model for setting up and verifying trust relationships. The key concept in WS-Trust is a *Security Token Service (STS)*. An STS is a distinguished Web service that issues, exchanges, and validates security tokens. WS-Trust allows Web services to set up and agree on which security servers they trust, and to rely on these servers.

Some Web service scenarios involve a short sporadic exchange of a few messages. WS-Security readily supports this model. Other scenarios involve long, multimessage conversations between the Web services. WS-Security also supports this model, but the solution is not optimal.

Protocols such as HTTP/S use public keys to perform a simple negotiation that defines conversation-specific keys. This key exchange allows more efficient security implementations and decreases the amount of information encrypted with a specific set of keys. *WS-SecureConversation* provides similar support for WS-Security. Participants often use WS-Security with public keys to start a conversation or session, and they use WS-SecureConversation to agree on session specific keys for signing and encrypting information.

WS-Federation allows a set of organizations to establish a single, virtual security domain. For example, a travel agent, an airline, and a hotel chain might set up such a federation. An end user who logs into any member of the federation has effectively logged into all of the members. WS-Federation defines several models for providing federated security through protocols between WS-Trust and WS-SecureConversation topologies. In addition, customers often have "properties" when they deal with an enterprise, and WS-Federation allows the setting up of a federated property space. This allows each participant to have secure controlled access to each member's property information about the end users.

The WS-Security family of specifications is discussed in detail in Chapters 12, "Security," and 13, "Advanced Security."

3.6.2 Reliable Messaging

In the Internet world, communication channels are typically unreliable. Connections break, messages fail to be delivered or are delivered more than once, and perhaps in a different sequence to that in which they were sent. Communication can become even more of an issue when the exchange of messages spans multiple transport layer connections. Although techniques for ensuring reliable delivery of messages are reasonably well understood and available in some messaging middleware products today (such as IBM WebsphereMQ), messaging reliability is still a problem. If messaging reliability is addressed by Web service developers who are incorporating techniques to deal with this directly into the services they develop, there is no guarantee that developers of different Web services will make the consistent choices about the approach to adopt. The outcome might not guarantee end-to-end reliable interoperable messaging. Even in cases in which the application developers defer dealing with the reliable messaging to messaging middleware, different middleware products from different suppliers do not necessarily offer a consistent approach to dealing with the problem. Again, this might preclude reliable message exchange between applications that are using different message-oriented middleware.

WS-ReliableMessaging addresses these issues and defines protocols that enable Web services to ensure reliable, interoperable exchange of messages with specified delivery assurances. The specification defines three basic assurances:

- **In-order delivery**—The messages are delivered in the same order in which they were sent.

- **At least once delivery**—Each message that is sent is delivered at least one time.

- **At most once delivery**—No duplicate messages are delivered.

You can combine these assurances to give additional ones. For example, combining at least once and at most once gives exactly one delivery of a message. The protocol enables messaging middleware vendors to ease application development and deployment for Web services by providing services that implement these protocols, possibly layered over their existing proprietary message exchange protocols. WS-Reliable Messaging protocols allow different operating and middleware systems to reliably exchange messages, thereby bridging different infrastructures into a single, logically complete, end-to-end model for Web services reliable messaging.

WS-ReliableMessaging is discussed in detail in Chapter 10, "Reliable Messaging."

3.6.3 Transactions

Dealing with many of today's business scenarios necessitates the development of applications that consist of multiple Web services exchanging many messages. An example might be a group of financial institutions setting up a financial offering that involves insurance policies, annuities, checking accounts, and brokerage accounts. Such applications can be complex, executing across heterogeneous, loosely coupled distributed systems that are prone to failure, and introducing significant reliability problems. For such applications, you must deal with the failure of any component Web service of the application within the context of the whole application. A coordinated orchestration of the outcome of the participating services that make up the business application is essential so that a coherent outcome of the whole business application can be agreed upon and guaranteed. Therefore, it is important that the Web services involved are able to do the following:

- Start new tasks, the execution and disposition of which are coordinated with other tasks.

■ Agree on the outcome of the computation. For example, does everyone agree that the financial packages were set up?

WS-Coordination, WS-AtomicTransaction, and *WS-BusinessActivity* define protocols that are designed specifically to address these requirements.

WS-Coordination is a general mechanism for initiating and agreeing on the outcome of multiparty, multimessage Web service tasks. WS-Coordination has three key elements:

■ **A coordination context**—This is a message element that is associated with exchanges during the interaction of Web services. This coordination context contains the WS-Addressing endpoint reference of a coordination service, in addition to the information that identifies the specific task being coordinated.

■ **A coordinator service**—This provides a service to start a coordinated task, terminate a coordinated task, allow participants to register in a task, and produce a coordination context that is part of all messages exchanged within a group of participants.

■ **An interface**—Participating services can use the interface to inform them of an outcome that all of the participants have agreed upon.

Although WS-Coordination is a general framework and capability, WS-AtomicTransaction and WS-BusinessActivity are two particular protocols that compose with and extend the WS-Coordination protocol to define specific ways to reach overall outcome agreement. They extend this framework to allow the participants in the distributed computation to determine outcome robustly .

WS-AtomicTransaction defines a specific set of protocols that plug into WS-Coordination to implement the traditional two-phase atomic ACID transaction protocols. However, traditional atomic transactions and the WS-AtomicTransaction protocol are not always suitable. For example, this protocol is generally not appropriate for use with many types of business transactions. Transaction protocols for business transactions have to deal with long-lived activities. These differ from atomic transactions in that such activities can take much longer to complete. Therefore, to minimize latency of access by other potential users of the resources being used by Web services participating in the activity, you need to make the results of interim operations visible to others before the overall activity has completed. In light of this, you can introduce mechanisms for fault and compensation handling to reverse the effects of tasks that were completed previously within a business activity (such as compensation or reconciliation). *WS-BusinessActivity* defines a specific set of protocols that plug into the WS-Coordination model to provide such long-running, compensation-based transaction protocols. For example, although WS-BPEL defines a transaction model for business processes, it is WS-BusinessActivity that specifies the corresponding protocol rendering. This, again, is an example for the composeability of the Web services specifications.

WS-Coordination and Transaction specifications are covered in detail in Chapter 11, "Transactions."

3.7 Service Components

The existing Web services standards do not provide for the definition of the business semantics of Web services. Today's Web services are isolated and opaque. Overcoming this isolation means connecting Web services and specifying how to jointly use collections (compositions) of Web services to realize much more comprehensive and complex functionality—typically referred to as a *business process*. A business process specifies the potential execution order of operations from a collection of Web services, the data that is shared between these composed Web services, which partners are involved, and how they are involved in the business process, joint exception handling for collections of Web services, and so on. This composition especially allows the specification of long-running transactions between composed Web services. Consistency and reliability are increased for Web services applications. Breaking this opaqueness of Web services means specifying usage constraints of operations of a collection of Web services and their joint behavior. This, too, is similar to specifying business processes.

3.7.1 Composition of Web Services

Business Process Execution Language for Web services (WS-BPEL, often short-ened to BPEL) provides a language to specify business processes and process states and how they relate to Web services. This includes specifying how a business process uses Web services to achieve its goal, and it includes specifying Web services that a business process provides. Business processes specified in BPEL are fully executable and are portable between BPEL-conformant tools and environments. A BPEL business process interoperates with the Web services of its partners, whether these Web services are realized based on BPEL or not. Finally, BPEL supports the specification of business protocols between partners and views on complex internal business processes.

BPEL supports the specification of a broad spectrum of business processes, from fully executable, complex business processes over more simple business proto-cols to usage constraints of Web services. It provides a long-running transaction model that allows increasing consistency and reliability of Web services appli-cations. Correlation mechanisms are supported that allow identifying statefull instances of business processes based on business properties. Partners and Web services can be dynamically bound based on service references.

WS-BPEL is discussed in detail in Chapter 14, "Modeling Business Processes: BPEL."

3.8 Composeability

One of the key guiding principles that has governed the specification of the Web services discussed in this book is that of *composeability*. Each of the Web service specifications addresses one specific concern and has a value in its own right, independently of any other specification. For example, developers of applica-tions can adopt reliable messaging to simplify development of their business application, use transactions as a method of guaranteeing a reliable outcome of their business application, or use BPEL to define their complex business applications. However, although each of these specifications stands on its own, all the specifications are designed to work seamlessly in conjunction with each other. The term *composeable* describes independent Web service specifications that you can readily combine to develop much more powerful capabilities. Composeability facilitates the incremental discovery and use of new services; consequently, developers must implement only that which is necessary at any given point in time. The complexity of a solution is a direct consequence of the specific problem that is being addressed.

The basic Web service specifications, WSDL and SOAP in particular, have been designed to support composition inherently. An important characteristic of a Web service is the multipart message structure. Such a structure facilitates the easy composition of new functionality. You can add extra message elements in support of new services in such a way that does not directly alter the processing of and pre-existing functionality. For example, you can add transaction protocol information to a message that already includes reliable messaging protocol information and vice versa without the protocols conflicting with each other, and in a way that is compatible with the pre-existing message structure.

```
 1 <S:Envelope...>
 2   <S:Header>
 3    <wsa:ReplyTo>
 4       <wsa:Address>http://business456.com/User12</wsa:Address>     ⎫
 5    </wsa:ReplyTo>                                                    ⎬ WS-Addressing
 6    <wsa:TO>HTTP://Fabrikam123.com/Traffic</wsa:To>                  │
 7    <wsa:Action>http://Fabrikam123.com/Traffic/Status</wsa:Action>  ⎭
 8    <wssec:security>
 9       <wssec:BinarySecurityToken                                  ⎫
10          ValueType="wssec:x509v3"                                 │
11          EncodingType="wssec:Base64Binary"   ⎬ WS-Security
12          dXJcY3TnYHB....Ujmi8eMTaW                                │
13       </wssec:BinarySecurityToken                                 ⎭
14    </wssec:Security>
15    <wsrm:Sequence>                                                            ⎫
16       <wsu:Identifier>http://Fabrikam123.com/seq1234</wsu:Identifier> ⎬ WS-Reliable Messaging
17       <wsrm:MessageNumber>10</wsrm:MessageNumber>                           │
18    </wsrm:Sequence>                                                          ⎭
19 </S:Header>
20 </S:Body>
 •   <app:TrafficStatus
 •     xmlns:env="http//highwaymon.org/payloads">
23          <road>520W</road>
24          <speed>3mph</speed>
25    </app:TrafficStatus>
26 </S:Body>
27 </S:Envelope>
```

Figure 3-2   Web service message composeability.

Figure 3.2 illustrates this by way of a simple Web service message that contains elements associated with three different Web services specifications. Lines 3–7 are associated with WS-Addressing, lines 8–14 with WS-Security, and lines 15–18 with WS-ReliableMessaging. Each of these elements is independent and can be incorporated and used independently without affecting the processing of other elements present. This enables transactions, security, and reliability of Web services to be defined in terms of composeable message elements.

A good example of the power of composeable Web services in practice is the requirement for service consumers to determine the assurances that are provided by a particular service that they might want to use. This enables the consumer to ascertain whether a particular service meets desired expectations, and if so, in what way. The services must document their requirements in terms of their specific support for transactions, security and reliable messaging, and so on. WS-Policy enables Web services to incrementally augment their WSDL in an independent way to provide a more complete and flexible description of elements that have to be added to the SOAP message to interact with the service successfully.

3.9 Interoperability

SOA and Web services promise significant benefits: reduced cost and complexity of connecting systems and businesses, increased choice of technology suppliers leading to reduced cost of technology ownership, and increased opportunities for businesses to interact both with customers and suppliers in new and profitable ways. The fundamental premise of Web services is that standardization, predicated on the promise of easy interoperability, resolves many of the long-standing issues facing businesses today. However, Web services and the SOAs that are based upon them are an emergent market. As such, the technologies and specifications that various organizations are defining for Web services are in flux. Issues relate to ambiguity of interpretation of specifications or standards, in addition to differences and insufficient understanding of interactions between them. For Web services to be successful, these specifications must be able to truly provide interoperability in a manner that is conducive to running a business or producing products that can effectively leverage Web services technology. The IT leaders behind the Web services specifications realize that interoperability is in the best interests of all industry participants. In 2002, they created the Web Services Interoperability Organization (WS-I).

3.9.1 WS-I

WS-I [WSI] is an open industry organization that is chartered to promote Web services interoperability across differing platforms, operating systems/middleware, programming languages, and tools. It works across the varied existing industry and standards organizations to respond to customer needs by providing guidance and best practices to help develop Web service solutions. Membership of WS-I is open to software vendors of all sizes, to their customers, and to any others who have interests in Web services. The work of WS-I is carried out by the members in WS-I working groups, generally consisting of individuals who have a diverse set of skills (developers, testers, business analysts, and so on). Members can actively participate in one or more WS-I working groups, based on their specific interest or expertise.

WS-I was formed specifically for the creation, promotion, and support of generic protocols for interoperable exchange of messages between Web services. Generic protocols are protocols that are independent of any actions necessary for secure, reliable, and efficient delivery. Interoperable in this context means suitable for and capable of being implemented and deployed onto multiple platforms. Among the deliverables that WS-I is creating are *profiles, testing tools, use case scenarios, and sample applications.*

A *profile* consists of a list of Web services specifications at specified version levels, along with recommended guidelines for use, or the exclusion of inadequately specified features. WS-I is developing a set of profiles that support interoperability. Profiles facilitate the discussion of Web service interoperability at a level of granularity for those people who have to make investment decisions about Web services and in particular Web services products. WS-I focuses on compatibility at the profile level. To avoid confusion, it is likely that only a few profiles will be defined. There is already a consensus on those standards that form the most basic Web services profile, and it is likely—although not manda-tory—that as additional profiles emerge, they will indeed be based on this basic profile. In addition to references to industry standards and emerging specifica-tions, a profile might contain interoperability guidelines that can resolve ambi-guities. Such guidelines constrain some of the specifications or standard MAYs and SHOULDs, often the source of interoperability problems, such that they become MUSTs or MUST NOTs to satisfy the requirements of the use cases and usage scenarios. The first, or *Basic*, WS-I profile pertains to the most basic Web services, such as XML Schema 1.0, SOAP 1.1, WSDL 1.1, and UDDI 2.0.

The *testing tools* monitor and analyze interactions with and between Web ser-vices to ensure that exchanged messages conform to the WS-I profile guide-lines. *Sample applications* are being developed to demonstrate the implementation of applications that are built from *Web Services Usage Scenarios*, which conform to a given set of profiles. Implementations of the same sample application on multiple platforms, using different languages and development tools, allow WS-I to show interoperability and provide readily usable resources for Web services developers and users.

WS-I is committed to building strong relationships and adopting specifications developed by a wide array of organizations, such as the Internet Engineering Task Force (IETF), Open Applications Group (OAGi), OASIS, OMG, UDDI, W3C, and many others. These organizations serve the needs of a vast range of communities and customer bases. It is the plan of WS-I to engage these groups and work together to meet the needs of Web services developers and customers.

3.10 REST

Despite the name, Web service technology offers several advantages in non-Web environments. For example, Web service technology facilitates the integra-tion of J2EE components with .NET components within an enterprise or department in a straightforward manner. But as shown, Web services can be implemented in Web environments, too, on top of basic Web technologies such as HTTP, Simple Mail Transfer Protocol (SMTP), and so on. Representational State Transfer (REST) is a specific architectural style introduced in [F00]. Simply put, it is the architecture of the Web.

Consequently, the question arises about how Web services compare to the Web, or how the corresponding underlying architectural styles SOA and REST compare.

3.10.1 "Representational" in REST

The basic concept of the REST architecture is that of a resource. A resource is any piece of information that you can identify uniquely. In REST, requesters and services exchange messages that typically contain both data and metadata. The data part of a message corresponds to the resource in a particular representation as described by the accompanying metadata (format), which might also contain additional processing directives. You can exchange a resource in multiple representations. Both communication partners might agree to a particular representation in advance.

For example, the data of a message might be information about the current weather in New York City (the resource). The data might be rendered as an HTML document, and the language in which this document is encoded might be German. This makes up the representation of the resource "current weather in New York City." The processing directives might indicate that the data should not be cached because it changes frequently.

3.10.2 "State Transfer" in REST

Services in REST do not maintain the state of an interaction with a requester; that is, if an interaction requires a state, all states must be part of the messages exchanged. By being stateless, services increase their reliability by simplifying recovery processing. (A failed service can recover quickly.) Furthermore, scalability of such services is improved because the services do not need to persist state and do not consume memory, representing active interactions. Both reliability and scalability are required properties of the Web. By following the REST architectural style, you can meet these requirements.

3.10.3 REST Interface Structure

REST assumes a simple interface to manipulate resources in a generic manner. This interface basically supports the create, retrieve, update, and delete (CRUD) method. The metadata of the corresponding messages contains the method name and the identifier of the resource that the method targets. Except for the retrieval method, the message includes a representation of the resource. Therefore, messages are self-describing.

Identifiers being included in the messages is fundamental in REST. It implies further benefits of this architectural style. For example, by making the identifier of the resource explicit, REST furnishes caching strategies at various levels and at proper intermediaries along the message path. An intermediary might determine that it has a valid copy of the target resource available at its side and can satisfy a retrieval request without passing the request further on. This contributes to the scalability of the overall environment.

If you are familiar with HTTP and URIs, you will certainly recognize how REST maps onto these technologies.

3.10.4 REST and Web Services

At its heart, the discussion of REST versus Web services revolves around the advantage and disadvantages of generic CRUD interfaces and custom-defined interfaces.

Proponents of REST argue against Web service technology because custom-defined Web service interfaces do not automatically result in reliability and scalability of the implementing Web services or cacheability of results, as discussed earlier. For example, caching is prohibited mainly because neither identifiers of resources nor the semantics of operations are made explicit in messages that represent Web service operations. Consequently, an intermediary cannot determine the target resource of a request message and whether a request represents a retrieval or an update of a resource. Thus, an intermediary cannot maintain its cache accordingly.

Proponents of Web service technology argue against REST because quality of service is only rudimentally addressed in REST. Scenarios in which SOA is applied require qualities of services such as reliable transport of messages, transactional interactions, and selective encryption of parts of the data exchanged. Furthermore, a particular message exchange between a requester and a service might be carried out in SOA over many different transport protocols along its message path—with transport protocols not even supported by the Web. Thus, the tight coupling of the Web architecture to HTTP (and a few other transport protocols) prohibits meeting this kind of end-to-end qualities of service requirement. Metadata that corresponds to qualities of services cannot—in contrast to what REST assumes—be expected as metadata of the transport protocols along the whole message path. Therefore, this metadata must be part of the payload of the messages. This is exactly what Web service technology addresses from the outset, especially via the header architecture of SOAP.

From an architectural perspective, it is not "either REST or Web services." Both technologies have areas of applicability. As a rule of thumb, REST is preferable in problem domains that are query intense or that require exchange of large grain chunks of data. SOA in general and Web service technology as described in this book in particular is preferable in areas that require asynchrony and various qualities of services. Finally, SOA-based custom interfaces enable straightforward creation of new services based on choreography.

You can even mix both architectural styles in a pure Web environment. For example, you can use a regular HTTP GET request to solicit a SOAP representation of a resource that the URL identifies and specifies in the HTTP message. In that manner, benefits from both approaches are combined. The combination allows use of the SOAP header architecture in the response message to built-in quality of service that HTTP does not support (such as partial encryption of the response). It also supports the benefits of REST, such as caching the SOAP response.

3.11 Scope of Applicability of SOA and Web Service

As indicated throughout the first three chapters of this book, Web service technology provides a uniform usage model for components/services, especially within the context of heterogeneous distributed environments. Web service technology also virtualizes resources (that is, components that are software artifacts or hardware artifacts). Both are achieved by shielding idiosyncrasies of the different environments that host those components. This shielding can occur by dynamically selecting and binding those components and by hiding the communication details to properly access those components.

Furthermore, interactions between a requester and a service might show configurable qualities of service, such as reliable message transport, transaction protection, message-level security, and so on. These qualities of services are not just ensured between two participants but between any number of participants in heterogeneous environments.

Given this focus, the question about the scope of applicability of SOA in general and Web service technology in particular is justified. As with most architectural questions, there is no crisp answer, no hard or fast rule to apply. Given this, common sense should prevail. For example:

- SOA is not cost effective for organizations that have small application portfolios or those whose new interface requirements are not enough to benefit from SOA.

- SOA does not benefit organizations that have relatively static application portfolios that are already fully interfaced.

- If integration of components within heterogeneous environments or dynamically changing component configurations is at the core of the problem being addressed, consider SOA and Web service technology. SOA offers potentially significant benefits to organizations with large application portfolios that undergo frequent change (lots of mergers and acquisitions or frequent switching of service providers).

- If reusability of a function (in the sense of making it available to all kinds of requesters) is important, providing the function as a Web service is a good approach.

- Currently, the XML footprint and parsing cost at both ends of a message exchange does take up time and resources. If high performance is the most important criterion for primary implementation, consider the use of Web service technology with care. Use of binary XML for interchange might help this, but currently there are no agreed-upon standards for this.

- Similarly, if the problem in hand is within a homogeneous environment, and interoperation with other external environments is not an issue, Web service technology might not have significant benefit.

3.12 Summary

This chapter provided a high-level overview and understanding of the structure and composition of a Web services platform. This overview was presented as a rendering of the fundamental concepts of service orientation that were introduced in Chapter 1, with a specific set of Web services specifications that IBM, Microsoft, and other significant industry partners developed. This platform represents the basic core of a new Web-based distributed computing platform that overcomes some of the problems of earlier distributed computing technologies. Although the platform is not complete, it certainly forms a viable foundation on which to build additional higher-level, value-added infrastructure and business services. It also seeks to address other aspects of a more complete distributed computing platform. Some additional potential future topics therefore may need to be addressed to provide this more complete platform, and these are covered in Chapters 17, "Conclusion," and 18, "Futures."

Part 2

Messaging Framework

This part of the book deals with the lowest layers of the Web services stack:

- SOAP

- WS-Addressing

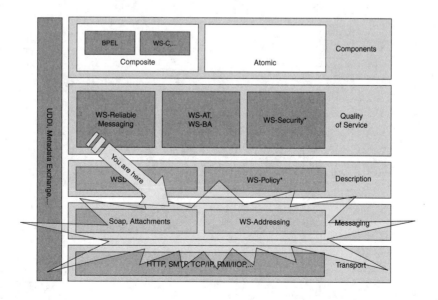

SOAP, discussed in Chapter 4, "SOAP," is the lingua franca of Web services. It is the message format that used to send Web services messages. SOAP is an XML-based format offering a simple message envelope structure that allows powerful features (described later in this book) to be built on top of it.

WS-Addressing, discussed in Chapter 5, "Web Services Addressing," gives SOAP a set of headers to route messages. The functionality that it offers is very much analogous to e-mail headers such as From, To, Subject, ReplyTo, and so on, incarnate as SOAP headers.

Chapter 4

SOAP

SOAP is the fundamental messaging framework for Web services. With SOAP, you can access Web services through loosely coupled infrastructure that provides significant resilience, scalability, and flexibility in deployment using different implementation technologies and network transports.

SOAP provides four main capabilities:

- A standardized message structure based on the XML Infoset

- A processing model that describes how a service should process the messages

- A mechanism to bind SOAP messages to different network transport protocols

- A way to attach non-XML encoded information to SOAP messages

Before discussing these capabilities, it's important to cover some of the history of SOAP.

4.1 A Brief History of SOAP

SOAP started off as the Simple Object Access Protocol, developed by Microsoft, Developmentor, and Userland. Subsequently, IBM and Lotus contributed to a revised specification that resulted in SOAP version 1.1 [SOAP 1.1] published in April 2000. This specification was widely accepted throughout industry and formed the basis of several open source interoperable implementations. WS-I.org adopted it as part of its basic profile.

The authors submitted the SOAP 1.1 specification to the World Wide Web Consortium (W3C) in May 2000, where it was treated as an input document for the formation of the XML Protocol (later becoming known as SOAP) Working Group in September 2000. The charter of this working group was to bring about the standardization of SOAP.

People were confused about what the SOAP acronym represented with several popular interpretations being used. In early deliberations, the working group decided that SOAP would no longer be an acronym; from then on, it was simply known as SOAP—period. The W3C working group finally produced the SOAP 1.2 Recommendation in June 2003. The Recommendation consisted of a primer [SOAP 1.2 Part 0], messaging framework [SOAP 1.2 Part 1], and adjuncts [SOAP 1.2 Part 2]. The working group has also developed specifications for attachments [MTOM], [XOP].

4.2 Architectural Concepts

The SOAP version 1.2 specifications—simply called SOAP for the rest of this chapter—introduce a set of concepts to describe the protocol together with the transmission and receiving of encapsulated data. First, it's important to define some of the terms that are used later on to describe SOAP in more detail.

4.2.1 Defining Some Terms

SOAP is a set of conventions that specify a message format together with a set of rules that govern the processing of the message as it passes along a message path. The conventions describe how a message is assembled and what interactions SOAP nodes processing SOAP messages along the message path can perform.

A SOAP message is the basic unit of communication between SOAP nodes. It consists of a SOAP envelope that contains zero or more SOAP headers. The SOAP headers are targeted at any SOAP receiver that might be on a SOAP message path. The SOAP envelope also contains a SOAP body that contains the message payload or business information. A SOAP body might contain, for example, a service request and input data for the service to process. While processing a SOAP message, a SOAP node might generate a fault condition. If this happens, a SOAP node returns a SOAP message containing a SOAP fault. These nested elements are illustrated in Figure 4-1.

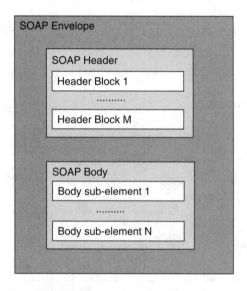

Figure 4-1   The nested elements of a SOAP message.

A SOAP node is an implementation of the processing rules described within the SOAP specification that can transmit, receive, process, or relay a SOAP message. Although the SOAP node implements the SOAP processing model, it can also access any services that underlying network protocols might provide. It does this through a SOAP binding that specifies the rules for carrying a SOAP message on top of some other underlying network protocol. These transport protocols might be other standards, such as HyperText Transport Protocol (HTTP), Simple Mail Transfer Prototol (SMTP), or Transmission Control Protocol (TCP). However, they might also include proprietary protocols, such as IBM WebSphereMQ.

SOAP nodes can send and receive SOAP messages. If a SOAP node transmits a message, it is called a SOAP sender; if it receives a message, it is called a SOAP receiver. Some SOAP nodes might both receive and transmit messages. In this case, they are called SOAP intermediaries. The SOAP sender that first builds the SOAP message is called the initial SOAP sender. The final destination of the message is called the ultimate SOAP receiver. This SOAP node is responsible for processing the payload of the message that is contained in the SOAP body.

Usually, a SOAP message passes through several SOAP nodes. An initial SOAP sender creates the message; the message then passes through various SOAP intermediaries before arriving at the ultimate SOAP receiver. This set of SOAP nodes is called a SOAP message path. In some cases, a SOAP message might not reach its intended ultimate SOAP receiver because the SOAP intermediary errs in processing the message. This is illustrated in Figure 4-2.

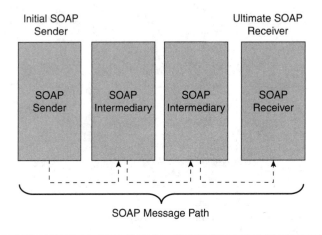

Figure 4-2   The SOAP message path.

4.2.2 The SOAP Processing Model

The SOAP message specification is expressed as an XML Infoset. This means that a SOAP sender has to create an Infoset that a SOAP receiver can reconstruct. To do this, the SOAP sender has to serialize the Infoset in a way that the SOAP receiver can use to reconstruct the original. The standard way of serializing is to use XML 1.0 syntax, but the specification allows other, potentially more optimized representations for more efficient network traffic. Any examples of SOAP messages used here employ the standard XML 1.0 syntax.

Let's start by looking at a basic SOAP message and its nested elements.

```
<env:Envelope xmlns:env="http://www.w3.org/2003/05/soap-envelope">
  <env:Header>
    <pns:qualityOfService xmlns:pns="http://example.org/qos">
      <pns:priority>3</pns:priority>
      <pns:timestamp>2004-02-25T01:00:00-00:00</pns:timestamp>
      <pns:persist>true</pns:persist>
    </pns:appHeaderBlock>
  </env:Header>
  <env:Body>
    <bmns:businessPO xmlns:env="http://example.org/po">
      <bmns:description>Widgets</bmns:description>
      <bmns:quantity>100</bmns:quantity>
      <bmns:price>20.5</bmns:price>
    </bmns:businessPO>
  </env:Body>
</env:Envelope>
```

The outermost element is the env:Envelope that includes the namespace URL for SOAP. Enclosed within this are two subelements that SOAP defines. These are the env:Header and env:Body elements. SOAP does not define their contents. The elements are specific to the application that creates and processes the SOAP message. However, the SOAP specification does define how a SOAP node processes these elements.

The env:Header element is optional in SOAP, but it has been included in the sample to illustrate its use. The SOAP header is an extension mechanism that provides a way for information to be passed within a SOAP message that is not part of the business message payload. In the previous example, the env:Header includes an immediate child element that contains a set of quality of service parameters. This immediate child is called a *header block* within the SOAP specification. A header can contain many header blocks. The header block has its own XML namespace in which the priority, timestamp, and persist elements appear. The SOAP specification allows header blocks to be targeted at specific SOAP nodes for processing as the message travels along its message path. The SOAP headers control and process a message as it moves along a message path. They include information that controls messaging qualities of service such as security, reliability, and addressing. By specifying new headers, you can create interoperable protocols based on SOAP. These form the basis of the services architecture. This is shown in the following example.

```
<env:Envelope xmlns:env="http://www.w3.org/2003/05/soap-envelope"

xmlns:wsa="http://schemas.xmlsoap.org/ws/2003/03/addressing"

xmlns:wssec="http://schemas.xmlsoap.org/ws/2002/04/secext"

xmlns:wsrm="http://schemas.xmlsoap.org/ws/2003/03/rm">
  <env:Header>
    <wsa:ReplyTo>

<wsa:Address>http://business456.com/User12</wsa:Address>
    </wsa:ReplyTo>
    <wsa:To>http://fabrikam123.com/Traffic</wsa:To>
    <wsa:Action>http://fabrikam123.com/Traffic/Status
</wsa:Action>
    <wssec:Security>
      <wssec:BinarySecurityToken
        ValueType="wssec:X509v3"
        EncodingType="wssec:Base64Binary">
        dWJzY3JpYmVyLVBic.....eFw0wMTEwMTAwMD
      </wssec:BinarySecurityToken>
    </wssec:Security>
    <wsrm:Sequence>

<wsu:Identifier>http:fabrikam123.com/seq1234</wsu:Identifier>
      <wsrm:MessageNumber>10</wsrm:MessageNumber>
    </wsrm:Sequence>
  </env:Header>
  <env:Body>
    <app:TrafficStatus xmlns:env="http://highwaymon.org/payloads">
      <road>520W</road>
      <speed>3MPH</speed>
    </app:TrafficStatus>
  </env:Body>
</env:Envelope>
```

The SOAP processing model means that you can use different service specifications, each with its own header definitions, to assemble a message that has more complex qualities of service. For example, a message that has to be delivered reliably, encrypted, and acknowledged can be composed with three headers, each with its own unique namespace. One defines the reliable delivery, the second defines the security mechanism, and the third requests an acknowledgement from the messaging middleware. The extensible SOAP structure and its processing rules allow the services architecture to be composeable in such a flexible way.

The application or middleware designer must architect header blocks within SOAP messages unless one is being used that is defined by an existing Web service specification. Any header should have a formal specification stating what the subelements are and how a SOAP node should process them with an appropriate role. The header specification should also define fault conditions that can occur, together with what impact they have on application-level processing.

The env:Body element within the SOAP message is mandatory. It contains the payload of the message, which is the information that is being transferred from the initial SOAP sender to the ultimate SOAP receiver. The choice of what information goes into the env:Header and what goes into the env:Body elements is a matter of business application and system design. In a typical enterprise environment, middleware that supports a defined set of service policies mandates what headers are required in a SOAP message. The env:Body is then used to contain necessary application-specific information, which is processed by the ultimate receiver of the remote service implemention.

4.2.3 SOAP Roles

When a SOAP node processes a SOAP message, the node is said to act in one of several roles. A SOAP role identifies how a SOAP node should process a message. A URI identifies the SOAP role. It might be one of the three roles within the SOAP specification or one that systems designers assign to meet the needs of some applications. It appears as an attribute on the parent header block element. Consider the following example.

```
<env:Envelope xmlns:env="http://www.w3.org/2003/05/soap-envelope">
  <env:Header>
    <hb1:firstHeaderBlock xmlns:hb1="http://example.org/hb1"
        env:role="http://example.org/Qos">
      .....
    </hb1:firstHeaderBlock>
    <hb2:secondHeaderBlock xmlns:hb1="http://example.org/hb2"
        env:role="http://www.w3.org/2003/05/soap-envelope/
➡role/next">
      .....
    </hb2:secondHeaderBlock>
    <hb3:thirdHeaderBlock xmlns:hb1="http://example.org/hb3">
      .....
    </hb3:thirdHeaderBlock>
```

```
  </env:Header>
  <env:Body>
    .....
  </env:Body>
</env:Envelope>
```

The hb1:firstHeaderBlock element in the example has a role attribute set to a value of http://example.org/Qos. The system designer assumes that the SOAP node that plays this role uses the information within the header block to manage message delivery quality of service in some specified way. The second header block hb2:secondHeaderBlock has its role attribute set to one of the roles defined within the SOAP specification. The specification defines three roles:

- http://www.w3.org/2003/05/soap-envelope/role/none

- http://www.w3.org/2003/05/soap-envelope/role/next

- http://www.w3.org/2003/05/soap-envelope/role/ultimateReceiver

If a header block has a role set to the "none" URI, no SOAP node should process the contents of the header block. Nodes might need to examine the header contents if another header block references them, but they should not be processed.

Every SOAP node must be capable of processing a header block with its role attribute set to the "next" URI, because this is a role that every node should assume. A header block with a role set to the "next" URI is one that the next SOAP node in the message path should examine and possibly process. In the previous example, the hb2:secondHeaderBlock has its role attribute set to "next."

Finally, a SOAP node that assumes the role of an ultimate SOAP receiver processes a header block with its role attribute set to the "ultimateReceiver" URI. A header block that has no role attribute is targeted at the SOAP node that is acting as an ultimate SOAP receiver. In the example, the hb3:thirdHeaderBlock is targeted at the ultimate SOAP receiver because it doesn't have a role attribute.

The SOAP env:Body doesn't have a role attribute. This is because the body element is always targeted at the SOAP node that assumes the "ultimateReceiver"
role. The SOAP specification says nothing about the structure of the env:Body
element. However, it does recommend that good XML design practices are employed so that, for example, subelements of the body are qualified for the XML
namespace.

Enforcing SOAP Roles—The "mustUnderstand" Attribute

Sometimes a SOAP node must process a particular header completely if it is
acting in that SOAP role. The SOAP specification signals this condition by introducing a "mustUnderstand" attribute that can be added to a header block.

```
<env:Envelope xmlns:env="http://www.w3.org/2003/05/soap-envelope">
  <env:Header>
    <hb1:firstHeaderBlock exmlns:hb1="http://example.org/hb1"
         env:role="http://example.org/Qos"
         env:mustUnderstand="true">
      .....
    </hb1:firstHeaderBlock>
    <hb2:secondHeaderBlock xmlns:hb1="http://example.org/hb2"
         env:role="http://www.w3.org/2003/05/soap-
envelope/role/next">
      .....
    </hb2:secondHeaderBlock>
    <hb3:thirdHeaderBlock xmlns:hb1="http://example.org/hb3">
      .....
    </hb3:thirdHeaderBlock>
  </env:Header>
  <env:Body>
    .....
  </env:Body>
</env:Envelope>
```

In the modified example, the SOAP node that is targeted by the
hb1:firstHeaderBlock element must process the header block because a
"mustUnderstand" attribute is set to true. This is commonly referred to as
a mandatory header block. The SOAP processing model states that processing
of a SOAP message must not start until a SOAP node has identified all the
mandatory header blocks targeted at it and is prepared to process them in
accordance with the specification for those header blocks. If a header block

has a "mustUnderstand" attribute set to false, or there is no such attribute, a SOAP node might choose to ignore and not process the header block, even though it might be targeted at it. If a header block has a "mustUnderstand" attribute and is targeted at a SOAP node, the SOAP node is obliged to generate and return a SOAP fault if it is unable to process the header block.

Passing Headers—The "relay" Attribute

The SOAP processing model states that a node that processes a header must remove it from the message before passing it to another node along the message path. This is because the SOAP specification errs on the side of caution, making sure that an intermediary makes no assumptions about what will happen to the message header it has processed later in the message path. The SOAP specification does, however, allow a node to reinsert a header into an outbound message with its contents unchanged or altered in some way, but the default behavior of the node is to remove the header after processing.

Sometimes, however, a systems designer wants a particular header to be targeted at any or all nodes within a message path. To allow this, SOAP introduces the "relay" attribute. If this attribute is set to true, a SOAP node that detects a header targeted at itself can forward the header block to the next node if it chooses not to process it.

```
<env:Envelope xmlns:env="http://www.w3.org/2003/05/soap-envelope">
  <env:Header>
    <hb1:firstHeaderBlock xmlns:hb1="http://example.org/hb1"
        env:role="http://example.org/Qos"
        env:mustUnderstand="true">
      .....
    </hb1:firstHeaderBlock>
    <hb2:secondHeaderBlock xmlns:hb1="http://example.org/hb2"
        env:role="http://www.w3.org/2003/05/
➥soap-envelope/role/next"
        env:relay="true">
      .....
    </hb2:secondHeaderBlock>
    <hb3:thirdHeaderBlock xmlns:hb1="http://example.org/hb3">
      .....
    </hb3:thirdHeaderBlock>
  </env:Header>
  <env:Body>
    .....
  </env:Body>
</env:Envelope>
```

In the previous example, the second header block is targeted at the "next" node in the message path. It also has the "role" attribute set to true. This means that a SOAP node that receives this message can process the header if it understands it. If it does so, the SOAP processing rules must be obeyed and the header removed before forwarding the entire message. A "role" attribute set to true means that the node, if it chooses to, can ignore the header block and forward it to the next node. Remember that if a header block also has the "mustUnderstand" attribute set to true, this over-rules a "relay," and the node must process the header block if it understands its meaning.

4.2.4 SOAP Faults

When an error occurs in processing a SOAP message, the specification provides a model for handling faults. The SOAP fault handling differentiates between the reasons that the fault occurred and the mechanisms that signal the presence of a fault. The signaling depends on the underlying transport mechanism. It is described in the SOAP binding specification.

SOAP fault information is placed within the env:Body element. All faults, both application and middleware generated, must use this structure. A sample SOAP fault is shown next.

```
<env:Envelope xmlns:env="http://www.w3.org/2003/05/soap-envelope"
              xmlns:flt="http://example.org/faults">
  <env:Body>
    <env:Fault>
      <env:Code>
        <env:Value>env:Receiver</env:Value>
        <env:Subcode>
          <env:Value>flt:BadValue</env:Value>
        </env:Subcode>
      </env:Code>
      <env:Reason>
        <env:Text>A Fault occurred</env:Text>
      </env:Reason>
      <env:Detail>
        <flt:MyDetails>
          <flt:Message>Something went wrong at the Receiver
➥</flt:Message>
          <flt:ErrorCode>1234</flt:ErrorCode>
        </flt:MyDetails>
      </env:Detail>
    </env:Fault>
  </env:Body>
</env:Envelope>
```

SOAP faults are reported within a single env:Fault element that is the child of the env:Body. The env:Fault element must contain two child elements: env:Code and env:Reason. It might also contain three other optional elements: env:Detail, env:Node, and env:Role.

The env:Code subelement must contain an env:Value that matches one of the five SOAP fault codes defined in part 1 of the specification. These codes are as follows:

- **VersionMismatch**—The message does not match the SOAP versioning mode.

- **MustUnderstand**—The targeted node does not understand its header in the message containing a "mustUnderstand" attribute.

- **DataEncodingUnknown**—The targeted node does not understand the message's data encoding.

- **Sender**—The message was incorrectly formed when a processing node received it.

- **Receiver**—The receiving node or ultimate SOAP receiver could not process the message.

You can further expand the env:Code element by using the optional env:Subcode element.

The env:Reason element within the fault structure is intended as a human-readable description rather than an element for automatic processing. If required, the env:Text element might contain language attributes to allow alternative national languages to be used for the fault text message.

The optional env:Detail element can contain namespace-qualified elements to provide additional information about the generated fault. Finally, the optional env:Node and env:Role elements can identify the URI of the node that generated the fault, along with its role.

4.2.5 Documents and RPC

SOAP supports two programming models: document literal and remote procedure call (RPC). For document literal, the env:Body contains a business document such as a purchase order or airline reservation that the requesting service
processes. After the service processes the document, it returns another document that might contain, for example, confirmation information that the order
or reservation has been completed. For RPC, the env:Body on a request message contains a procedure name to be invoked in addition to a set of encoded
arguments to the procedure. After the procedure has been invoked, a result and
a set of return values are returned.

Web services have standardized on the use of the document literal model.
For further information on the RPC model, look at the SOAP Primer [SOAP 1.2
Part 0].

4.2.6 Message Exchange Patterns

SOAP describes a one-way messaging model for transferring information between an initial SOAP sender and an ultimate SOAP receiver. The information is
described in terms of a SOAP Infoset that is created by the initial SOAP sender
and re-created by the ultimate SOAP receiver. For practical use, this simple one-
way model can be extended to provide more useful interactions between Web
services. These interactions are called message exchange patterns (MEPs).

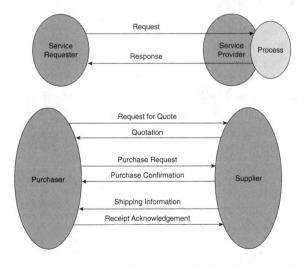

Figure 4-3   Message exchange patterns.

Request/Response MEP

Most Web services operate using the request/response MEP. In this pattern, a requesting service sends a message to a provider. The provider then processes the message and returns a response to the original requester. Because of the stateless nature of Web services, no "session" state is preserved, as in other network protocols such as HTTP. Therefore, the requesting service needs some way to correlate the response to the request that caused it. There are two possible solutions to this:

- Application-based correlation

- Middleware-based correlation

In the first solution, the correlation of requests and responses is carried out at the application level. This relies on the design of the business messages that are to be carried in the SOAP env:Body element. For example, a purchase order application might be designed that includes a unique purchase order number as an element within its document schema. The initial SOAP sender application sets the value of this element and sends it to the purchase order service that acts as the ultimate SOAP receiver. When the purchase order service assembles its response, it inserts the purchase order number from the request into the document. The purchase order service then becomes the initial SOAP sender to return its response to the originating service, which then acts as an ultimate SOAP recipient to receive the response. The original requester can then, using the purchase order number inserted in the response document, tie together the request and response.

In the second solution, an env:Header element in the SOAP message contains correlation information. This might be a header designed specifically for a particular set of applications or the Message Information Header elements defined as part of WS-Addressing. If WS-Addressing is used, a request message might have the following information in its headers:

```
<env:Envelope xmlns:env="http://www.w3.org/2003/05/soap-envelope"

xmlns:wsa="http://schemas.xml.org/ws/2004/03/addressing"
                xmlns:app="http://example.org/app">
  <env:Header>
    <wsa:MessageID>uuid:aaaabbbb-cccc-dddd-eeee-ffffffffffff
➥</wsa:MessageID>
```

```
    <wsa:ReplyTo>
        <wsa:Address>
           http://mybusiness.com/poRequest</wsa:Address
        </wsa:Address>
    </wsa:ReplyTo>
    .....
  </env:Header>
  <env:Body>
    .....
  </env:Body>
</env:Envelope>
```

The request message has a unique identifier that the wsa:MessageID element provides. It also has a wsa:ReplyTo element that identifies where response messages should be sent. The response message that the service provider generates is then structured as follows:

```
<env:Envelope xmlns:env="http://www.w3.org/2003/05/soap-envelope"

xmlns:wsa="http://schemas.xml.org/ws/2004/03/addressing"
                xmlns:app="http://example.org/app">
  <env:Header>
    <wsa:MessageID>uuid:uuuuvvvv-wwww-xxxx-yyyy-zzzzzzzzzzzz
➡</wsa:MessageID>
    <wsa:RelatesTo>uuid:aaaabbbb-cccc-dddd-eeee-ffffffffffff
➡</wsa:RelatesTo>
    .....
  </env:Header>
  <env:Body>
    .....
  </env:Body>
</env:Envelope>
```

In the response message, the wsa:RelatesTo element contains the wsa:MessageID of the request message that triggered the response, allowing the two messages to be related. The way that this correlation information is passed to the application layer depends on the interface between the Web services and application layers.

Long-Running Conversational MEP

Some business operations require more complex message exchanges between services than a single request/response. This can result in message exchanges that continue between two Web services for an extended period of time. These long-running conversational MEPs require additional correlation information to ensure that the state of the message is retained between the communicating services.

An example of a long-running conversational MEP might be a purchase order request and fulfillment process.

1. A purchaser requests a quotation for some items.

2. The supplier responds with a quotation.

3. The purchaser places an order against the quotation.

4. The supplier responds with a confirmation of the order.

5. Some time later, the supplier provides details of shipping information.

6. The purchaser acknowledges the receipt of the order to the purchaser.

Note that although most of the interchanges can be expressed as request/ response MEPs, the supplier initiates some interchanges (such as the supplier providing shipping information).

Just as with the request/response MEP, the application or the Web service middleware layers can be assigned the task of ensuring that all the messages in a long-running conversational MEP are managed correctly. These layers might need to differentiate many instances of a long-running conversation between the same two services. Therefore, it might be helpful to use a conversation identifier within the business document inside the SOAP env:Body element or a separate header containing a conversation identifier that is inserted in each SOAP message that is part of the conversation.

4.2.7 SOAP Bindings

So far, this book has only looked at the SOAP envelope and processing model. It hasn't considered how the message is transmitted over a network. This is where the SOAP binding specifications are used. They allow a SOAP message to be transmitted over different network protocols such as HTTP, e-mail, and proprietary transports such as IBM WebSphereMQ. The purpose of a particular binding specification is to define a serialization of the SOAP Infoset such that it can be conveyed to the next node in a message path and the Infoset can be reconstructed without loss of information.

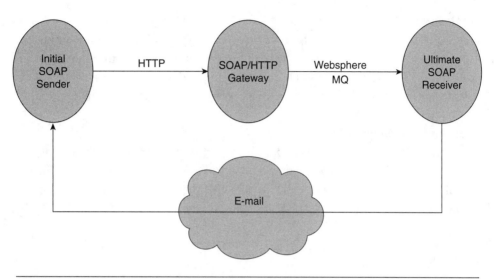

Figure 4-4   SOAP bindings.

A binding specification is valid only for a single hop between SOAP nodes, not the entire message path. A complete message path should be able to use the same binding specification, but it doesn't have to. The first hop might be to an HTTP server, so that will need the SOAP Infoset to be serialized and deserialized to and from HTTP. However, if the HTTP server is acting as an enterprise gateway, the SOAP message might continue along its message path using another network protocol such as IBM WebSphereMQ and a different binding mechanism. The important point is that the information that is held within the SOAP message Infoset is preserved as the message moves from node to node, regardless of how it is serialized at the network layer.

If the SOAP message is part of an MEP such as request/response, the request and response messages can be sent via different transport protocols. To extend the previous example, if the request is sent along a message path bound to HTTP for one hop and WebSphereMQ for another, the response can use another binding, such as e-mail. Remember that the information contained within the env:Body of a SOAP message is business application information and has nothing to do with the underlying network infrastructure. Therefore, a business scenario such as placing an order at a Web site and receiving an order confirmation by e-mail would match the example described previously.

SOAP and HTTP

The SOAP specification provides a normative binding to HTTP 1.1. In addition, it provides application designers with a SOAP Web method feature that supports the GET, POST, PUT, and DELETE operations described in the HTTP 1.1 specification. See the SOAP primer for a complete description of this binding.

SOAP and WebSphereMQ

This section shows how a nonstandard transport such as IBM WebSphereMQ can transport SOAP messages within a Web services infrastructure. It provides a reliable network transport mechanism for SOAP messages and has been implemented for either Apache Axis or Microsoft .NET environments.

Figure 4-5 shows how the WebSphere transport for SOAP fits into a Web services infrastructure.

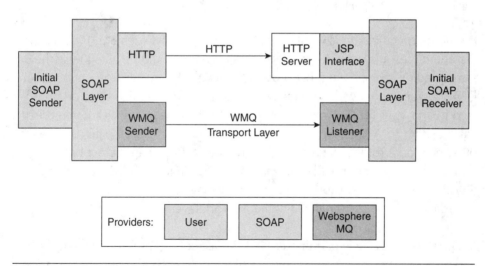

Figure 4-5   WebSphereMQ as a SOAP transport.

Considering the single-hop case in which HTTP is used as the network transport between an initial SOAP sender and the ultimate SOAP receiver, the sending application passes details of the required service invocation to its SOAP layer, which prepares a SOAP message for transmission. This message is sent to the server system, where an HTTP server receives the request and passes it through the SOAP layer for processing by the ultimate SOAP receiver. The response can be returned to the service requester either synchronously or asynchronously.

The WebSphereMQ transport provides an alternative network transport to HTTP, as shown in Figure 4-5. It provides an enhanced transport mechanism and allows Web services to be invoked over an existing WebSphereMQ infrastructure. The transport is implemented as plug-in modules that connect to the SOAP layer. The SOAP layer forwards the message via the WebSphereMQ transport whenever the target URI contains a wmq: protocol prefix in the target endpoint URI. The WMQ sender writes the SOAP request message to a WebSphereMQ request queue. A WMQ listener retrieves messages from the request queue, invokes the required service, and then passes any response back to the service requester via a WebSphereMQ response queue.

4.3 SOAP Attachments

In many use cases, applications need to send large amounts of binary data in a SOAP message. Binary data usually means nontextual information such as audio, images, or executables. Using the standardized serializations for SOAP, only characters that XML allows are permitted. Therefore, the only possible solution is to transform the binary data into characters using the Base64 content encoding scheme specified in the IETF RFC 2045. This solution has two major problems:

- Encoding and decoding between binary and characters take a long time.

- The message size increases substantially when the binary data is encoded as characters.

The result is degraded performance, particularly over low-bandwidth network links or when SOAP nodes have minimal processing power.

A solution to this problem is provided by two additional SOAP specifications: the SOAP Message Transmission Optimization Mechanism (MTOM) and the XML-binary Optimized Packaging (XOP). MTOM provides a way to identify any element information item in the SOAP message Infoset as a candidate for optimization. XOP specifies a way to serialize the various optimized elements and package them in the message to be transmitted.

To illustrate the use of MTOM, consider the following SOAP message Infoset:

```
<?xml version='1.0' ?>
<env:Envelope xmlns:env="http://www.w3.org/2003/05/soap-envelope">
 <env:Header>
   :::
 </env:Header>
 <env:Body>
  <m:myLogo
xmlns:m="http://example.org/logo">HNoem0KA893nbnmsWNms9HWMOmeoNSA
PSAAQbAQSbgUbA0WbAEZbAYbbAodbA8fbAAQkAQSkAgUkA0WkAEZkAYbkAodkA8fkAA
➡gtAQitAgkt
A0mtAEptAYrtAottA8vtAAg2AQi2Agk2A0m2AEp2nmsndkNSK678nnmsjkanwbrhjkr
➡eHJKDL8LKj
          :::
qG4dSiwpp2eK4LZLr6tuqTWump4H4xSz6G1dioPCqT5eWq5EtdUdJSSoYLAMjqasWYL
➡ZYmTOrz+o
7aJOt+aM9rWrxut4DAArILM9t0kShRgCFJaUk+uvAgshVRaPlXebGyv67APwKb9qw/r
➡0di/a6Cxn
1ELvZYABAsD==</m:myLogo>
          :::
    <p:myPhoto
xmlns:p="http://example.org/photos">HlkR4kTYMCgoAQMAAAA
AA8///ru6q/8zPzMzM/7v/CLsw6pne+4jPCIgACHcwFWYhBFUQBEQABDM
AEBAsAAAAAjAIKAAUw/gRRCFlmnopqrFHJvvNyyLw2Ji56789+/ADKcHia30iMpSEo
➡EobgKHDnS
          :::
w83hCNkr0gECT1bgEaJigpDmwFEvYOkDCgYQLMus1QDgFUYOoGGN+gtPdYYgOMDZLhw
➡yA+BHyDMR
qweAJoAgAcYHvzTQktoAsODhl4LYBIDMevgtHPUDiAmg5gSQTUB8ETxO1HKAJRj4OI7
➡0AMeKgriF
LOECAAwO=</p:myPhoto>
 </env:Body>
</env:Envelope>
```

In the message env:Body, two elements contain Base64 encoding of binary data. Element m:myLogo and p:myPhoto contain my logo and photograph, respectively. If these binary elements are small, it's all right to include them in the SOAP message. However, if the binary data is large (such as a set of medical images), it is necessary to find an alternative way of sending them via SOAP.

The SOAP processing model requires that a SOAP receiver reconstruct identically the Infoset that the SOAP sender generates. MTOM assumes that the receiving application requires the binary data and not the Base64 representation that is reflected in the Infoset. Therefore, MTOM provides an optimization feature that can bypass the Base64 encoding and decoding of binary data implied by the binary representation within an Infoset. To implement a SOAP feature, it's necessary to provide a protocol binding. MTOM provides an enhancement to the SOAP HTTP binding to transfer the optimized serialization. This enhancement is XOP.

The following example shows a SOAP message that is serialized using XOP.

```
MIME-Version: 1.0
Content-Type: Multipart/Related; boundary=example-boundary;
  type=application/xop+xml;
  start="<myInfo.xml@myCompany.example.org>";

startinfo="application/soap+xml;action=\"http://myCompany.
➡example.org/Action\""
Content-Description: Optimized SOAP message example

—example-boundary
Content-Type: application/xop+xml; charset=UTF-8
type="application/soap+xml;action=\"http://myCompany.example.org/
➡Action\""
Content-Transfer-Encoding: 8bit
Content-ID: myInfo.xml@myCompany.example.org>

<?xml version='1.0'?>
<env:Envelope xmlns:env="http://www.w3.org/2003/05/soap-envelope"
      xmlns:xmlmime='http://www.w3.org/2004/06/xmlmime'>
 <env:Body>
  <m:myLogo xmlns:m="http://example.org/logo"
      xmlmime:contentType='image/jpg'><xop:Include
xmlns:xop='http://www.w3.org/2003/12/xop/include'
       href="cid:logo.gif@myCompany.example.org"/>
  </m:myLogo>
     :::
  <p:myPhoto xmlns:p="http://example.org/photos"
      xmlmime:contentType="image/jpg"><xop:Include
xmlns:xop='http://www.w3.org/2003/12/xop/include'
          href="cid:johnPhoto.jpg@myCompany.example.org"/>
  </p:myPhoto>
 </env:Body>
</env:Envelope>
```

```
—example-boundary
Content-Type: image/jpg
Content-Transfer-Encoding: binary
Content-ID: <logo.gif@myCompany.example.org>

::: the binary data :::

—example-boundary
Content-Type: image/jpg
Content-Transfer-Encoding: binary
Content-ID: <johnPhoto.jpeg@myCompany.example.org>

::: the binary data :::

—example-boundary—
```

The MIME multipart/related package includes a compound document broken
into related parts. The root part of the document contains the original SOAP
message with one major difference. The Base64 encoded data is replaced by an
xop:Include element that points to other parts of the MIME package that include
the raw binary octets. It does this by referencing the content-id of the MIME part
with the binary data. This mechanism allows the costly encoding and decoding
between binary and Base64 to be eliminated.

4.4 Differences Between SOAP 1.1 and 1.2

The SOAP 1.2 Recommendation and SOAP 1.1 are different in a couple of
ways. The W3C working group has spent most of its time clarifying and compo-
nentizing SOAP. The SOAP 1.1 specification contained a processing model,
HTTP binding, a pattern for remote procedure calls (RPCs), and encoding all
within the same specification. This might have led implementers to believe that
SOAP was intended only for interacting with services over HTTP using RPC.
That is why the working group decided to restructure and extend the specification into a set of documents that underline the flexibility of SOAP and its usefulness for different use cases.

The resulting SOAP 1.2 Recommendation consists of three documents. The first,
Part 0, is a primer that reviews the complete SOAP Recommendation, including
the support for attachments. The second document, Part 1, describes the core

SOAP specification as a messaging framework. Part 1 describes the SOAP message in terms of the XML Infoset, together with its associated processing model. The use of the XML Infoset in describing the SOAP message allows the message structure to be documented without referring to its serialization. The messaging framework also describes SOAP's extensibility with a framework that allows SOAP bindings to be described to different underlying network protocols.

The third document, Part 2, contains the remainder of the specification as a set of optional features. This includes a description of a data model and encoding mechanism in addition to patterns for SOAP's use for RPC. The document then describes mechanisms for extending SOAP with further features and a framework for binding to network protocols. The core SOAP specification describes a one-way message, which is why the third part also includes descriptions of how to combine the one-way message into more complex message exchange patterns, such as request/reply. Finally, Part 2 includes a binding to HTTP as an example of a request/reply pattern.

This restructuring emphasizes the flexibility of SOAP and is intended to solve the perceived restrictions of the SOAP 1.1 specifications. For a detailed listing of the differences between SOAP 1.1 and 1.2, review section 6 of the SOAP 1.2 primer [SOAP 1.2 Part 0].

4.5 Summary

This chapter described SOAP, which is the underlying messaging framework for Web services. It covered the SOAP processing model and the way its extensibility mechanisms allow the specification of interoperable protocols. The extension mechanisms enable the specifications that underpin the Web service architecture to compose and process complex messages.

SOAP can be bound to different underlying transports, such as HTTP and IBM WebSphereMQ. This allows the deployment of the Web services architecture on a heterogeneous network and infrastructure. You can use SOAP messages to send large amounts of binary data by using an attachment mechanism.

Chapter 5

Web Services Addressing

SOAP introduces an extensible message format and a common processing model with the purpose of enabling different protocols and interaction patterns. Other specifications define, in a modular, composeable way, the additional artifacts and conventions required to support specific behaviors and protocols. First and foremost, mechanisms must be provided to ensure that messages are correctly delivered to the appropriate destination, or service endpoint. Web Services Addressing defines these mechanisms.

To provide these mechanisms, it's necessary to resolve at least two different problems. The first is how to identify Web service endpoints. Before this chapter can begin to discuss how the Web services infrastructure will direct messages to their destinations, one must understand how to represent such "destinations" using a certain XML dialect. This problem is more subtle than it might appear at first sight, when it's approached from a Web-only perspective, as opposed to a Web services or service-oriented perspective. That's because of the rich and dynamic nature of Web service interactions as compared to traditional Web requests. The second problem is how to communicate these endpoint identifiers (or "endpoint references") in the course of a Web services exchange. For example, how to encode endpoint references in a SOAP message as SOAP headers, and what is the precise meaning and processing model for those endpoint references? Here, again, the rich nature of the service-oriented interaction model calls for careful design.

The goal of the WS-Addressing specification is to provide the means to identify a Web service endpoint and a way to use such identifiers in SOAP messages for the delivery and exchange of messages between Web service providers and Web service requesters. Together, these two mechanisms define a simple yet powerful solution to the problem of how to address a Web service endpoint.

5.1 Addressing Web Services

In a first approach, one could build a simple solution to the addressing problem by using the mechanisms that the current Web architecture provides to identify and address Web "resources" (that is, Web pages and any other Web-accessible resource). This would essentially mean borrowing the addressing model used by the HyperText Transport Protocol (HTTP). A uniform resource identifier (URI) identifies a Web resource, and the HTTP protocol clearly defines how to use these identifiers to direct requests to the resource. This is a powerful and well-understood mechanism that supports the operation of the Web. Following this model, one could assign a unique URI to each service endpoint and use HTTP headers to encode any additional information required in the course of the interaction. There are, however, important differences between traditional Web interactions and Web services interactions, which render the URI-HTTP addressing and interaction model insufficient as a solution for the Web services addressing problem. Following are some important characteristics of Web services interactions to take into account when considering the addressing problem:

- Access to services is not limited to a single protocol. SOAP messages might be, and are likely to be, carried over protocols different from HTTP. These protocols can include proprietary messaging protocols. Several different protocols may even be used in the course of a single service interaction.

- Service interactions are not restricted to simple synchronous request-response exchanges. Typically, they involve asynchronous messages, too, and they are rich in quality of service properties, such as security and transactions.

■ Web services support business interactions that are typically long running and stateful. That is, they comprise several related message
exchanges over a potentially long period.

These characteristics are a direct reflection of the kind of real-world problems
that Web services intend to address. SOAP messages that one enterprise sends
to another are typically carried over different transport protocols along their
path. Initially sent by the originating application (possibly using a proprietary
protocol), these messages are transmitted over HTTP between the two enterprises and then delivered to the target application, possibly over a third protocol. Similarly, asynchronous interactions (over e-mail or other messaging
protocols), are a fact of the day-to-day interaction between businesses and their
customers. Existing messaging protocols already define a specific mechanism to
support the asynchrony of the interactions. For example, they provide reply-to
addresses for follow-up correspondence and allow for the identification of messages so that future responses can be correlated to the original message.

Note also that when business interactions are automated, quality of service
guarantees become essential. For example, it is necessary to ensure that transmission errors and application failure situations are appropriately addressed,
unauthorized access is prevented, confidentiality of the interaction adequately
protected, etc. In short, quality of service guarantees a fundamental aspect of
the interaction with a service endpoint, to an extent not found in regular Web
interactions.

The stateful character of business interactions is particularly important. Service
and business interactions usually comprise several interrelated message
exchanges with each of the involved parties. These messages are logically
related and are processed within a common context, even if they are not exchanged consecutively. The term used to describe this type of interaction is
stateful. Individual applications can manage themselves the stateful character of
a service interaction, but a cleaner and more efficient model results if the basic
interaction framework directly embeds support for stateful interactions.

URIs and the HTTP protocol have proven their value in supporting today's Web.
However, central as they are to the architecture of the Web, they were not designed to support rich, flexible interactions, such as the ones just described. The

requirement that can be derived from these characteristics is for an addressing mechanism that is protocol independent, well structured, aware of Web service metadata standards, and compatible with the SOAP messaging model.

5.2 Architectural Concepts

WS-Addressing defines two fundamental concepts: endpoint references as a general-purpose way of encoding the addressing information needed to reach service endpoints, and message information headers to support the use of endpoint references in addressing and exchanging Web service messages.

5.2.1 Endpoint References

An endpoint reference is a data structure that is defined to encapsulate all the information that is required to reach a service endpoint at runtime. A service endpoint in WS-Addressing is any potential source or destination of Web services messages. In view of this definition one can consider a Web Services Description Language (WSDL) port as a service endpoint. A WSDL port, however, is a descriptive abstraction that cannot (and, in fact, does not attempt to) capture the runtime character of service endpoints. The dynamic nature of service interactions often implies a more subtle relationship between the concepts of port and endpoint. In some cases, endpoints are dynamically generated and lack a WSDL description altogether. In other common situations, multiple endpoints share the same WSDL port representation, such as in the case of interactions with a service that provides the functions for processing multiple stateful resources. From the WS-Addressing point of view, a service endpoint maps to at most one WSDL port. As WSDL ports, endpoints can support at most one WSDL interface. Also, like WSDL ports (and with similar semantics), endpoints can have policies attached to them. On the other hand, endpoint references might carry additional runtime information (not present in the WSDL port definition) that is required to properly address and interact with an endpoint.

An endpoint reference contains two types of information: runtime information required for the interaction with the endpoint, and associated metadata. Runtime interaction information consists of three fields within an endpoint reference:

- A mandatory address field (or "address property" in the terminology of the WS-Addressing specification)—This is the only mandatory required field; its value is a URI that represents the address at which the service endpoint can be reached.

- A set of endpoint "reference properties"—These are information fields that are represented as XML elements; together with the endpoint address, they are used to help deliver messages to endpoint.

- A set of "reference parameters"—These are information fields, also represented as XML elements, which are necessary to successfully interact with the endpoint but are not required to identify the endpoint when routing messages to it. The endpoint issuer provides them to facilitate the interaction.

The runtime information in the endpoint reference supports the routing of messages to the endpoint. The issuer of the endpoint reference (typically the service-side middleware infrastructure) defines the runtime information within the endpoint reference. This information is otherwise opaque to consumer applications; that is, a consumer application should not attempt to introspect or interpret the runtime information contained within an endpoint reference it receives. Applications (usually the service requester middleware) are simply required to include these fields in messages that are addressed to the endpoint according to the specific data representation and protocol used. In the case of SOAP, the WS-Addressing specification defines how these properties are incorporated as headers of a SOAP message. SOAP binding is discussed later in this chapter (Section 5.2.4).

In addition to runtime information, an endpoint reference can include metadata associated with the endpoint. The metadata helps consuming applications configure their interaction with the endpoint. It has three fields:

- The qualified name of the port type that the endpoint supports. This is an optional field. It might be omitted either because it is undefined (that is, no WSDL port type definition of the interface of the endpoint is available) or because it is assumed that the consumer of the endpoint reference has this information available through some out-of-band mechanism.

- The WSDL service name (a qualified name) and port name that provide the static representation of the endpoint. Again, this is an optional field.

- Policies that are applicable to the endpoint, represented by an optional set of WS-Policy policy elements that need to be followed when interacting with the endpoint.

Following is an example of an endpoint reference:

```
<wsa:EndpointReference>
    <wsa:Address>http://www.example.com/stq</wsa:Address>
    <wsa:ReferenceProperties>
        <exp:customer-id>xgtopsnlk-0001<exp:customer-id>
    </wsa:ReferenceProperties>
    <wsa:ReferenceParameters>
        <exp:model-id>llp-11<exp:model-id>
    </wsa:ReferenceParameters>
    <wsa:PortType>tns:StockQuotePortType</wsa:PortType>
    <wsa:ServiceName PortName="StockQuotePort">
        tns:StockQuoteService
    </wsa:ServiceName>
</wsa:EndpointReference>
```

5.2.2 Comparing Endpoints

Among the runtime information included in an endpoint reference, the address and reference properties determine the message destination and the expected behavior of the endpoint. Two endpoint references with identical addresses and sets of reference properties must be assumed to represent the same endpoint in the sense that both point to the same location and follow the same behavior. In particular, both endpoints support the same interfaces and the same protocol binding and comply with the same policies. Thus, two endpoint references with different reference parameters represent the same endpoint as long as their address and reference properties match.

The runtime consequence of this distinction is that when the reference properties of an endpoint reference change, one must assume that a different set of polices applies to the endpoint, and the runtime infrastructure should make sure it has updated information about the applicable policy set for the new endpoint. One can accomplish this, for example, by using the metadata exchange service, described later in this book (see Chapter 9, "Web Services Metadata Exchange"). A change in the reference parameters does not imply a change in the set of applicable policies.

5.2.3 Message Information Headers

WS-Addressing introduces a set of message headers to allow messages to be directed to service endpoints and to provide the information necessary to support a rich bidirectional and asynchronous interaction. WS-Addressing explicitly recognizes the basic forms of interaction supported in WSDL 1.1 (one-way messages and request-reply interactions) and describes how message headers are used and processed in those cases. However, the use of WS-Addressing message headers is not limited to the two interactions and can support more complex message interactions as well.

Only two message headers are required on every message: one to identify the destination of the message, and a second one to indicate how to process the message:

- The "To" header contains the URI address of the target endpoint.

- The "Action" header contains a URI identifying the intent or semantics of the message.

Note that the identification of the target endpoint relies on the values of the endpoint reference properties as much as on the "To" URI address. If reference properties appear in the endpoint reference, they must be present on messages that are targeted to the endpoint. The way they appear on the message depends on the specific serialization (encoding) of the message. The next section presents the encoding rules that apply to SOAP messages. Not all endpoint references contain reference properties, however.

The "Action" header of a message identifies the message's intent. The content (body) of a message is described by a certain document type, typically an XML Schema definition, but this is not enough to uniquely identify its intent since one can use the same document type with different purposes. For example, one might use a "CustomerInformation" document in one interaction to create a new record in a customer database and to update an existing record in another. In both cases, the document that is contained in the body of the message is the same, but each message must be processed differently. The Action header contains a URI value that indicates how the sender of the message intended the message to be processed. In this example, messages that are sent as input to the

"CreateRecord" and "UpdateRecord" operations contain the same document type but carry different URI values in the Action header. This allows the receiving side to decide how to deal with messages that arrive at the endpoint.

The value of the Action URI is naturally related to the WSDL operation to which the message is related. In fact, because the Action URI indicates the intent of an individual message, it is naturally mapped to each of the messages that appear in the definition of a WSDL operation, rather than to the operation itself. Therefore, the input, output, and possible fault messages of a WSDL operation typically are assigned distinct, unique Action URIs. WS-Addressing provides two mechanisms to assign these URIs to the messages of a WSDL operation—one explicit and another implicit. WS-Addressing defines an attribute in the WS-Addressing namespace, "wsa:Action", which one can encode on the input, output, and fault elements of a WSDL operation definition to explicitly assign an Action value to them. The example that follows, from Section 3.3 of the WS-Addressing specification, shows how this is done.

```
<portType name="StockQuotePortType">
  <operation name="GetLastTradePrice">
    <input message="tns:GetTradePricesInput"
           wsa:Action="http://example.com/GetQuote"/>
    <output message="tns:GetTradePricesOutput"
           wsa:Action="http://example.com/Quote"/>
  </operation>
</portType>
```

To deal with WSDL documents that don't explicitly assign Action values to messages and to relieve WSDL authors from the burden of creating and encoding Action URIs for all their WSDL operation messages, WS-Addressing defines an implicit encoding scheme. When no explicit statement is made about the value of the Action URI for a message, it is implicitly assumed that the value is derived from a combination of the target namespace of the WSDL document and the port type and message names (the reader should refer to the WS-Addressing specification for a detailed definition of the corresponding algorithm to use for that purpose). If, in the preceding example, all the wsa:Action attributes were removed (and assuming the target namespace given next), the Action values for the input and output messages would be set by default to the following values:

```
Target namespace: http://www.example.com/wsdl/stockquote
  Input message Action:
http://www.example.com/wsdl/stockquote/StockQuotePortType/
GetLastTradePriceRequest
  Output message Action:
http://www.example.com/wsdl/stockquote/StockQuotePortType/
GetLastTradePriceResponse
```

- The "ReplyTo" header contains the endpoint to send reply messages. The reply message is required when the message is the request in a request-reply exchange; it is optional in other cases.

- The "FaultTo" header (should there be one) contains the endpoint where fault messages should be sent. If "FaultTo" is absent, one may use the ReplyTo endpoint instead.

- The "Source" endpoint indicates the endpoint that originated the message. The use of the Source header is optional in all cases, but it is useful in many situations, for example when no endpoint is explicitly provided to send replies to, or when it is different from the endpoint that originated the message. The Source header also allows the receiving endpoint to keep track of who is sending the message, regardless of who needs to receive the answer or whether there will be an answer at all.

Two additional headers are provided to allow defining relationships between individual messages.

- The "MessageId" header contains a URI value that uniquely identifies the message that carries it. Message identifiers make it possible to reference individual messages and define relationships between them. The MessageId field is only required when the message is the request in a request-reply exchange.

- The "RelatesTo" header contains a URI value that must be the MessageId of a previously exchanged message. It defines the current message relationship to the message that is being identified. The "RelationshipType" attribute in this header specifies what type of correlation between the two messages is being asserted.

The relationship type is represented by a qualified name. WS-Addressing defines one such relationship to be represented by the qualified name "wsa:Reply." It indicates that the message is the reply to a prior request, as part of a request-reply message exchange. Other relationship types will be defined in the future to support more complex relationships between messages derived from other message exchange patterns.

To illustrate how these headers are used together, this chapter examines how a service endpoint manipulates headers in the course of a request-reply interaction and uses the endpoint references provided in an incoming message to direct the response to the appropriate target. Before going into that, however, it's necessary to examine how to formulate a SOAP message addressed to an endpoint using the information contained in the endpoint reference.

5.2.4 Binding Endpoint References to SOAP Messages
WS-Addressing defines how to encode the fields of an endpoint reference as SOAP headers when directing a SOAP message to the endpoint. In the message one must only encode the runtime information from the endpoint reference:

1. The URI value of the Address field in the endpoint reference is copied as the value of the To header in the SOAP message.

2. Each reference property element is copied as an individual SOAP header.

3. Each reference parameter element is copied as an individual SOAP header.

The sender of the message (the "consumer" application for the endpoint reference) treats reference properties and parameters as opaque tokens and limits its manipulation to steps 2 and 3. On the receiving side, headers that originate from reference properties are extracted by the service middleware and used to route the message to the appropriate processing endpoints. Reference parameters are made available but are not required for routing. Even though reference properties are not identified as such on a SOAP message, they are always known to the receiving side, because the service middleware defines and encodes them when issuing the endpoint reference.

The relationship among the information in the endpoint reference, the WSDL definition, and the WS-Addressing message headers that appear in a SOAP message is illustrated in Figure 5-1.

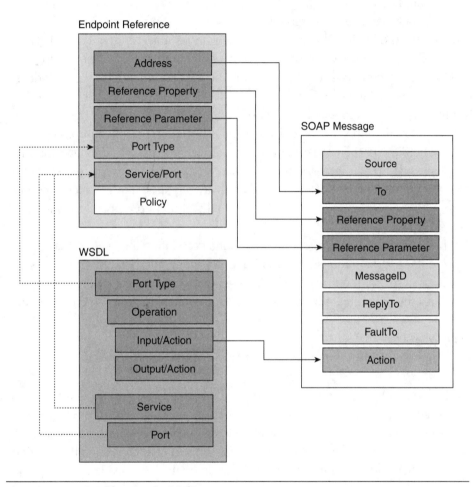

Figure 5-1   WS-Addressing in SOAP messages.

5.2.5 Request-Reply Pattern in WS-Addressing

Even though WS-Addressing can support many other message exchange patterns, the request-reply pattern is particularly prevalent. For that reason, the request-reply pattern is explicitly discussed in the WS-Addressing specification. The specification provides normative guidance for the encoding of the request and reply messages.

Request Message

In the formulation of a request message, the ReplyTo and MessageID headers are mandatory. A ReplyTo header is naturally required when asynchronous responses are needed to indicate where to send the asynchronous reply. In the case of synchronous request-reply interaction, the reply message is sent back through the open channel used by the synchronous transport (typically HTTP) to deliver the request. WS-Addressing requires that the ReplyTo header also be included in synchronous request-reply interactions and mandates the encoding of an endpoint reference whose address URI is a predefined URI introduced by the specification to represent anonymous endpoints. Although the ReplyTo header is strictly unnecessary in this case, the resulting simplification has significant value. One of the consequences is to allow the service middleware on the receiving side to infer from the message headers whether a reply is expected, permitting more efficient processing of one-way requests. (For instance, one may close a connection as soon as it is determined that that no reply is expected.)

The presence of a message identifier supports correlating the asynchronous reply to the original request. Again, although it's not strictly required in the synchronous case, the requirement provides a uniform model for all requests and simplifies the encoding at the requester side and processing at the provider side.

Reply Message

To formulate a reply, the endpoint must follow three mandatory steps:

1. Extract the ReplyTo endpoint reference and use its contents to address the new reply message. In the case of a SOAP message, the rules to map its contents of the endpoint reference to SOAP headers are the ones defined before: the Address field is copied into the To header, while all reference properties and parameters become additional SOAP headers.

2. The RelatesTo header must be included, and the message identifier of the request is copied as its value. This allows the correlation of the reply with the original request.

3. The RelationshipType field is set to a value of "wsa:Reply" indicating that the message is a response message to the one identified by the value of the RelatesTo header.

Figure 5-2 illustrates how rules map the information that is contained in the request message and the WSDL definition of the invoked operation into the reply message.

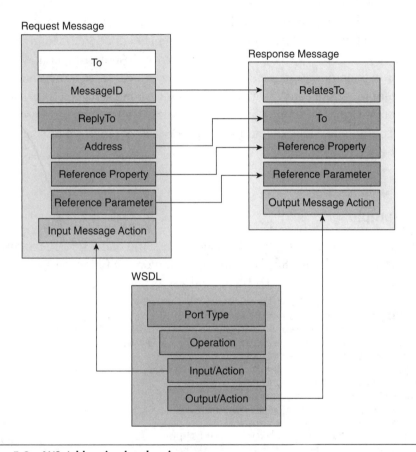

Figure 5-2   WS-Addressing headers in response messages.

One interesting consequence of WS-Addressing and its normative support for request-reply interactions is the introduction of a more dynamic model for service interactions. Consider a service that, according to its WSDL service description, offers a request-reply operation over a synchronous protocol such as HTTP. Requesters who invoked the service would assume that the service returned its responses over the open HTTP channel. Assuming WS-Addressing compliance implies that requesters now have full control over where and how the service will send its response. If the requester wants to receive the response in the traditional way, a ReplyTo header with the anonymous URI address would be encoded. However, if the requester encoded a different endpoint reference in the ReplyTo header, the service provider would accordingly change its usual behavior. Upon receiving the request, it would close the incoming HTTP connection, open a new one to the address encoded in the ReplyTo, and use it to send its reply message. The result is that WS-Addressing endows the requester with an unprecedented degree of control over service behavior, which might seem to violate the WSDL binding contract of the service. Of course, after a service states its support for WS-Addressing, users of the services must assume conformance with the normative processing of request-reply patterns as part of the service behaviors.

5.3 Example

As an example of the concepts just presented, assume that a service requester intends to invoke the "GetStockQuote" operation on the following endpoint reference:

```
<wsa:EndpointReference xmlns:exp="..." xmlns:tns="..."
xmlns:wsa="http://schemas.xmlsoap.org/ws/2004/08/addressing">
    <wsa:Address>http://www.example.com/stq</wsa:Address>
    <wsa:ReferenceProperties>
        <exp:customer-id>xgtopsnlk-0001<exp:customer-id>
    </wsa:ReferenceProperties>
    <wsa:ReferenceParameters>
        <exp:model-id>llp-11<exp:model-id>
    </wsa:ReferenceParameters>
    <wsa:PortType>tns:StockQuotePortType</wsa:PortType>
    <wsa:ServiceName PortName="StockQuotePort">
        tns:StockQuoteService
    </wsa:ServiceName>
</wsa:EndpointReference>
```

Using the information on the endpoint reference (Address, Reference Properties, and Reference Parameters) and the Action values encoded in the operation definition (as in the preceding example), a SOAP request message would be as follows (assuming that the port "StockQuotePort" provides a standard SOAP binding):

Example   101

```
<S:Envelope xmlns:S="http://www.w3.org/2003/05/soap-envelope"
xmlns:wsa="http://schemas.xmlsoap.org/ws/2004/08/addressing"
   xmlns:exp="... ">
   <S:Header>
     <wsa:MessageID>uuid:aaaabbbb-cccc-dddd-eeee-ffffffffffff
     </wsa:MessageID>
     <wsa:ReplyTo>
        <wsa:Address>
          http://stq-services.com/requester
        </wsa:Address>
     </wsa:ReplyTo>
     <wsa:To>http://www.example.com/stq</wsa:To>
     <wsa:Action>http://example.com/GetQuote</wsa:Action>
     <exp:model-id>llp-11<exp:model-id>
     <exp:customer-id>xgtopsnlk-0001<exp:customer-id>
   </S:Header>
   <S:Body>
   ... <!—ticker symbol —>
   </S:Body>
</S:Envelope>
```

Observe how the reference properties and parameters are serialized as SOAP
headers in the SOAP envelope. The response from the endpoint is formulated
using the values of the ReplyTo and MessageId headers in addition to the Action
for the output message provided by the WSDL definition of the operation. It
would be as follows:

```
<S:Envelope xmlns:S="http://www.w3.org/2003/05/soap-envelope"
xmlns:wsa="http://schemas.xmlsoap.org/ws/2004/08/addressing"
   xmlns:exp="... ">
   <S:Header>
     <wsa:RelatesTo> uuid:aaaabbbb-cccc-dddd-eeee-ffffffffffff
     </wsa:RelatesTo>
     <wsa:To>http://stq-services.com/requester</wsa:To>
     <wsa:Action>http://example.com/Quote</wsa:Action>
   </S:Header>
   <S:Body>
   ... <!—quote —>
   </S:Body>
</S:Envelope>
```

5.4 Future Directions

WS-Addressing is a base specification on which many of the most fundamental Web services protocols, described later in this book, must rely. For that reason, the stability of the specification is of paramount importance. No extensions or major modifications are expected. WS-Addressing has been submitted to the World Wide Web Consortium and will undergo a fast-track standardization process with the goal of producing a standard that is closely aligned with the current specification by the end of 2005.

5.5 Summary

The SOAP messaging model is the basic framework that supports runtime Web services interoperability. SOAP, however, does not define the mechanisms to unambiguously address messages to Web services endpoints, and it does not provide explicit support for rich service interactions such as asynchronous or stateful interactions. The WS-Addressing specification discussed in this chapter defines an Infoset representation of the information required to address service endpoints (the endpoint reference) and provides the rules and mechanisms needed to use that information (as headers in a SOAP message envelope) to support a rich set of services.

Part 3

Describing Metadata

This part of the book explains the technologies that are available for describing services. The immediate and pervasive nature of this metadata distinguishes the Web services platform from many other distributed computing systems. The figure that follows shows where you are in the Web services stack.

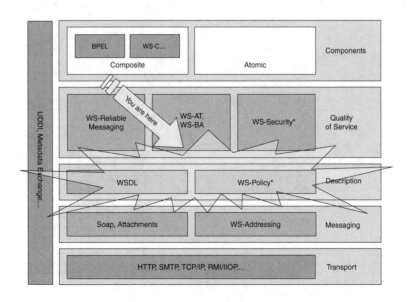

Chapter 6, "Web Services Description Language," discusses the Web Service Description Language (WSDL). WSDL allows you to describe a service in terms of what it does and then specify where the users of the service can locate it and how they should interact with it. This chapter discusses both the currently popular WSDL 1.1 version and the up-and-coming WSDL 2.0 version.

Chapter 7, "Web Services Policy," discusses the WS-Policy family of specifications. WS-Policy is a framework of specifications for defining and associating policies with Web service descriptions. The actual policies are domain specific, but the framework offers standard mechanisms to combine policies and to attach them to WSDL documents and other Web service components.

Chapter 6

Web Services Description Language (WSDL)

Web Services Description Language (WSDL) is in many ways what makes Web services interesting. Although SOAP is a message format that everyone understands in the Web services world, WSDL is what everyone uses to tell others what they can do.

WSDL is an XML vocabulary to describe Web services. It allows service authors to provide crucial information about the service so that others can use it. WSDL is designed to be highly extensible and adaptable to enable the description of services using different type systems (such as XML Schema, RelaxNG, or even Java) and services that communicate over SOAP and various other protocols (such as RMI/IIOP or in-memory calls).

A WSDL document consists of two parts: a reusable abstract part and a concrete part. The abstract part of WSDL describes the operational behavior of Web services by recounting the messages that go in and out from services. The concrete part of WSDL allows you to describe how and where to access a service implementation.

WSDL carefully does not cross into describing semantics of Web services. A WSDL document tells, in syntactic or structural terms, what messages go in and come out from a service. It does not provide information on what the semantics of that exchange are. That limitation was intentional in WSDL; semantic descriptions must be described in natural language or other evolving semantic description languages, such as DAML+OIL and OWL-S.

The World Wide Web Consortium (W3C) is standardizing the widely used version of WSDL, which is version 1.1. Although the standard version, 2.0, will be ready shortly, it probably won't become widely deployed for several years.

This chapter discusses both versions of WSDL, considering the differences between them and how to use WSDL in a future-proof manner.

6.1 Role of WSDL in WS-*/SOA

WSDL is the foundation of a set of specifications in the area of describing a service—that is, for capturing service metadata. As such, WSDL plays a critical role in enabling many of the advantages of Web services and service orientation, such as loose coupling and future proofing. In particular, designing systems around service contracts as defined by WSDL gives those systems flexibility to apply late or dynamic binding and overall looser coupling.

WSDL is used in Web services in two distinct scenarios:

- **Describing a service for its clients**—In this case, the WSDL document describes a published service for its clients. The description contains message declarations, operation or message exchange declarations, and the location of a service that processes those messages, in addition to mechanisms for interacting with that service. The primary purpose of WSDL in this scenario is to enable a client of that service to use that service effectively.

- **Describing a standard service for service implementors**—In this case, the WSDL documents a standard service. An example is a vertical market segment, such as manufacturers of automotive tires, getting together and agreeing on what the tire-buying service that is offered to car manufacturers looks like. After the message formats and the interactions involved with tire buying have been agreed to by the tire manufacturers, a WSDL document describes them. Then a specific tire manufacturer can start with that WSDL and offer the service, which results in another WSDL. This other WSDL plays the role of a WSDL from the previous scenario: Its clients (automotive manufacturers) can use it.

6.2 History

WSDL was created in one month in September 2000 by combining two service description languages: NASSL (Network Application Service Specification Language) from IBM and SDL (Service Description Language) from Microsoft. NASSL had a structure similar to WSDL in terms of an abstract part that was bound to specific concrete wire protocols and formats. However, NASSL was heavily focused on describing remote procedure call (RPC)–style interactions rather than message-oriented interactions. NASSL was focused on enabling not only XML-based interaction with a service, but also other formats and protocols, such as IIOP and in-memory method calls. NASSL did not constrain itself to what most people consider the Web, which is the graph of servers that support the HTTP protocol; rather, it wanted to support any network connected, accessible service.

SDL, on the other hand, had almost the opposite structure. A service that was offered over multiple protocols was described as if each was a completely different service, without a common underlying abstract service description. It was, however, much more message-centric than NASSL.

The combined language WSDL was designed to marry RPC and messaging while supporting multiple protocols and message formats. Details of WSDL and how that was achieved are discussed later in this chapter.

Since the release of WSDL 1.0 in September 2000, a slightly updated version, 1.1, was released later that year and submitted to the W3C for standardization in 2001. WSDL 1.1 is now widely used and is a *de facto* standard for describing Web services. The Web Service Description Working Group of the W3C is almost finished with a new version of WSDL. It will be called WSDL 2.0 to reflect the significant changes and improvements that have been incorporated to it.

6.3 Architectural Concepts

WSDL is designed around a few core concepts. These core concepts are discussed next.

6.3.1 Extensibility

It is easy to get carried away with a machine-processable language for describing a service. Some things are absolutely critical, such as the format of the data to be exchanged, the way those messages should be sent, and their destination. Going beyond such minimalist thinking, you could argue that a description language worth its weight should allow you to describe how much it costs to use the service, what the security characteristics are, and so on. The problem, of course, is where to stop.

WSDL avoids this problem by limiting itself to being a language to describe a few key aspects of a service: the message formats, the message interaction patterns, the way the messages should be represented "on the wire," and where those messages should be sent. Everything else is left out.

However, those elements are not omitted forever. WSDL (and, in fact, many of the Web services specifications) carefully supports the notion of extensibility. That is, someone who wants to indicate the price for using the service can do so with WSDL. He must invent the appropriate language syntax and insert it at the right place in WSDL. The problem of how to indicate the price for an arbitrary service is left for others to solve.

Thus, the principle of extensibility in WSDL has allowed it to be as tightly defined as possible without excluding many other (perfectly valid and interesting) description capabilities.

6.3.2 Support for Multiple Type Systems

Within the world of XML schema definition languages are several candidates, including Document Type Definitions (DTDs), W3C XML Schema, and RelaxNG. Today, W3C XML Schema is a W3C recommendation and clearly the dominant XML schema definition language. However, in the days of WSDL 1.0, XML Schema was still a work in progress, and an even wider array of choices was available.

Coming from the NASSL legacy, it was WSDL's intent to be able to describe services whose data representation had nothing to do with XML. WSDL has even been used to describe services offered by mainframe computers in which the data is structured using COBOL copybooks. It has also been used to describe services whose data is structured using the widely popular MIME type system. In such cases, describing the services by first generating an XML representation of the data and then describing the XML form is a secondary form of description.

WSDL holds as a fundamental tenet that the messages the service can consume or produce might be described in just about any schema (or structure definition) language. As illustrated later, this tenet is achieved by the flexibility that is de-signed into the <types> and <message> elements of WSDL 1.1 and the Description and Interface Operation components of WSDL 2.0.

At the same time, to support the creation of an interoperable universe of Web services, WSDL directly supports the W3C XML Schema language. If a service is to be offered for public consumption, it should be described using W3C XML Schema, because that greatly increases the likelihood that an interested consumer will understand the service description.

6.3.3 Unifying Messaging and RPC

The world of system integration can be broken down into two broad camps: those that believe distributed object systems are the key, and those that believe message-oriented middleware is the key. Web services, as a unifying integration architecture, has to support both. That is, the description language has to support describing services that are of the RPC flavor in addition to those that are of the messaging flavor. In addition to implications for how the messages are defined, this requirement brings additional complexity in terms of the kinds of interactions that occur between the client and the server.

RPC systems are rather straightforward to describe. They are perfectly good languages for describing such systems that exist in the form of OMG IDL and MS IDL, for example. Messaging systems by themselves are also relatively straightforward to describe. The challenge is to cover both in one language without being overly clumsy. WSDL 1.1 and 2.0 have taken different approaches in solving this problem. WSDL 1.1 uses the `<message>` construct, and WSDL 2.0 prefers to layer the RPC interaction as a pattern of usage of a pure message system. Later sections of this chapter explain these in some detail.

6.3.4 Separation of "What" from "How" and "Where"

The first thing a client needs to know about a service is what it does. Then it needs to know how to use a service and where it is offered. That is the basic principle behind the way WSDL is structured. It separates what the service does (expressed in the form of `<portType>` in WSDL 1.1 and `<interface>` in WSDL 2.0) from how the service is to be interacted with (expressed in the form of `<binding>` in WSDL 1.1 and 2.0) and where the service is offered (expressed in the form of `<port>` in WSDL 1.1 and `<endpoint>` in WSDL 2.0).

This separation allows one description of what a service does to be offered in different forms of interaction at different locations. By describing the service first in terms of what it does (which is called the abstract service description) and then in terms of how to interact with it and where it is available, you maximize the opportunity to reuse the abstract service description and even the description of how to interact with a service.

6.3.5 Support for Multiple Protocols and Transports

Although many people think of SOAP as the only message format in Web services, WSDL carefully supports multiple ways to interact with a service. For example, the same service might be available over SOAP messages sent via HTTP at one location and over RMI/IIOP messages sent over TCP at another location.

The `<binding>` construct of WSDL exists to support this separation. A binding tells how to access a service via a specific communication protocol. WSDL does not restrict the set of protocol and transport bindings. It provides an extensible architecture to support any number of them. Even the protocol and transport bindings that are part of the standard specification are expressed using this extension architecture.

6.3.6 No Ordering

Services that WSDL describes typically offer some number of operations. However, the description does not indicate in what order to execute the operations. For example, if the operations are to log in, execute a query, and log out, only the human semantics of those words indicate the order in which to invoke the operations.

Such ordering is sometimes called the *public process* or *abstract process* of the Web service. WSDL does not address that problem. Business Process Execution Language for Web services, or BPEL (see Chapter 14, "Modeling Business Processes: BPEL"), includes the concept of abstract processes, which you can use for this purpose.

6.3.7 No Semantics

The scope of WSDL as a language for describing services is carefully limited to expressing what the service does only at a structural level. There is no attempt to capture service semantics—that is, nothing is said about what the service does with the information that is sent. For example, if a service offers an operation called getQuote, just looking at the WSDL, you don't know whether this operation returns stock quotations, insurance quotations, or quotations for building a house.

The motivation for omitting semantics completely was that the field of semantic description is only at a research stage. What WSDL contains directly are things that are concrete and that have practical and well-defined usage patterns. Although semantic descriptions are omitted from WSDL accordingly, they are not left out forever because of extensibility.

6.4 WSDL 1.1

WSDL 1.1 is the *de facto* standard for describing Web services. Many vendors widely support it, both in development tools and in runtimes. After SOAP, WSDL is the most widely adopted Web services specification. This section first discusses the language structure of WSDL and presents some of the design rationale that went into it. Then it discusses the processing model for WSDL and offers some do's and don'ts as best practices for using WSDL 1.1.

6.4.1 Language Structure

WSDL documents typically contain two groups of definitions: an abstract part and a concrete part. The abstract part describes what the Web service does in terms of the messages it consumes and produces without considering how and where that service is offered. The "what" part of the description is covered by the `<types>`, `<message>`, and `<portType>` elements. The "how" and "where" parts are covered by the `<binding>` and `<service>` elements. Figure 6-1 summarizes the language syntax.

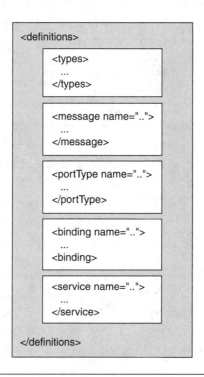

Figure 6-1   Syntactic structure of the WSDL 1.1 language.

A WSDL document consists of a set of definitions contained within a `<definitions>` element. The definitions define data structures (`<types>`), messages (`<message>`), interfaces (`<portType>`), bindings (`<binding>`), and services (`<service>`). The following sections consider each of these in some detail.

Definitions

Similar to XML Schema, a WSDL `<definitions>` element defines a bag of definitions for a single namespace, called the target namespace. The namespace is like an ownership or relationship assertion among the definitions within that document. Note that although the "targetNamespace" attribute is defined to be optional, you cannot really omit it for a nontrivial use of WSDL because omitting the namespace would make the definitions within `<definitions>` unreferenceable, even within the same document.

More than one definition's element might exist with the same value for the targetNamespace attribute, which demonstrates the idea that more than one physical document can define items for a single namespace. The "name" attribute of `<definitions>` was meant to distinguish a given collection of definitions for a namespace from another collection for the same namespace. However, because you cannot refer to that name while importing other WSDL documents, the name does not offer much value and has in fact been dropped in WSDL 2.0.

The items that can be described within `<definitions>` are messages, portTypes, bindings, and services. Note that a single `<definitions>` element can contain any number of portTypes. Therefore, it is possible for one organization to place all the portTypes offered by one entity (identified by the target namespace) within a single document.

Types

The `<types>` element is used to contain data structure declarations that are referred to later to define the messages that a service exchanges. Keeping to WSDL's design principle of minimality, WSDL does not define a data structure declaration language of its own. Instead, it uses extensibility to allow other languages to be used. Languages that can define XML data include XML Schema, RelaxNG, and DTDs. Languages that can define non-XML data include the MIME type system, OMG IDL, or COBOL copybooks.

For the case of XML Schema in particular, you can embed a schema directly by including an `<xsd:schema>` element inside `<types>`. The WSDL fragment that follows shows an element being declared inside the schema:

```
<types>
  <xsd:schema targetNamespace="http://foo.com"
        xmlns:xsd="http://www.w3.org/2001/XMLSchema">
   <element name="ServicePacValidationData">
    <complexType>
     <sequence>
       <element name="Header" type="ServicePacData:Header"/>
       <element maxOccurs="20" minOccurs="1"
            name="LineItemSegment"
            type="ServicePacData:LineItemSegment"/>
     </sequence>
    </complexType>
   </element>
  <xsd:schema>
</types>
```

If another type description language is used, you must employ an extension element to contain those definitions. Although this is how WSDL was designed, that capability is not often used. Instead, most users have utilized XML Schema as the type system language and converted whatever their native type system is to XML Schema. Although that is the most flexible in terms of understandability by consumers of the service (as more people will understand XML Schema), it is not the only way to WSDL.

Messages

The `<message>` construct allows you to describe the messages that the Web service is exchanging. In WSDL, messages can consist of one or more parts, where a part represents a single item that is to be sent or received. For example, a medical record that is sent from a hospital to an archiving service might include some information encoded in XML and a set of images representing X-Rays and other scans. A WSDL description of that message would have one part for the XML document and one part for each of the images.

Each part of a message must be described in some manner: whether the part is an XML document, an image, or a Java object. Thus, the general problem of describing a part is coupled to the language that defined data structures in the <types> element. Hence, the mechanism for describing parts is necessarily extensible.

Recognizing that XML Schema plays a central role in Web services, WSDL has built-in support for describing parts whose content was defined using XML Schema's top-level modeling constructs of global elements and complex types. To indicate that a message part is of a certain complex type, you must ensure that the optional attribute "type" is present on the <part> element. Similarly, to indicate that a message part is a certain global element, you must ensure that the optional attribute "element" is present on the <part> element. An example is given next:

```
<message name="ValidationMessage">
    <part name="count" type="xsd:int"/>
    <part name="items" type="tns:ItemType"/>
</message>
```

Although XML Schema support appears to be deeply integrated to <part>, it is actually an extension attribute of <part>. In fact, during WSDL's design, the designers considered whether to use an attribute from a namespace other than the WSDL namespace to indicate XML Schema–defined elements and attributes. However, given the expected widespread use of XML Schema, designers decided that option would be unnecessarily burdensome to users.

The design of <part> envisioned that if a type system other than XML Schema were used to define the structure of the part, a different extension attribute should be introduced to indicate the type of that part. For example, for a MIME part of type image/gif, the expectation was to use the following:

```
<part name="xray" mime:type="image/gif"/>
```

However, for describing MIME parts in particular, the usage did not go this way. In fact, even the WSDL 1.1 specification neglected to follow through with this design and used XML Schema to describe the content abstractly and employed the MIME binding to indicate that the part was sent or received over a MIME binding (such as SOAP with Attachments, as you will be see later in the "HTTP & MIME Binding" section). Instead of the `<message>` and `<part>` construct defining MIME-typed parts in a first-class manner as MIME-typed, the specification described the parts in XML Schema and used the binding to indicate their actual MIME types. The actual part would then be defined using the "type" or "element" attribute that referred to the mapped XML Schema description of the MIME-typed part.

PortTypes

A `<portType>` construct defines a set of related `<operation>`s that a Web service supports. As a processor of messages, there is nothing intrinsic to a Web service called an "operation." Instead, an operation is simply a grouping of a related set of messages that are exchanged. In WSDL 1.1, operations are named and defined by the messages that the service receives or sends; each operation can send or receive at most one message in each direction. Thus, WSDL 1.1 has four kinds of operations:

- **One-way**—A message comes to the service, and the service produces nothing in response.

- **Request-response**—A message comes to the service, and the service produces a message in response.

- **Solicit-response**—The service sends a message and gets a response back.

- **Notification**—The service sends a message and receives nothing in response.

The WSDL fragment that follows illustrates how these four kinds of operations are indicated in a WSDL document.

```
<portType name="p1">
    <operation name="op1">
        <input message="x:m1"/>
    </operation>
    <operation name="op2">
```

```
      <input message="x:m1"/>
      <output message="y:m2"/>
   </operation>
   <operation name="op3">
      <output message="x:m1"/>
      <input message="y:m2"/>
   </operation>
   <operation name="op4">
      <output message="x:m1"/>
   </operation>
</portType>
```

The first operation, op1, is a one-way operation; it declares an input message only. The second is a request-response operation; the server expects message x:m1 to be sent and responds with message y:m2. The third, op3, is a solicit-response operation; the server sends the message x:m1 and expects to receive a response of message y:m2. Finally, the fourth operation is a notification operation; the server sends the message x:m1 and does not expect a response.

The first two kinds of operations are sometimes called *inbound operations* because they are offered by the service and triggered by a message coming into the service. Similarly, the latter two are typically called *outbound operations*. Although WSDL 1.1 defined all four of these operations, only the inbound operations are fully supported. That's because the bindings that are defined by the specification only support those two styles. Outbound operations are not bound in the standard bindings in WSDL 1.1 because it's difficult for the server to decide where to send the outbound operations. With the advent of WS-Addressing (see Chapter 5, "WS-Addressing"), it is now possible to bind these properly.

A common confusion about WSDL is that request-response and solicit-response operations are automatically synchronous. In other words, the programming models that are suitable for using such operations and the bindings that are possible for such operations must be blocking and synchronous. However, no such assumption was made in WSDL 1.1's design. Request-response operations can be bound to asynchronous protocols such as SMTP and programmed either with a blocking style or a nonblocking callback style. In fact, it's not even assumed that the response will be sent back to the same party that sent the request. Bindings might offer mechanisms for a requester to direct responses to some other party. Thus, request-response operations are in many ways a composition of a one-way operation and a notification operation. They are composed to indicate that the application message pattern is such that the message is first received by the service (the one-way operation), and then it responds with the response message (the notification operation). Without this coupling, the service description would not be explicit about the ordering of the messages.

For request-response operations, the service might also indicate faults that can occur during the message exchange. Such faults are messages that might be sent in place of the response message if a faulty condition arises during the execution of the service. These faults are typically application-level faults and not infrastructure-level faults. Therefore, from the point of view of the Web service consumer, additional faults can occur because of infrastructure issues, such as network problems. It is not WSDL's intent to document all possible errors that might occur when invoking a Web service.

The WSDL 1.1 specification allows faults to be declared for solicit-response operations. However, no bindings are given for them, and it is not clear what such faults mean. Because the service generates faults, it is not immediately obvious why a service would send a fault to start an operation.

Bindings

The `<types>`, `<message>`, and `<portType>` constructs describe what a service does in terms of which messages are exchanged. The purpose of the `<binding>` element is to describe how to format those messages to interact with a particular service.

WSDL does not assume one standard way to format messages. Instead, it uses extensibility to define how to exchange messages using SOAP, HTTP, or MIME.

SOAP Binding

The SOAP binding of WSDL is an extension of WSDL that describes how to format the messages using SOAP 1.1. In summary, the SOAP binding specifies how to take the input or output `<message>` of an operation and create a SOAP envelope from it. To support the unification of describing message-oriented and RPC-oriented Web services, the binding introduces the concept of operation styles. The SOAP binding defines two operation styles:

- **Document style**—Document style basically means that all the parts of the `<message>` are directly inserted into the SOAP envelope as children of the `<Body>` element.

- **RPC style**—RPC style basically means that all the parts of the `<message>` are wrapped in some outer element representing the RPC. Then that resulting single wrapper element is inserted as the single child of SOAP's `<Body>` element.

The SOAP binding supports even greater flexibility by introducing the notion of encoding: the mapping of an abstract data structure definition into a concrete XML representation. Given that there are often many ways in which you can map an abstract structure into XML, the encoding style selects the appropriate mapping algorithm.

The following fragment shows a simple SOAP binding.

```
<binding name="ServicePacValidationBinding"
         type="tns:ServicePacValidationPortType">
   <soap:binding style="document"
          transport="http://schemas.xmlsoap.org/soap/http"/>
   <operation name="validateServicePac">
      <input>
         <soap:body use="literal"/>
      </input>
      <output>
         <soap:body use="literal"/>
      </output>
   </operation>
</binding>
```

HTTP & MIME Binding

The HTTP & MIME bindings that are defined by WSDL 1.1 allow you to bind a restricted set of portTypes to HTTP and MIME. The allowable set is restricted because not all XML structures can be easily represented in HTTP GET and POST operations.

The MIME binding assumes that the MIME parts have been described using XML Schema as Base64-encoded strings and then indicates how that is mapped to a MIME part. You can combine the HTTP and MIME bindings to form SOAP-with-Attachments-compatible SOAP messages.

Services

The `<service>` element in WSDL is the final part of a service description. It indicates where to find a service using its `<port>` element children. A single `<service>` can contain any number of `<port>` elements. Each `<port>` describes where a single portType is offered via a given binding. Thus, each `<port>` refers to a binding element by name and adds the address at which that binding is offered. The fragment next shows a simple `<service>`.

```
<service name="ServicePacValidationService">
   <port binding="tns:ServicePacValidationBinding"
         name="ServicePacValidationPort">
      <soap:address
           location="http://foo.com/services/SPVPort"/>
   </port>
</service>
```

6.4.2 Best Practices

WSDL 1.1 offers flexibility in how you can describe a service. Although that flexibility makes the language quite powerful, applying all of that flexibility can lead to interoperability problems. In particular, if a service is meant for public consumption, you must take into account specific considerations. If the service is to be used within a single organization, the organization can define the particular patterns of WSDL usage.

This is where the Web Services Interoperability Organization (WS-I) fits in. The role of WS-I is to define profiles of various Web service specifications to enable maximum interoperability. For WSDL, the WS-I Basic Profile [WS-I BP 1.0 in App. A] defines a set of constraints; adhering to them undoubtedly offers the greatest interoperability.

The specific requirements of the WS-I Basic Profile for WSDL include the use of only "literal" encodings with both document style and RPC style operations. Furthermore, for document style operations, the `<message>` constructs are required to have only one part. These rules were carefully constructed based on user experience and other interoperability problems. You should adhere to them unless the services are not meant for general public consumption.

Looking forward to WSDL 2.0, you should follow some additional constraints when using WSDL 1.1. In particular, WSDL 2.0 requires a service to implement exactly one interface. Thus, it is best to avoid defining WSDL 1.1 services with multiple ports when those ports offer different portTypes.

6.4.3 Problems and Limitations

Despite its phenomenal success in terms of wide adoption, WSDL 1.1 has several fundamental problems and limitations. Many of these issues are addressed in WSDL 2.0.

6.4.3.1 Messages

The problem with the `<message>` construct is that it was both too powerful and too weak simultanouesly.

One of the common requirements for describing services is to be able to say that a variable number of items needs to be sent or received. Unfortunately, the `<part>` mechanism of `<message>` doesn't support that. You can list only a fixed number of parts of a message. Another common need is to be able to indicate that a choice of responses exists. That is not supported by `<message>` either.

One of the main values of `<message>` and `<part>` was to enable description of parts in other systems, such as MIME. However, the WSDL specification neglected to use this mechanism to describe MIME parts.

To address these restrictions of `<message>` properly, you need to make it as functional as XML Schema's complexType construct. WSDL 2.0 solves this problem by doing away with `<message>` and `<part>` completely and using XML Schema constructs directly and carefully defining how other type systems will work.

6.4.3.2 SOAP Binding

The concept of operation styles and encodings has caused numerous difficulties for users. Originally created as a solution to bridge messaging-oriented and RPC-oriented service descriptions under one abstract form, SOAP binding has become a focal point of criticism against WSDL. This, too, is addressed in WSDL 2.0 by focusing only on "document/literal" style cases directly and allowing others to be built on top of that by convention.

6.4.3.3 Services

The problem with the `<service>` element is that it lacks clarity and crispness. When offering a service that has multiple interfaces, `<service>` offers no real guidelines as to whether to group all of it into one `<service>` element or multiple `<service>` elements within the same document. Furthermore, no semantics are given for the set of all ports that are found within a single `<service>` element. This leads to lack of interoperability because different people might choose differently.

6.5 WSDL v2.0

WSDL 1.1 was submitted to the W3C in late 2001, and the W3C Web Service Description Working Group was formed in early 2002 to standardize WSDL. WSDL 2.0 is the standard version of WSDL that the W3C is currently finalizing.

In many ways, WSDL 2.0 is a much simpler, less powerful, yet more usable service description language than WSDL 1.1.

6.5.1 Overall Language Structure

The basic structure of WSDL 2.0 is similar to WSDL 1.1, but it has some important and subtle differences. First, the language of 2.0 is defined in a syntax-independent manner using a WSDL component model. Although that does not directly affect end users of WSDL 2.0, it does affect tool builders and implementers. The overall syntactic structure is shown in Figure 6-2.

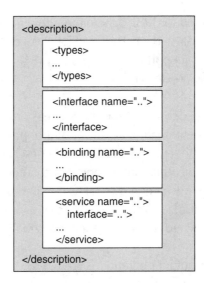

<description>

    <types>
    ...
    </types>

    <interface name="..">
    ...
    </interface>

    <binding name="..">
    ...
    </binding>

    <service name="..">
       interface="..">
    ...
    </service>

</description>

Figure 6-2   Syntactic structure of the WSDL 2.0 language.

A WSDL 2.0 document consists of a set of definitions contained within a
<description> element. The biggest immediate syntactic difference is the elim-
ination of the <message> construct. Instead, operation definitions now
directly refer to XML Schema element declarations. Some of the more important
changes are discussed in detail next.

6.5.2 Interface Extensions

Interface extensions in WSDL 2.0 allow you to define a new interface by extending one or more interfaces. This is similar to interface extensions in traditional object-oriented programming languages. One difference is that there is
no notion of overloaded operations. However, this feature is likely to be used
heavily, especially because of the change that a service must now implement
exactly one interface. (See Section 6.5.5.)

6.5.3 Elimination of <message>

The <message> problems were dealt with by eliminating that construct. Instead,
XML Schema global element declarations represent the information to be exchanged. Although that at first appears to support only XML structured data,

extensions are also defined for XML Schema to allow first-class description of binary formats, such as MIME data. Thus, WSDL 2.0's default data structuring mechanism provides full support for XML and MIME structured data. Other forms must be handled via extensibility.

Eliminating the `<message>` construct has made it easy to bind WSDL operations to SOAP messages, thus eliminating a major point of pain from WSDL 1.1. At the same time, RPC-style operations must now be described with a somewhat second-class form (by indicating that the input and output element schemas have been defined to follow a certain style) as compared to WSDL 1.1. That was a conscious trade-off made with the belief that as Web services evolves, it will be centered more toward document exchanges than RPCs.

An example of an input-output operation is shown next.

```
<interface name="ExampleInt">
    <operation name="op1">
        <input element="x:input-element"/>
        <output element="y:output-element"/>
    </operation>
</interface>
```

6.5.4 Message Exchange Patterns

WSDL 1.1 had somewhat arbitrarily chosen four message exchanges (one-way, request-response, output-only, and solicit-response) as the only interesting patterns of message exchange. In WSDL 2.0, this issue is completely clarified with the concept of message exchange patterns. An operation now conforms to a message exchange pattern and indicates one or more messages that will be sent or received during that exchange. The definition of the pattern indicates the order of the messages in addition to the source and destination.

WSDL 2.0 defines eight sets of patterns. However, only two are bound by the bindings included in the specification (in-only and in-out, which correspond to the one-way and request-response patterns of WSDL 1.1, respectively).

6.5.5 Services

Services in WSDL 2.0 have been defined with specific semantics to avoid the problems of WSDL 1.1. A service is now a collection of endpoints, in which all the endpoints implement the same single interface. An endpoint is what used to be called a port, but with cleaner semantics.

Restricting a service to support only one interface has given it strict semantics, but at the loss of some functionality. However, the introduction of interface extensions has recovered much of that loss.

An example of a service that offers an interface via two different bindings at two endpoints is given next.

```
<service name="ExampleService" interface="x:ExampleInt">
    <endpoint name="b1" binding="y:Binding1"
              address="http://foo.com/bar1"/>
    <endpoint name="b2" binding="z:Binding2"
              address="mailto:bar1.service@foo.com"/>
</service>
```

6.5.6 Features and Properties

Features and properties are a controversial feature of WSDL 2.0. Features and properties associate nonfunctional characteristics of a service description to its WSDL description. For example, features and properties can indicate that a service requires authentication or that its messages must be sent reliably.

The controversy arises because of overlap with the WS-Policy family of specifications. (See Chapter 7, "Web Services Policy.") The authors of WS-Policy feel that such characteristics go beyond WSDL and are beyond the scope for the WSDL working group to produce.

As WS-Policy moves toward standardization, this overlap of functionality is expected to be resolved in favor of the WS-Policy approach for describing nonfunctional characteristics.

6.6 Future Directions

With the completion of WSDL 2.0, it is unlikely that the WSDL specification will be further evolved. Of course, errata will be issued, but it is not expected that a version 3.0 is likely. Because WSDL is a base specification, changing it impacts many other specifications. Therefore, unless some unusual new requirement is identified in the future, it is unlikely that WSDL 2. 0 will be further developed.

Even the adoption of WSDL 2.0 will take some time because WSDL 1.1 is now firmly entrenched in the developer community. Almost every major software industry player now supports WSDL 1.1 in tooling and runtimes, and it will be a while before WSDL 2.0 replaces that. In fact, it is likely that something similar to HTTP adoption will happen here. WSDL 1.1 will probably never go away completely, just like HTTP 0.9 and 1.0 have never really gone away.

6.7 Summary

WSDL allows service authors to describe the key characteristics of their services so that others can use them. This chapter explained the underlying architectural concepts of WSDL and how they are realized in WSDL 1.1 and WSDL 2.0.

Chapter 7

Web Services Policy

There is a broad set of historical work in the area of computer systems and information policy. This includes different perspectives on how technical (IT) staff and business managers maintain and manage information systems. As the underlying technology evolves, so does the ability to use meta-information about those systems to help businesses and customers do more with the systems they have.

Much of the historical policy work has concentrated on the data management, systems configuration, and security areas. A business' need to manage the information and resources under its control often drives this focus. As businesses depend more on technology, their ability to control access to resources and enforce their administrative policies become central requirements. In a dynamic distributed environment, this includes the need to manage and distribute these policies only to authorized entities. Recently, government regulations have increased businesses' responsibility to protect consumer information from being distributed to third parties without the individual's consent. This new privacy legislation adds to the existing set of business requirements and introduces access to customer data (and metadata) as part of the information that is critical to the day-to-day management of the business.

In a service-oriented environment, service policies have a fundamental impact on interoperability. It's important to communicate to potential requesters any policies that a service provider enforces when those policies impact the interaction either because they require requesters to follow a specific behavior or a protocol or because they imply service-side behavior that impacts requester requirements or expectations (such as following a particular privacy policy). Service policies become a critical part of service descriptions, augmenting the basic WSDL functional description with a statement of nonfunctional service behaviors. As such, Web service policies support the development of service applications and provide the means to perform both development time and runtime service discovery and selection based on nonfunctional capabilities. For example, a service can be selected from among a list of functionally equivalent services based on its support for a specific privacy policy or the security guarantees it provides. The descriptive capability of policies, however, cannot be confined to services alone (although that will be the main focus of this chapter), but is required to annotate resources of different kinds, such as documents or document schemas.

The first set of Web Services Policy documents [WS-Policy, WS-PolicyAttachment, and WS-PolicyAssertions] was published in 2002. An updated set of two documents [WS-Policy and WS-PolicyAttachment] was published in September 2004. The modifications that were introduced into the new set clarify the processing and attachment models, while simplifying the policy syntax and defining how service policies can be represented and attached to services or resources in the context of the Web services framework. This chapter refers to these two specifications collectively as WS-Policy.

7.1 Motivation for WS-Policy

The need for an interoperable, standardized representation of nonfunctional capabilities and requirements of service endpoints should be clear, in view of the discussion in the previous section. It is necessary, however, that you understand why WS-Policy was created as a separate specification from WSDL, which already provides the basis for functional service descriptions. There are three major reasons for this.

First, there is the benefit of clearly separating concerns, avoiding a single monolithic specification to deal with all the diversity of service description information. WSDL has a clear focus on functional descriptions. Nonfunctional descriptions and quality of service aspects are naturally dealt with in a composeable, reusable specification, such as WS-Policy. Additional service description aspects, such as semantics, are best left to a different description language (such as OWL-S).

Second, the use of policies is not limited to service endpoints, but encompasses a variety of possible subjects, even when considering the service-oriented environment. XML documents, stateful resources of every kind, reliable messaging sessions, and so on can be legitimate subjects on which policies will need to be asserted to ensure interoperability among services. For this reason, WS-Policy strives to provide a flexible, extensible policy attachment mechanism for associating policies with subjects. WSDL is concerned only with service endpoints.

The flexibility of the attachment mechanism satisfies a third requirement that WSDL is not designed to support. That requirement involves representing the incremental addition of capabilities to an existing service. From a development and systems management perspective, it is common to incrementally modify a service offering by endowing it with additional capabilities available within a deployment environment. For example, confidentiality, authentication, support for reliable messaging protocols, and so on might be added to a service without impacting an application. In this way, services can be positioned to offer different qualities of service to different targeted audiences. In those cases, the service description also needs to be updated. WS-Policy Attachments provides support to flexibly add policies to preexisting services.

To fulfill this vision, WS-Policy must be able to encode capabilities and requirements that are derived from any discipline or application domain. Because of this, WS-Policy is intrinsically extensible, relying on discipline-specific assertions to represent discipline-specific properties, such as security policies, transaction policies, and business-specific policies. Domain experts, such as industry or standard groups, will define these domain dialects, which will then be used within the WS-Policy framework, leveraging a common, domain-independent processing model.

The simplicity of assertion expressions does not preclude additional semantics being defined for policy domains through technology such as Resource Description Framework (RDF) and the Web Ontology Language (OWL). The Web services community is interested in adding semantics to WSDL. Semantics for policy domains could also annotate policy assertions, allowing a policy container to aggregate a set of related assertions for a particular endpoint.

Web services policies are relevant in several scenarios. Following are three of particular relevance:

- **Development and deployment of interoperable service requester applications**—Together with WSDL, WS-Policy provides a declarative description of the requirements that services make on requesters, which guide the development and deployment of those applications.

- **Service discovery and selection**—WS-Policy descriptions enable service requesters to locate services based on their nonfunctional capabilities in addition to their functional properties. This way, it is possible to locate services that provide a given level of security or support for specific reliability guarantees.

- **Dynamic update of requester configuration**—Interacting endpoints can exchange policies using the WS-MetadataExchange port types. This way, services can update their configuration at runtime and customize each specific interaction. Requesters then retrieve updated policy information from the service provider and use it to reconfigure their runtime accordingly.

7.2 Architectural Concepts

The WS-Policy framework consists of two specifications: WS-Policy and WS-PolicyAttachment. The WS-Policy specification describes the grammar for expressing policy alternatives and composing them as combinations of domain assertions. The WS-Policy specification also describes the basic mechanisms for the merging of multiple policies that apply to a common subject and the intersection of policies to determine compatibility.

The WS-PolicyAttachment specification describes how to associate policies with a particular subject. It gives normative descriptions of how this applies in the context of WSDL and UDDI, and it provides an extensible mechanism for associating policies with arbitrary subjects through the expression of scopes. The next section explores attachment in more detail.

7.2.1 Policy Framework

A policy in the WS-PolicyFramework is the expression of a set of valid policy alternatives. Policy alternatives describe the acceptable combinations of constraints and requirements, which govern the interaction between a service and a requester or the access to a resource. A policy assertion represents each behavior (a discipline-specific constraint or requirement, such as following a reliable messaging protocol of encrypting messages). Therefore, a policy alternative is a combination of assertions, possibly from multiple disciplines. The policy does not specify to which subject the policy must be applied (the policy subject). It is merely a self-contained description of the constraints and requirements.

You can express the set of policy alternatives in a given policy in a compact form using policy operators, as described next. These choices enable you to group assertions or optionally include them within a group. You then define a normative algorithm for the translation of an arbitrary policy into its normal or enumerated form to facilitate the intersection of policy sets to find viable policy options for two parties that are trying to determine if they have comparable policies.

The Policy Container

The primary component of the WS-Policy Framework is the policy container, which is represented by the Policy element. This element is a container for collections of assertions or combinations of assertions that represent a set of valid policy alternatives. Assertions are combined through policy operators. Policies can be named using the Id attribute to enable referencing and reuse.

Policy Operators

The WS-Policy specification defines two operators and a modifying attribute to enable policy authors to group assertions into valid combinations.

ExactlyOne Operator

This operator means that one—and only one—of its contained assertions or operators might be considered as part of an alternative at any one time. Consider the following:

```
<wsp:Policy>
   <wsp:ExactlyOne>
       <wsse:SecurityToken>
           <wsse:TokenType
               wsse:x509v3
           </wsse:TokenType
       </wsse:SecurityToken>
       <wsse:SecurityToken>
           <wsse:TokenType>
               wsse:kerberosV5TGT
           </wsse:TokenType>
       </wsse:SecurityToken>
   </wsp:ExactlyOne>
</wsp:Policy>
```

This policy represents two valid policy alternatives: one that specifies the constraint that an X.509 security token needs to be presented, and another that specifies the constraint that a Kerberos token needs to be presented. No policy alternative allows both tokens to be presented simultaneously.

All Operator

This operator is a simple aggregation of assertions. All children must be considered part of the combined behavior.

As an example, consider the following policy.

```
<wsp:Policy>
   <wsp:All>
       <wsse:SecurityToken>
           <wsse:TokenType>wsse:x509v3</wsse:TokenType>
       </wsse:SecurityToken>
       <wsrm:RMAssertions>
           ......
       </wsrm:RMAssertions>
   </wsp:All>
</wsp:Policy>
```

This policy has a single valid policy alternative. This alternative combines reliable messaging behavior with the requirement to present an X509 security token.

"Optional" Operator

This attribute is encoded on policy assertions to indicate that the inclusion of an assertion in the combined behaviors is optional.

```
<wsp:Policy>
<wsse:Integrity wsp:optional="true">
...
</wsse:Integrity>
</wsp:Policy>
```

Here, the policy contains two valid policy alternatives: one that includes the use of a digital signature, and one that does not (and does not specify additional behavior). The absence of the optional attribute has the default interpretation of optional="false." In other words, the assertion is required.

You can include the use of these operators and optional attributes in various combinations within a policy by nesting assertions and operators inside another operator. A policy is said to be in "normal form" when it is composed of a single ExactlyOne operator containing one or more All operators. Every policy in normal form follows this template. The WS-Policy specification describes the rules for converting a policy into normal form.

```
<wsp:Policy>
<wsp:ExactlyOne>
<wsp:All>...<wsp:All> +
</wsp:ExactlyOne>
</wsp:Policy>
```

In a normal form policy, each valid policy alternative is contained within an All element, and all of the alternatives are contained under a single ExactlyOne operator. This means you can choose only one alternative, and that alternative is a complete expression of the combined behaviors. In other words, where any particular assertion included in the policy appears in an alternative, you must apply its behavior, and where it does not appear in an alternative, you must not apply its behavior.

The WS-Policy specification defines a normative algorithm for translating any policy expression into a normal form policy. The meaning of a policy as a collection of alternatives is defined by its corresponding normal form, as defined by the normative transformation algorithm. An example of such a transform is illustrated next, using fictitious assertions A, B, C, and D.

```
<wsp:Policy>
    <A/>
    <B optional=true>
    <wsp:ExactlyOne>
            <C/>
            <D/>
    </wsp:ExactlyOne>
</wsp:Policy>
```

The normal form is as follows:

```
<wsp:Policy>
  <wsp:ExactlyOne>
            <wsp:All> <A/> <B/> <C/> </wsp:All>
            <wsp:All> <A/> <C/>      </wsp:All>
            <wsp:All> <A/> <B/> <D/> </wsp:All>
            <wsp:All> <A/> <D/>      </wsp:All>
  </wsp:ExactlyOne>
</wsp:Policy>
```

Policy Vocabulary

The vocabulary of a policy is the set of all assertions that appear in the policy. Every assertion that is declared in a policy is considered part of the policy's overall vocabulary. For instance, in the last example of the previous section, the vocabulary of the policy would include assertions A, B, C, and D. As policies are merged through inclusion or through attachment to a common policy subject, so, too, are their vocabularies.

Because the vocabulary represents all the behaviors that the policy, considered as a whole, is making a statement about, each policy alternative is cast within this context. Consequently, each alternative is making an explicit statement of which behaviors within the vocabulary are part of the alternative, and (implicitly through their absence) which behaviors are not. This is the absence is negation rule of policy expressions.

It is important to note, however, that policies make no statement about behaviors whose assertions are not part of the policy vocabulary (because they are never mentioned in the policy). When intersecting policies to determine compatibility, the "absence is negation" rule applies within the scope of the policy's vocabulary.

Policy Identification and Inclusion

You can name policies using the wsp:Id attribute on the policy that is contained. Policy identifiers are unique absolute URIs. You need to assign an identifier to a policy so that other documents and definitions can reference it.

You need to reference policies in two main situations. In the first one, the contents of a policy expression can be embedded into a new policy by reference, using the PolicyReference element. The policy reference element is used within a Policy container; it carries the URI of the policy to be included, and its semantics are equivalent to textual substitution of the PolicyReference element by the contents of the included policy.

PolicyReference provides a means of aggregating policies, and it supports modularizing complex policy definitions into reusable policies that represent individual disciplines or concerns. For example, for manageability purposes, a service provider might find it desirable to model its separate quality of service domains, such as security, transactions, and reliability, as separate policies. A service provider can then combine these separate domains as required for each deployed service by including the appropriate policies under a single policy container.

Policy identifiers are also required when policies are attached to specific policy subjects. The different attachment mechanisms are discussed in more detail in section 7.2.2.

Policy Intersection

The intersection of policies is defined in the WS-PolicyFramework specification as a mechanism to help determine the potential compatibility between two policies. This situation arises every time the policies of a service need to be checked against the capabilities or requirements of the service requester. For instance, during the service discovery phase, a potential service user can express his quality of service requirements in the form of a policy that services need to support. Although an exact match might not be possible (between the policy advertised by the service and the one representing the requester's requirements), the question arises of whether there is a set of compatible settings that both policies support. That alone would be enough to support the interaction from the quality of service compatibility point of view. By inspecting the structure of the two policies, you can determine whether such a compatible set might exist. The process by which this determination is done is called *policy intersection*, because it involves identifying the set of policy alternatives that appear in both policies. You cannot decide on actual compatibility by the intersection of policies alone; intersection simply discards clear nonmatches and returns possible matches (matching the element names of the XML representation of the assertions). You must validate the resulting common alternatives by discipline-specific engines to ensure technical compatibility.

Policy intersection selects a subset of matching alternatives that appear in both policies. Policy assertions are compared to their element-qualified names and are considered equivalent if the names match. A match in the qualified names of the assertions does not imply that the assertions match (because attributes and children of the two assertion elements might not match) but provides a first check of compatibility that needs to be further refined by checking the assertions for compatibility. In the general case, this second comparison step requires the use of discipline-specific knowledge, which is not available at the policy framework level. This is, for example, the case in the assertions that include parameters (in the form of attribute values of additional nested elements). Without an understanding of the meaning of each parameter, you cannot judge the compatibility of two parameter values. Policy intersection provides a first pass at establishing the compatibility of policies by preselecting possible matches between alternatives. Therefore, intersection is a domain-independent process for explicitly ruling out incompatible policy alternatives.

This mechanism is expected to be used in various ways. In a simple scenario, a service requester uses it to determine which of the policy alternatives that a service offers are compatible with its own technical capabilities and requirements. To do this, the requester formulates a policy that represents the type of service interactions it supports and intersects it with the actual policy offered by the service it wants to access. This process can result in one or more potential alternatives. It is advisable that you follow the intersection with validation of the matching alternative(s) using assertion-specific knowledge.

7.2.2 Attaching Policies to Web Services

In the context of Web services, policies describe the constraints on an interaction between two or more Web service endpoints—typically a service provider and a service requester. However, policies that were created using the Policy container do not indicate the subject to which they apply. In WS-Policy, the association of policies with subjects is clearly separated from policy definition. That allows you to associate policies with multiple subjects and encourages you to reuse policy definitions.

WS-PolicyAttachment is concerned with the introduction of various mechanisms to associate policies with subjects. In a Web services scenario, several things might constitute a subject: a particular document, a document type, a message, a message exchange, a port type, an endpoint, a whole service, or a collection of services. The important point is that the set of possible subjects is not a closed set. Extensibility of attachment mechanisms is a fundamental requirement in WS-Policy. Two different mechanisms are introduced in this specification to satisfy this requirement:

- A generic policy annotation to be used in arbitrary XML documents. A policy annotation allows direct attachment of policies to specific subjects that are defined or described within the document. The annotation directly identifies the applicable policies.

- An external attachment mechanism that associates policies with subjects from outside the documents where the subject is defined or described.

You create policy annotations using the PolicyURIs attribute or the PolicyReference element. (Both are global definitions within the WS-Policy namespace.) The value of the PolicyURIs attribute is a list of whitespace-separated policy identifiers. The PolicyReference element contains one policy identifier. You use multiple elements when you need to attach more than one policy. You can encode the PolicyURIs attribute or the PolicyReference element, or you can nest it under an XML element to indicate that the referenced policies apply to the subject that element identifies.

WS-PolicyAttachments describes in detail how to use policy annotation in WSDL service description documents. Annotation of WSDL descriptions is a primary mechanism by which policies are attached to a service endpoint. (It is not the only mechanism, however, because you can also attach policies to a service endpoint using the external attachment method, as explained next.) Several types of WSDL definitions can constitute a policy subject. They include the message definitions, port type definitions, and WSDL bindings, among others. An attachment to a WSDL message binding using the PolicyReference element is shown in the next example.

```
<binding name="stockQuoteSoapBinding"
    type="tns:StockQuotePortType">
  <soap:binding style="document"
      transport="http://schemas.xmlsoap.org/soap/http"/>
  <operation name="GetLastTradePrice">
    <soap:operation soapAction=
     "http://example.comGetLastTradePrice"/>
    <input>
        <wsp:PolicyReference URI=
           "http://www.example.com/StdSecurityPolicy1"/>
        <soap:body use="literal"/>
    </input>
    <output>
        <soap:body use="literal"/>
    </output>
  </operation>
</binding>
```

Here, a security policy is attached to the input message of the "GetLastTradePrice" operation by including the PolicyReference element with the policy name URI under the `<input>` element of the binding. Because the scopes of WSDL definitions are naturally overlapping, the scopes of the corresponding policies overlap, too. Consider, for example, policies that are attached to a message and to a port type that contains an operation that uses the message. Both the message policy and the port type policy apply to the message as a subject, because the message is included in the scope that the port type definition defines. In general, when policies are associated with the WSDL definitions of overlapping scopes, the policy for a subject is the aggregation of all applicable in-scope policies. This is known as the *effective policy* of the subject. To clarify the possible usage cases and provide guidance to service developers, WS-PolicyAttachment defines a normative set of possible policy subjects in a Web service, identifies the corresponding WSDL elements that make up the overall policy description of each of them, and provides the policy aggregation mechanism that computes the effective policy.

External association of policies with subjects is done using the PolicyAttachment element. A PolicyAttachment contains a subject scope expression that identifies the set of subjects to which policies are being attached in addition to the policy to be attached. PolicyAttachment either provides an inline definition or uses one or more PolicyReference elements. The scope expression is an extensible part of the PolicyAttachment construct that allows various scenarios and disciplines to define their own expressions for describing policy subjects.

```
<wsa:EndPointReference>
   <wsa:Address>
       http://www.example.com/StockQuote
   </wsa:Address>
</wsa:EndpointReference>
```

WS-PolicyAttachment introduces the use of one such domain expression. As shown in the preceding example, you can encode a WS-Addressing endpoint reference as a scope expression to attach policies to the referenced endpoint.

The external attachment mechanism is particularly useful for communicating policy associations at runtime, via a message exchange. For example, in the course of their interaction, two endpoints might agree to use a certain conversational protocol during part of the interaction. The constraints on this protocol are specific to the interaction and relate to specific message instances, identifiable by their unique message identifier URIs, their sequence number if available, or by some other conversation-specific identifier. You cannot communicate this information prior to the dialogue through attachment to WSDL or UDDI; you can only communicate at runtime because that's when the identifiers are established. With the introduction of the WS-MetadataExchange specification, an endpoint can also request a policy at runtime. This late binding allows policies to reflect a finer level of granularity because the MEX request might identify the requester or the instance of a service via an EPR, which allows the provider to offer a policy expression that is targeted toward the individual requester.

WS-PolicyAttachment describes a normative use of UDDI for associating policies with Web service endpoints, giving service requesters and providers the ability to leverage the query capabilities of UDDI for discovery of endpoints based on their policy descriptions.

7.3 Future Directions

At the time of this writing, WS-Policy is at the start of the path toward standardization. The current WS-Policy document focuses on expressing two types of metadata: capabilities (things a service can do) and constraints (things a service requires). One of the next tasks is to gather domain-specific experts and have them specify domain-specific expression languages to express the constraints and capabilities that are relevant for each domain in the form of assertion dialects. Examples of proposals in this area comprise WS-SecurityPolicy, which includes requirements for authentication and message-level security, and WS-ReliableMessaging, which includes capabilities for RM and WS-Transactions (WS-AtomicTransaction and WS-BusinessActivity).

When multiple service assurance protocols exist, it is important for a Web service to be able to indicate which one it supports and what requirements it places on potential requesters.

As Web services gain adoption and more complex Web services applications are deployed, the WS-Policy framework might need to be extended to express and support service agreements (such as WS-Agreements) and specification profiling for interoperability (WS-I conformance claims). Service agreements don't just require a language for expressing goals and objectives. They also need a mechanism for negotiating and associating an agreement with a service endpoint and the parties that are governed by the agreement terms.

It may be necessary to clarify the relationship between WS-Policy and full-fledged semantic description frameworks. Just as WSDL extensions have been proposed to allow semantic expressions to extend the definition of a service interface, individual policy assertions can be annotated with semantic expressions and reasoned about as the semantic Web moves from theory to practice.

7.4 Summary

Ensuring the quality of service of Web services interactions is one of the most critical requirements of the Web services stack of specifications. Several specifications described later in this book—such as WS-Security, WS-Reliable messaging, and WS-Transactions—define the protocols that support specific aspects of this requirement. In a service-oriented environment, where loose coupling between applications is a fundamental property, the quality of service capabilities and requirements of a service must be declaratively expressed in standardized vocabularies so that you can properly configure and maintain partner services and avoid unnecessary coupling. WS-Policy defines a general-purpose framework for representing and combining statements about the quality of service properties. WS-Policy is an extensible framework that can accommodate domain-specific dialects to represent these assertions and allow the attachment of policies to arbitrary types of subjects though the generic attachment mechanisms that WS-PolicyAttachments define.

Part 4

Discovering Metadata

This part of the book answers the question of how to go about discovering all the important metadata (the explicit service description information) that supports service orientation. The figure that follows shows where metadata falls in the Web services stack.

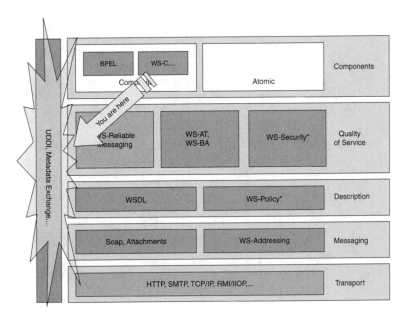

This part presents two approaches for discovering metadata: via a centralized registry (UDDI) or by distributed discovery (Metadata Exchange). UDDI, which is discussed in Chapter 8, "Universal Description, Discovery, and Integration," provides a centralized registry of metadata that can reference all kinds of information, including WSDL documents, policies, and others, and offers several powerful and flexible techniques for querying the registry.

WS-Metadata Exchange, which is discussed in Chapter 9, "Web Services Metadata Exchange," is a protocol for querying a Web service endpoint for its own metadata. This simple protocol allows an application to ask any service endpoint for its WSDL document, for its policies, for any schemas, or for any other kind of metadata.

Chapter 8

Universal Description, Discovery, and Integration (UDDI)

This chapter covers the Universal Description, Discovery, and Integration (UDDI) specifications and associated documents, focusing on UDDI version 3 [UDDI301], which is the most recent UDDI version.

The chapter begins with a brief history of the development of UDDI, followed by a description of the role of a service registry like UDDI in service-oriented architectures (SOA) and the WS Stack and a summary of the motivation for UDDI.

The majority of this chapter looks at the architectural concepts of UDDI, including the UDDI data model and how it is used to model WSDL descriptions, in addition to the UDDI architecture and APIs.

The final part of the chapter discusses the major topics that are being worked on for the next version of the UDDI specification.

8.1 Role of UDDI in SOA and the WS Stack

One of the main benefits of a SOA is the ability to reuse services through the process of "service composition," the process in which existing services are assembled to create new services and applications. To realize this benefit, designers and developers need to know what existing services are available and how to interact with them. UDDI has an important role to play in providing a single well-known place that can be searched for services and provide pointers to more detailed information about the services, including the WSDL description of the service if one exists.

A second benefit is the ability to dynamically select an implementation of a service at runtime. Either the application or the infrastructure that is hosting it can perform this selection. UDDI also enables service providers to publish their service implementations, and service users to find the one that provides the best match with their requirements.

These two roles of the UDDI registry are described in the following sections.

8.1.1 Use of UDDI During Design and Development

In a typical development-time use case of UDDI, a developer will require a specific service, such as a service that supports renting a car, when building a new application. To find this service, the developer would send to the UDDI registry a query for all service providers (instances of "businessEntity," which we describe later in this chapter) that are categorized as supporting the car rental function. The categorization can use a well-known category system, such as UNSPSC, a proprietary category system, or a combination of both. After the developer obtains the list of providers, she can choose to issue further queries to find out more details about those that interest her, in particular, the actual services they provide. Having selected a provider and a particular service, the developer can then use the pointers in the UDDI data structures to find additional details about the service, including the WSDL description for the service if that is appropriate. She can then use development tools to generate the code artifacts necessary to invoke the service.

8.1.2 Use of UDDI at Runtime

UDDI has always been intended for use at runtime, not only during design and development. Runtime usage is referred to as the *invocation pattern* in the UDDI specifications.

One of the key attributes of an SOA is the ability to dynamically bind to a service, and UDDI is a key component in enabling this behavior. Rather than bind a client to a particular implementation of a service at a particular location, one can use UDDI to find an implementation of a service at runtime and then retrieve the location of the service to configure the client dynamically.

8.2 Motivation for UDDI

The original motivation for UDDI was to provide the specifications and a set of actual implementations of a registry of Web services and of the businesses that provide them. The specifications were intended to enable product implementations of UDDI, and the implementations were intended to provide a registry that businesses could use to advertise themselves and any services they wanted to make available to the general public. This public registry, known as the *UDDI Business Registry*, is a single logical registry composed of implementations of UDDI from multiple companies. A second public registry, the test registry, was made available so that developers could experiment with UDDI in advance of product implementations becoming available.

A UDDI registry provides a well-known shared registry or index where clients can search for businesses and services that they want to interact with. UDDI offers a standard way for businesses to describe themselves, including categorizing themselves in as many ways as are appropriate, such as geographic location and industry sector(s) serviced, and for potential clients to search for them based on their particular requirements.

Even within a single enterprise, it can be difficult to identify and describe existing services in a way that allows other developers to discover them, and the benefits of UDDI are applicable within an enterprise. This type of deployment of UDDI allows for much greater control over the content of the registry.

Another use of UDDI is between cooperating enterprises, in which case an enterprise might host a UDDI registry containing details of services that approved business partners provide.

8.3 Architectural Concepts

This section describes the concepts in the UDDI V3 architecture.

8.3.1 UDDI V3 Data Model

Following are the main elements of the UDDI data model:

- businessEntity

- businessService

- bindingTemplate

- tModel

- publisherAssertion

Each of these is described in a section that follows, following a description of categorization.

Categorization

Categorization is one of the most important aspects of UDDI. Categorization is represented in the UDDI data model by the categoryBag element. This element can contain multiple keyedReferences, with each keyedReference indicating one categorization from a particular category system. A tModel represents each category system, and one element of a keyedReference is the key of the tModel that represents the category system. The keyedReference can contain two other pieces of information. The first is a keyName, which for most category systems is for documentation purposes only; it is not used in queries other than with one predefined category system. The second is a keyValue, which is the particular value to be used for this instance of the category system.

As an example, one of the category systems described in the UDDI specification is the ISO 3166 geographical category system. The key of the tModel that represents this category system is uddi:uddi.org:ubr:categorization:iso3166. If a business wants to indicate that it operates in the state of California in the U.S., it includes a keyedReference with this tModelKey and a keyValue of "US-CA."

If a client wants to search for a business in California, it includes the same keyedReference in its search request. When matching a keyedReference such as this, the default is to do a case-sensitive exact match. However, one also has the option of performing a case-insensitive match (on "us-ca"), or an approximate match using wildcards, for example "US-%" to match against any U.S. state.

businessEntity

A businessEntity represents any provider of a service, not just a business. Other examples include departments and project teams. A businessEntity contains information about the service provider as a whole, including names and descriptions, in multiple languages if desired, and specific contact information for the service provider. A businessEntity can be categorized with multiple keyedReferences. A businessEntity contains zero or more businessServices. A businessEntity might have zero or more digital signatures.

As described later, a businessEntity can be related to another businessEntity through a publisherAssertion.

businessService

A businessService represents a single service or set of related operations that can be invoked in different ways. A businessService is owned or contained by a single businessEntity but can be projected to more than one additional businessEntity if one service provider wants to offer a service owned by a different service provider. A businessService can have multiple names and descriptions, in different languages if required. A businessService can be categorized with multiple keyedReferences. A businessService has no contact information; only a businessEntity has contact information. The businessService contains the key of its parent businessEntity so that it can retrieve the contact information if necessary.

A businessService contains zero or more bindingTemplates. If a businessService has more than one bindingTemplate, each one represents an alternative means of invoking the service, within the scope of the single provider of the service. Different providers of the same service are represented by different businessService entities. A businessService might have one or more digital signatures. Alternatively, the businessService might be included in the digital signature of its parent businessEntity.

bindingTemplate

A bindingTemplate represents a deployed implementation of a service or part of a service. It includes the URL that is the network endpoint that a client uses to communicate with the service. A bindingTemplate is contained by a single businessService. A bindingTemplate might have multiple descriptions, in different languages if desired, but it does not have a name.

New in UDDI V3 is the addition of a categoryBag to the bindingTemplate structure so that one can categorize a bindingTemplate in the same way that one can categorize a businessEntity or businessService. Also new in UDDI V3 is the provision for a bindingTemplate to have zero or more digital signatures, if separate signatures are required specifically for the bindingTemplate, rather than including the bindingTemplate in the digital signature(s) of its parent businessService.

A bindingTemplate might also include multiple instances of a tModelInstanceInfo structure, each of which represents some element of the technical information that is relevant to the deployed instance of the service or part of the service. A tModelInstanceInfo element consists of a tModel key, zero or more descriptions, and an instanceDetails element, if detailed information such as parameter settings is required. The collection of tModelInstanceInfo elements is known as the "technical fingerprint" of the bindingTemplate, and the tModel keys can be used in queries to search for bindingTemplates that contain at least one tModelInstanceInfo that refers to a particular tModel.

tModel

The tModel is used for a wide range of purposes in UDDI. In the UDDI specification, it is used for the following:

- Representing value sets such as identification systems, category systems, and namespaces.

- Structured categorizations known as categorization groups (new in UDDI V3).

- Representing transports such as HTTP.

- Postal address formats.

- Find qualifiers (both standard and user-defined, new in UDDI V3).

- Use type attributes when a new use for one of the elements that has a useType attribute is invented. The recommended approach in this case is to use a tModel key as the new useType value.

tModel also represents any concept that is not better represented by one of the other UDDI data structures.

A tModel must have a single name, which should be in the form of a URI, and it can have zero or more descriptions, in multiple languages if desired. A tModel can have multiple overviewDoc elements, each of which can refer to a detailed description of the tModel and its uses. Such descriptions are stored outside of UDDI. A tModel can be, and usually is, categorized with multiple keyedReferences in a categoryBag. A tModel might have zero or more digital signatures. Because a tModel is outside the containment hierarchy of the other main elements described so far, no parent entity can contain the signature of a tModel.

publisherAssertion

A publisherAssertion represents an association between two businessEntities. The owner of each businessEntity involved must assert the publisherAssertion before it is considered valid.

A publisherAssertion consists of the two keys of the relevant businessEntity elements, a keyedReference representing the relationship between the two businessEntity instances, and zero or more digital signatures.

Several relationships are defined in the UDDI specifications. One example is a parent-child relationship; therefore, if one businessEntity represents the parent business of another business represented by a second businessEntity, this relationship can be expressed in UDDI. One can query UDDI for related businesses.

8.3.2 UDDI and WSDL

The OASIS UDDI Specification Technical Committee (TC) has published a "V2 Technical Note" [UDDIWSDLTN] on using UDDI and WSDL that is intended to replace the existing V1 Best Practice [UDDIWSDLBP]. A *Technical Note* is a document produced by the TC that represents the consensus view of the TC on a topic for which there is insufficient implementation experience to publish a "Best Practice." The intention is that after sufficient implementation experience is obtained with the approach described in the technical note, it will become the new Best Practice specification for using WSDL and UDDI.

The V1 Best Practice captured little information from the WSDL; it required that a tModel be produced for all of the WSDL bindings in a particular file, or one per binding. The overview URL of the tModel contained the URL of the WSDL file, with a fragment identifier representing a particular binding if the tModel represented a single binding. These tModels were categorized as relating to WSDL, but no other information from the WSDL was captured.

The V2 Technical Note requires that every portType and binding have its own tModel. It extends the normative mapping to include WSDL services and ports.

This section describes the architecture of the mapping between WSDL 1.1 and UDDI described in the UDDI/WSDL Technical Note. The mapping to UDDI is intended to support both UDDI V2 and V3 clients. No use is mandated of the new features in UDDI V3, because such features are generally invisible to UDDI V2 clients. For example, the mapping doesn't require the use of the categoryBag on a bindingTemplate, which is new in UDDI V3. That's because if information were represented only in the categoryBag, it would not be visible to

V2 clients, and it would be inefficient to duplicate the same information in two different ways to support both V2 and V3 clients. If one knows that only V3 clients will publish to and inquire from the UDDI registry, one can use these new features of V3.

The Technical Note introduces several new tModels, which are expected to be supported by any UDDI implementation that supports the approach described in the Technical Note. One of the new tModels represents a new category system, known as the WSDL Entity Type category system that categorizes the UDDI elements in terms of the WSDL element they represent. This allows searches for businessServices, for example, to be restricted to those businessServices that correspond to a WSDL service, because not all businessServices in a UDDI registry necessarily relate to a service that has a WSDL description.

The mapping is summarized in Table 8-1.

Table 8-1   **Summary of Mapping from the UDDI/WSDL Technical Note**

WSDL Entity	Corresponding UDDI Entity
portType	tModel
binding	tModel
service	businessService
port	bindingTemplate

The details of the mapping for each of the WSDL entities are described in the following sections.

Mapping of WSDL portType Element

A WSDL portType is represented in UDDI as a tModel that is categorized as a portType in the WSDL Entity Type category system. The name of the tModel is taken from the local name of the portType. If a targetNamespace is associated with the portType, an additional keyedReference is added to the categoryBag of the tModel, with a keyValue that is the value of the targetNamespace. The tModelKey is the key of another of the new category systems that the Technical

Note introduced: the XML namespace category system. The location of the WSDL document that contains the definition of the portType is stored as the value of the overviewURL within the overviewDoc of the tModel.

The V1 Best Practice for UDDI and WSDL allows a fragment identifier to refer to an individual binding within a WSDL document, but no definitive standard for fragment identifiers with WSDL 1.1 has emerged. Therefore, the V2 Technical Note does not rely on fragment identifiers, and the URL that is stored is the base URL of the WSDL document. Sufficient information is captured in the UDDI model to allow the particular portType within the document to be identified.

This mapping allows tModels that represent portTypes to be queried based solely on the fact that they correspond to a WSDL portType, or based on any combination of namespace name and local name.

Mapping of WSDL Binding Element

The mapping of a WSDL binding is similar to, but more complex than, the mapping of a portType. A WSDL binding is represented by a tModel that is categorized as a WSDL binding using the WSDL Entity Type category system. For compatibility with the V1 Best Practice, the tModel is also categorized with the wsdlSpec value using the standard UDDI types category system. As with the portType, the name of the tModel is taken from the name of the binding. If a targetNamespace is associated with the binding, a keyedReference is added for that in the same way as for a portType. The location of the WSDL document that describes the binding is again stored in the overviewURL of the overviewDoc of the tModel.

The relationship between the WSDL binding and the portType it is a binding of is captured with another keyedReference in the categoryBag of the tModel corresponding to the binding. The tModelKey in this keyedReference is the key of another of the new tModels introduced in the Technical Note: the portType reference category system. The keyValue in the keyedReference is the key of the tModel that corresponds to the portType. This allows all tModels that represent bindings of the particular tModel to be queried using a standard find_tModel call, after the key(s) of the tModel(s) corresponding to the portType are known.

The protocol that the binding supports, such as SOAP, is represented by another keyedReference in the categoryBag of the tModel, referring to yet another new category system introduced by the Technical Note: the Protocol Categorization category system. The keyValue of the keyedReference is the key of a tModel that represents the protocol. This allows a query for bindings of a particular portType to be restricted to those that support a particular protocol.

Finally, if the binding supports a particular transport, such as HTTP, that information is modeled using yet another keyedReference, this time relating to the Transport Categorization category system introduced in the Technical Note. This allows a query for a binding tModel to be restricted to those that support a particular transport. When used in combination with the other keyedReferences in the categoryBag, this allows for bindings of a particular portType that support a particular protocol and transport to be found.

Mapping of WSDL Service Element

A UDDI businessService represents a WSDL service. One can use an existing businessService if a WSDL description is being defined for an existing service, or create a new one. The name of a newly created businessService should be easy to read. It does not have to have the name of the WSDL service, but the WSDL service name becomes the default if no other name is supplied. A UDDI businessService might represent only one WSDL service.

The businessService is categorized as a service using the WSDL Entity Type category system. The WSDL service name is modeled definitively using a keyedReference in the categoryBag of the businessService referencing the XML Local Name category system that the Technical Note defines. The keyValue of the keyedReference is the local name of the WSDL service. When querying for a service by name, one must specify that name in a keyedReference in the categoryBag of the query. Again, the name of the businessService name is not necessarily the same as the WSDL service name. The businessService's category bag contains a keyedReference that models the targetNamespace of the WSDL service, if one appears in the corresponding WSDL document.

Mapping of WSDL Port Element

The ports of a WSDL service are represented by a UDDI bindingTemplates inside the services's businessService. The WSDL binding of the port is modeled as a tModelInstanceInfo in the bindingTemplate for the port; the tModelKey is the key of the tModel that represents that WSDL binding. The local name of the port is modeled as the value of the instanceParms of this tModelInstanceInfo.

As an optimization, another tModelInstanceInfo is added with the tModelKey of the portType that the binding relates to. This allows a more efficient query of all implementations of a particular portType, rather than requiring multiple calls to find all bindings of the portType and then all implementations of any of those bindings.

UDDI and WSDL at Development Time

If a developer chooses a service that has a WSDL description, she imports the WSDL service definition or generates it directly from the information held in UDDI if that is sufficient. Then she generates whatever code artifacts needed to access the service.

When a developer knows some information about the WSDL description of the required service, she can issue queries to UDDI that are focused on WSDL elements of the service description, such as the namespace or the local name. She can also issue queries relating to the WSDL portType that is desired, or a particular binding of that portType.

UDDI and WSDL at Runtime

The modeling approach presented in the UDDI/WSDL Technical Note is sufficient to allow all implementations of a portType to be retrieved. This is appropriate if the environment that is hosting the client is flexible enough to be able to use any protocol and transport to invoke the service. If a particular protocol, such as SOAP, is required, a more precise query can be used, which will return only implementations that support that particular protocol. Finally, if there is a requirement to use a particular binding of a portType, perhaps because the use of some particular headers is required, one may query the implementations of that particular binding directly.

8.3.3 UDDI and WS-Policy

The WS-PolicyAttachment Specification [WS-Policy Attachment] describes how to attach policies to the following UDDI entities:

- businessEntity

- businessService

- bindingTemplate

- tModel

Two approaches are described in the WS-PolicyAttachment specification. The first is to reference remotely accessible policy expressions directly from the UDDI entities. This approach is convenient when the policy expression is referenced by only one UDDI entity. The second is to create a tModel to represent a policy expression and then to reference the tModel from a UDDI entities. This approach should be used when multiple UDDI entities reference the same policy expression.

Referencing Remote Policy Expressions Directly

The WS-PolicyAttachment specification defines a tModel to represent a category system called the Remote Policy Reference category system. The valid values of this category system are URIs that identify remote policy expressions.

In UDDI V3, the policy expression is associated with aUDDI entity. It includes a keyedReference in the categoryBag of the entity with a tModelKey value that is the key of the tModel representing this category system and a keyValue value that is the URI of the remote policy expression.

A different approach for a bindingTemplate is required for UDDI V2, because in the UDDI V2 data model, a bindingTemplate does not have a categoryBag.

Referencing Remote Policy Expressions Indirectly

To support the publication of tModels to represent individual remote policy expressions, the WS-PolicyAttachment Specification defines another tModel to represent a different category system: the WS-Policy Types category system. One must categorize a tModel that represents an individual remote policy expression with the WS-Policy Types category system. This category system has a single valid value of "policy." The URI that identifies the policy expression serves as the overviewURL of the tModel and as a direct reference to the policy expression, using the first approach.

A UDDI entity associates itself with the tModel for a policy expression using a third category system, the Local Policy Reference. The valid values of this category system are keys of tModels that are categorized using the WS-Policy Types category system. To make the association one simply adds a keyedReference to the categoryBag of the UDDI entity with a tModelKey value of the key of the tModel representing the Local Policy Reference category system and a keyValue value of the key of the tModel representing the individual remote Policy Expression.

Querying UDDI Using Policy Expressions

Queries to a UDDI registry can use the policy expression's URI to retrieve UDDI entities associated with that policy. If the association is direct, the query includes a keyedReference in the categoryBag, with a tModelKey value of the tModel representing the Remote Policy Reference category system and a keyValue value of the URI of the policy expression. If the association is indirect, the one needs to retrieve the tModel that represents the policy expression before the actual query for UDDI entities. The query must include a keyedReference in the categoryBag, with a tModelKey value representing the Local Policy Reference category system and a keyValue returned by the first query.

8.3.4 UDDI V3 Architecture and APIs

The UDDI V3 architecture is made up of the following components:

- A client
- One or more UDDI implementations (nodes) forming a registry
- Zero or more taxonomy servers

The client interacts with the UDDI registry using SOAP/HTTP requests and responses in a document/literal style, with the APIs defined in the UDDI specification.

One can combine multiple UDDI nodes to form a single UDDI registry, as long as the nodes have compatible policy definitions and they replicate data with each other to ensure that, after a replication cycle has completed, all nodes in the registry have the same data. The nodes communicate with each other using SOAP/HTTP to replicate the data. If one issues the same query to different nodes in the registry, the same information is returned. Each piece of data in a registry belongs to a single publisher; likewise, a single node has the custody of each individual piece of data in the resgitry. The data can only be updated or deleted by the publisher sending a request to the node that has custody of the data. Although the nodes are equivalent for reading from the registry, they are different when it comes to writing to the registry.

If a request to a node requires the use of a taxonomy that an external server provides, the node might make a SOAP/HTTP call to that server to validate the use of the taxonomy. An UDDI node might also cache taxonomy information from a remote server to avoid further remote calls to the taxonomy server.

Several APIs/portTypes are defined in the UDDI specification. They can be divided into the following groups:

- Operations that a client can invoke against a UDDI node

- Operations that a UDDI node can invoke against a client

- Operations that a UDDI node can invoke against another node

- Operations that a UDDI node can invoke against a taxonomy server

Each of these groups is described in more detail in the following sections.

Client to Node Operations

The following portTypes are available so that clients can invoke operations against an UDDI node:

- UDDI_Inquiry_PortType

- UDDI_Publication_PortType

- UDDI_Security_PortType

- UDDI_CustodyTransfer_PortType

- UDDI_Subscription_PortType

The UDDI_Inquiry_PortType has two kinds of operations: find operations and get operations. The find operations issue queries to the UDDI registry; the get operations retrieve full details of one or more entities of a particular type.

All of the "find" operations take a findQualifiers element. This element modifies which entities match the query and how they are sorted. The "find" operations return abbreviated information about the matching entities, typically the key of each entity and the name(s) and description(s) of the entity as appropriate. In UDDI V3, when too many results match a single call, only part of them are returned and one can use a mechanism called a listDescription to page through the results.

Another new feature in UDDI V3 is that some of the find operations can take a nested query as an argument, which can result in much more efficient queries. For example, the find_business operation can take a find_tModel query as an argument in addition to a find_relatedBusinesses query. These inner or nested queries are issued first by the UDDI registry that processes the find_business operation. The results of these nested queries are used to alter the original find_business operation. One can achieve the same effect by issuing the find_tModel or find_relatedBusinesses queries separately and then building up a more complex find_business query. However, this requires at least three calls to the UDDI registry if both nested queries are used, whereas being able to nest them within the find_business query means that only one call to the UDDI registry is required.

Each of the get operations takes one or more keys as input, typically from the result of one or more find operations, and returns the full information about each entity.

The UDDI_Publication_PortType contains all of the operations that add content to, update content in, or remove content from an UDDI registry. It also contains several specialized get operations.

A businessService can be added to a businessEntity either by being included in the definition of the businessEntity supplied in a save_business call or by being included in a save_service call. If a save_business call updates a businessEntity, any services that were part of the businessEntity but are not included in the updated definition of the businessEntity are implicitly deleted. One must be careful when adding or updating a businessService that is owned by a businessEntity that has at least one digital signature because the signature(s) can be invalidated by the change. Similar considerations apply to adding or updating a bindingTemplate within a businessService.

The function of delete_tModel is unique in that it does not completely remove a tModel; it only marks it as hidden. A find_tModel call does not return a hidden tModel, but a get_tModelDetail call can still retrieve its details. One can even publish new references to the tModel, although this practice is discouraged because the tModel is presumably not intended to be used for new publications. The reason for this design is that tModels are intended to represent stable concepts and standards that should continue to have value even when new versions become available. Such new versions are represented by new tModels.

The UDDI_Security_PortType portType defines the discard_authToken and get_authToken operations that are used if the authentication mechanism that UDDI defines is supported.

The UDDI_CustodyTransfer_PortType portType defines operations that allow for the custody or ownership of one or more businessEntity elements (and the associated businessService elements) and one or more tModel entities to be transferred to another node or owner.

The UDDI_Subscription_PortType portType defines operations that allow a user to register an interest in entities in an UDDI node that matches the information in the subscription request, and to retrieve details of events that involve those entities. Support for subscription is new in UDDI version 3 and is described in more detail in a later section.

Node to Client Operations

Only one portType is defined for nodes to invoke operations against an UDDI client: the UDDI_SubscriptionListener_PortType portType. A single operation is defined in this portType: notify_subscriptionListener.

If a client wants to receive asynchronous notifications when an event that matches a subscription request occurs, it can deploy a Web service that implements this portType and register that fact in the UDDI registry by creating a bindingTemplate for it. The key of this bindingTemplate is then supplied in the subscription request to indicate that this style of receiving notifications is required.

Node to Node Operations

Only one portType is defined for nodes to invoke operations against another node: the UDDI_Replication_PortType portType. The operations that are defined in this portType allow multiple nodes to operate together as part of a multinode registry.

Node to Taxonomy Server Operations

The following portTypes are available for a node to invoke operations against a taxonomy server:

- UDDI_ValueSetCaching_PortType

- UDDI_ValueSetValidation_PortType

Each of these portTypes defines a single operation. The operation in the UDDI_ValueSetCaching_PortType portType is get_allValidValues. When an UDDI node invokes get_allValidValues against a value set server, the value set server returns the entire set of valid values in a single response. The operation in the UDDI_ValueSetValidation_PortType portType is validate_values. When an entity such as a businessEntity is published to an UDDI node, and it references a value set that is externally verified, the UDDI node invokes the validate_values operation against the appropriate value set server, passing it the entire businessEntity element. The value set server checks that the uses of the value sets it provides are correct.

8.3.5 New Features in UDDI V3

The following are the main features that were added to UDDI with the V3 specification:

- Publisher-assigned keys

- Support for digital signatures

- Policy

- Subscription API

- Enhancements to categorization

- Changes in authentication

For full details, see the UDDI Version 3 Features List [UDDIV3Features].

Publisher-Assigned Keys

Prior to UDDI V3, UDDI entities had keys that were Universal Unique Identifiers (UUIDs). The UDDI registry assigned these keys when it first saved the entity. This meant that it was not possible using just the UDDI API to save the same entity to two different registries and have the same key be assigned to the entity in both registries. This made it difficult to move information between a test and production registry, for instance, without changing the keys used for the entities. With UDDI V3, a publisher can assign a key to an entity when it is first saved, and these keys can be based on a domain name, making them more meaningful. Taking one of the tModels defined in the V3 specification as an example, its V3 key is uddi:uddi.org:specification:v3_policy, whereas the corresponding V2 key (UUID) is uuid:d52ce89c-01f8-3b53-a25e-89cfa5bbad17. This ability to specify the key when the entity is saved means that one can use the standard UDDI API to republish the same entity into a production UDDI registry, keeping the same key that the entity had in a test registry.

A key in UDDI V3 must begin with "uddi:" and its total length must be no longer than 255 characters.

When using publisher-assigned keys, one needs to understand the concepts of key generators and key partitions. UDDI V3 keys are divided into nonKeyGeneratorKey and keyGeneratorKey keys.

A nonKeyGeneratorKey can be one of three types:

- A uuidKey similar to a V2 UUID key, such as uddi:4CD7E4BC-648 B-426D-9936-443EAAC8AE23

- A domainKey based on a DNS host name, such as uddi:tempuri.com

- A derivedKey, which is a nonKeyGeneratorKey with a string other than ":keygenerator" (or "keyGenerator" because all UDDI keys are case-folded to lowercase when an UDDI registry receives them) appended, such as uddi:tempuri.com:fish:buyingservice

A keyGeneratorKey is a nonKeyGeneratorKey with ":keygenerator" (or ":keyGenerator") appended. An example of a keyGeneratorKey is uddi:tempuri.com:keygenerator. The nonKeyGeneratorKey that this keyGenerator is based on is uddi:tempuri.com.

To establish a key partition, one must save a tModel categorized as a keyGenerator tModel. It must also have a publisher-assigned key that is a keyGeneratorKey. The partition associated with the tModel is named after the nonKeyGeneratorKey that is the basis of the keyGeneratorKey of the tModel. In the previous example, the tModel with key "uddi:tempuri.com:keygenerator" defines a partition named "uddi:tempuri.com." After the tModel is saved only its owner can propose keys such as "uddi:tempuri.com:fishbuyingservice," because this key is in the "uddi:tempuri.com" partition.

To allow multiple publishers to be able to propose keys, one can divide a partition into subpartitions. Continuing the tempuri.com example, the publisher that owns the tModel with key "uddi:tempuri.com:keygenerator" can publish another keyGenerator tModel with the key "uddi:tempuri.com:fish:keygenerator" to establish a "fish" subpartition of the "uddi:tempuri.com" partition. One may transfer ownership of this second tModel to another publisher, who can then assign keys only in this new subpartition, such as "uddi:tempuri.com:fish: buyingservice." Note that the original publisher cannot assign keys in this subpartition because the ownership of the tModel was transferred. A partition or subpartition can have only a single owner; therefore, only one publisher at a time can publish entities that have keys assigned from a partition.

If multiple registries have appropriate policies, they can form a group known as an affiliation, which enables UDDI entities to be copied between registries. An enterprise might establish an affiliation between a test or staging registry and a production registry so that data can be copied easily from the test or staging registry to the production registry. The main function of the affiliation is to ensure that keys used in one registry in the affiliation can safely be used by the same publisher in all other registries in the affiliation.

One can use a designated registry as a root registry, guaranteeing uniqueness of key partitions across all other registries that are affiliated to the root registry. A company such as tempuri.com can publish a keyGenerator tModel with the key uddi:tempuri.com:keygenerator in the root registry and then republish the same tModel into its own top-level internal UDDI registry and be sure that the same tModel cannot be claimed by any other business that uses the same root registry in the same way. By doing this, tempuri.com can be assured that any keys it generates internally can be used with any affiliated registry without risk of collision.

Support for Digital Signatures

To improve the trust in the quality and provenance of the data in an UDDI registry, UDDI V3 added the capability for publishers to digitally sign the information that they publish. The following entities might have a digital signature associated with them:

- businessEntity
- businessService
- bindingTemplate
- tModel
- publisherAssertion

One must be careful with businessEntity and businessService because they can have child elements (businessService and bindingTemplate) added separately, which might invalidate the original digital signature of the parent entity. For example, perhaps the businessEntity is saved with three child businessService elements, and the businessEntity is signed. If another businessService is added to the businessEntity later with a save_service call, the businessEntity would have four businessService elements, and the original digital signature would no longer be valid.

The support for digital signatures in UDDI V3 requires a particular canonicalization scheme known as *Schema Centric XML Canonicalization.* [SCC14N]

UDDI V3 queries can specify that results should be restricted to only those entities that have a digital signature.

Clients that use either the UDDI V1 API or the UDDI V2 API cannot assign a digital signature when publishing or see a digital signature when querying an UDDI V3 registry.

If an entity to be signed has a publisher-assigned key, it is possible to save the signed entity in a single call. If, however, the entity has a registry-assigned key, two calls are necessary. The purpose of the first call is to allow the registry to assign the key to the entity; only a limited amount of information needs to be sent with the first call. The second call updates the entity with the full information and includes the digital signature.

UDDI Policy

Another major new feature in UDDI V3 is the use of policy definitions to control the behavior of a UDDI node or registry and to communicate these behaviors to clients and potential registry users. One can define a policy for an individual node or for a registry in the case of a multinode registry.

The UDDI V3 specification defines two types of policies:

- Policies represented by an XML document
- Policies represented by UDDI data structures

UDDI data structures should be used to represent policies that affect a UDDI client so the client can retrieve them using the normal UDDI inquiry API. Following are examples of this type of policy:

- Support for a particular API, such as the security API

- Authorization policy

- Data confidentiality

Policies that are more concerned with the administration of a node or the registry are more likely to be represented in an XML document. Following are examples of this type of policy:

- A process for auditing the registry

- A process for adding nodes to the registry

- A process for synchronizing the clocks of the nodes in the registry

Subscription API

The subscription API allows clients to register an interest in UDDI entities that meet certain criteria and, optionally, be notified when new entities are published that meet the criteria or when existing entities that meet the criteria are altered or deleted. Support for the subscription API is optional.

The following types of entities can be used with subscription:

- businessEntity

- businessService

- bindingTemplate

- tModel

- Related businessEntity

- publisherAssertion (providing the subscriber owns at least one of the businessEntity elements mentioned in the publisherAssertion)

A subscriber can be notified of changes either synchronously or asynchronously, depending on the capabilities of the node. If a subscriber wants to be notified asynchronously, he either must have an e-mail address to which the information is mailed, or he must implement the UDDI_SubscriptionListener_PortType and define a bindingTemplate in the registry with the endpoint of the service that implements this portType.

The criteria that the subscriber is interested in are defined by a combination of standard inquiry APIs, both find and get requests. Registering an interest in new entities requires the use of a find request. One can use either type of request to register an interest in an existing entity.

The subscription API enables automatic copying of data between registries. When an event matching the subscription criteria takes place at the registry that owns the data, the registry sends a notification to the subscriber (another registry). The notification allows the subscriber to automatically update its copy of the data to match the original.

Categorization Enhancements

Following are the enhancements in UDDI V3 that relate to categorization:

- keyedReferenceGroup

- Extending category systems through derivation

The keyedReferenceGroup element allows one to group multiple keyedReferences together and consider them a single complex categorization, identified by an additional tModel for the group as a whole, separate from the tModel indicated in each keyedReference.

For example, one could describe the geographic location of an entity using the World Geodetic System 1984 (WGS 84). The keyedReferenceGroup will contain the key of the tModel representing the WGS 84 category system and the following keyedReferences:

- A keyedReference for the latitude of the location

- A keyedReference for the longitude of the location

- A keyedReference for the precision of the location

When a query includes a keyedReferenceGroup an entity matches the query with a keyedReferenceGroup if the tModel keys for the two groups are identical and the keyedReferences within the group in the query are a subset of the keyedReferences within the group in the entity.

Changes in Authentication

The UDDI V2 specifications required authentication for the publish API but did not allow authentication for the inquiry API. Authentication information was carried in the publish API explicitly in the form of an UDDI authentication token (the authToken element). The publish API also contained calls to acquire an authentication token, given a userid and password, and to discard an authentication token. Although the V2 specifications allowed an authentication token to be obtained other than through the UDDI authentication calls, the token still had to be passed explicitly to publish calls and could not be passed to inquiry calls.

In the UDDI V3 specification, the UDDI authentication token is optional on every call in the inquiry, publication, custody transfer, and subscription APIs. The mechanisms for authentication and identification are now part of the policy definitions of the registry and the particular node. The UDDI V3 specification allows the use of transport-level authentication as an alternative to explicit tokens carried in the UDDI request messages.

8.4 Future Directions

Work is underway in the OASIS UDDI TC on the next version of the UDDI specification. This section describes some of the major topics being considered at the time of writing.

8.4.1 Standardization of Taxonomy Language

Although most UDDI implementations support user-defined taxonomies, no standard syntax is currently available to represent the taxonomy in a way that multiple implementations can read it.

The current proposal being worked on in the OASIS UDDI TC is to support OWL [OWL] as the standard exchange syntax for taxonomies. In addition to providing a standard syntax for taxonomies designed specifically for UDDI, this approach allows emerging OWL tools to be used to develop taxonomies for UDDI. It also allows OWL ontologies to be produced without UDDI in mind for the purpose of UDDI taxonomies, although not all of the information in the OWL ontology will be reflected in the UDDI taxonomy.

8.4.2 Semantic Searching

UDDI searching based on semantics has attracted much attention. Most of the approaches developed to date have implemented the semantics either alongside UDDI or in a wrapper around UDDI, requiring each solution to invent its own nonstandard programming model. The OASIS UDDI TC is working on integrating some level of support into UDDI so that tools and applications can use the standard UDDI programming model.

8.4.3 Instance-Based Security

Currently, authorization in UDDI is limited to the individual APIs, such as the Publish API. Work has begun to extend the UDDI authorization support to individual entities within a UDDI registry.

8.5 Summary

This chapter introduces the main elements of the UDDI standard. UDDI defines a standard for service registries. Service registries are used at development time to support the development of service-based applications and support the dynamic discovery and binding of services by service clients. These are two of the fundamental characteristics of service oriented architectures. By defining an XML based realization of a service registry, UDDI plays a fundamental role in making the Web services framework a true instantiation of the service oriented architecture.

UDDI defines a data model for registering services, a query API and a set of protocols to be followed by implementers of UDDI registries. In addition, specific extensions of the basic standard define how WSDL and WS-Policy service descriptions are registered and used within the UDDI framework. The UDDI v3 set of specifications produced by the OASIS UDDI Technical Committee offers a complete solution for the problem of registering and discovering services in a Web services environment.

Chapter 9
Web Services Metadata Exchange

Metadata plays a fundamental role in Service-Oriented Architectures. The term *metadata* refers to explicit information about a service that is encoded in a machine-readable format. Explicit metadata encodes in an unambiguous way details about the interaction contract between service requesters and providers. Technical capabilities and requirements of service endpoints are encoded using XML Schema, Web Services Description Language (WSDL), and WS-Policy definitions. Service requesters are developed and configured to comply with these metadata specifications; service providers are selected according to the metadata that a requester expects. Explicit metadata is the key feature of SOAs that enables loose coupling between requesters and providers. As such, metadata is required in multiple steps of the application lifecycle (development, deployment, runtime) and in different scenarios. The central registry model, which is exemplified by the UDDI standard, covers one important set of scenarios. These scenarios and use cases were already discussed in Chapter 8, "UDDI."

Another set of scenarios is not completely addressed by the central repository model. These are dynamic scenarios in which requesters discover service endpoints at runtime, and the properties of the interaction are customized to fit a particular requester. These scenarios are served by the process of *bootstrapping* the interaction. In bootstrapping, the interacting endpoints exchange their service definition and configuration metadata prior to the actual interaction. Then they use the retrieved metadata to dynamically configure the endpoints' capabilities.

The bootstrapping approach allows much more flexible configuration of the interacting endpoints. You can customize the interaction to its specific conditions: the identity of the requester endpoint, the date and time, and any relevant business or technical conditions. You obtain the corresponding endpoint metadata just in time to refresh possibly stale cached copies and to update the endpoint's configuration.

The bootstrap works best when you can assume a direct, nonmediated interaction between requesters and providers. The service requester directly queries the service endpoint for its metadata and the requester gets a fresh, customized copy of it. However, to support this model, you have to assume that every endpoint supports a metadata retrieval interface in addition to its business interface. How this function is actually provided is essentially irrelevant. An endpoint might redirect requests for metadata to another endpoint or a URL providing the metadata on its behalf. Whether the endpoint supports the metadata exchange or the runtime environment transparently provides it is an implementation detail. The key point is the ability of the service requester to directly request from its target endpoint updated, customized metadata.

The Web Services Metadata Exchange specification (WS-MetadataExchange) defines a simple yet flexible interface to allow service endpoints to provide metadata information to requesters and support the bootstrapping of Web service interactions. The WS-MetadataExchange interface is flexible and could be used to retrieve general information from the endpoint, not necessarily constrained to metadata. However, the specification clearly states that the operations should be used only to retrieve metadata (that is, endpoint description) information, and that this information applies exclusively to the service endpoint or its associated resources. This limitation is important to maintain clear and distinct semantics of the bootstrap process.

9.1 Architectural Concepts

WS-Metadata Exchange builds around the notion of querying endpoints directly for their relevant metadata. To do so, it defines a simple WSDL interface that enables service requesters to query the services they intend to use for specific metadata properties. The WS-MetadataExchange interface follows two important design principles: extensibility of the set of metadata languages and definitions ("dialects"), and the ability to redirect metadata queries to dedicated endpoints.

9.1.1 Extensibility of Metadata Dialects

You can associate different types of metadata with an endpoint. Policies, service descriptions (in the form of WSDL documents), and associated XML Schemas are examples of metadata that you can associate with a service endpoint. However, you can define other forms of metadata to describe aspects of an endpoint as new industry standards are developed or higher forms of interaction are built on top of the basic Web services framework (such as semantically rich interactions, with the associated semantic description of services). The design of the WS-MetadataExchange interface takes this fact into account by assuming that the set of possible metadata dialects is naturally extensible. The WS-MetadataExchange specification recognizes certain metadata dialects (discussed in the next section) but also supports arbitrary metadata dialects. Service requesters and service providers can specify the type of metadata they intend on retrieving or providing, respectively.

Dialects and Identifiers

Metadata *dialects* are specific XML languages that represent properties of a service endpoint. Each metadata dialect is in turn represented by a unique URI. Typically, dialect identifiers correspond to the namespace URI that identifies the XML Schema definition of the language (the target namespace of its defining XML Schema). Following are the dialects that the WS-Metadata Exchange specification explicitly recognizes:

- The XML Schema dialect corresponds to the schema definition files for the messages that are exchanged by the endpoint.

- The WSDL dialect provides the WSDL description of the endpoint.

- The WS-Policy dialect encodes the set of policies that apply to the end-point using a WS-Policy expression.

- The WS-PolicyAttachment dialect encodes PolicyAttachment elements that associate a policy with a particular resource that relates to the endpoint.

- The WS-MetadataExchange dialect indicates an additional source of metadata for the endpoint, by using the "Metadata" element defined in the WS-MetadataExchange identification.

If the dialect URI determines the type of metadata exchanged, the metadata *identifier* indicates a specific metadata definition, such as a WSDL target name-space, an XML Schema target namespace, or a policy identifier. Identifiers allow requesters to ask for specific descriptions, as opposed to types of definitions (which are indicated by the dialect). Certain metadata dialects, such as the WS-PolicyAttachment dialect, might not support identifiers. It is important to observe that, when identifiers are supported, they are scoped to a specific dialect. For example, a WSDL and an XML Schema document might have the same target namespace. Therefore, the interpretation of the identifier is relative to the dialect within which it is used.

9.1.2 Use of Indirection: Metadata References and Locations

The amount of metadata that is associated with an endpoint can be large. In addition, even though the metadata exchange model has the service endpoint provide its own metadata to requesters, it is important that endpoints can offload this function to dedicated endpoints when required. WS-MetadataExchange allows service endpoints to provide their responses to metadata queries in the form of a dedicated endpoint (a "metadata reference") or a URL (a "metadata location") from which the actual metadata is to be retrieved, through a Web services or traditional Web request. The goal of this design is to allow endpoints and infrastructure deployers to deal flexibly with the load that is associated with the metadata exchange function.

9.1.3 Metadata Request Operations

WS-MetadataExchange introduces two metadata request operations: one for general-purpose metadata queries, and a second one for retrieval of metadata from metadata reference endpoints. Endpoints that support the WS-MetadataExchange specifications are required to support only the first one. Referenced endpoints that are given as metadata references are required to support the second.

GetMetadata Requests

The GetMetadata operation is the only required operation for WS-MetadataExchange-compliant endpoints. Requesters use it to solicit metadata from the service endpoint. GetMetadata allows several types of requests, enabling generic, dialect-specific, and definition-specific metadata requests.

A service requester uses a *generic metadata request* to ask for all metadata that is relevant to the interaction with the target endpoint, without imposing a restriction on the metadata to be returned. The service endpoint returns metadata that includes as many dialects as it considers relevant for the interaction with this requester. No additional parameters need to be specified in the request message.

A *dialect-specific request* retrieves applicable metadata of a single dialect, such as all policies or WSDL definitions that apply to the service. The requester only needs to specify the desired dialect with the request; it is up to the service endpoint to return as much information as is available and deemed relevant for the interaction.

A *definition-specific request* retrieves specific metadata definitions of a particular dialect as identified by a single metadata identifier. Recall that identifiers are scoped to a particular dialect. If the requested definition is available and relevant to the service endpoint, it will be returned with the response. Note that more than one definition might be returned corresponding to a given identifier.

The generic format of the GetMetadata request message is shown next. Observe that the generic request encodes an empty GetMetadata element, the dialect-specific request adds a nested element including the dialect URI, and the definition-specific one includes two elements—one with the dialect and a second one with the identifier.

```
<wsx:GetMetadata>
   [<wsx:Dialect>xs:anyURI</wsx:Dialect>
   [<wxs:Identifier>xs:anyURI</wsx:Identifier>]?
   ]?
</wsx:GetMetadata>
```

WS-MetadataExchange assigns a particular Action URI to this request, following the WS-Addressing model, in which the individual messages of an operation are assigned specific Action URIs.

GetMetadata Responses

The response that the service endpoint sends in response to a GetMetadataRequest can also take several forms to allow efficient communication of metadata and support scalability.

The information that is returned in a GetMetadata response is included within a "Metadata" element. The children of this element are a variable number of "metadata sections" as "MetadataSection" elements, each of them containing information about one metadata definition or set of related definitions (or "unit") of the same dialect and describing a particular aspect of the endpoint behavior. Each metadata section includes a "Dialect" attribute to indicate the type of metadata it contains. Multiple metadata sections of the same dialect are possible. An optional "Identifier" attribute on the MetadataSection element can identify the definition or set of definitions returned. This is typically the case when the original request contains a metadata identifier, and a matching metadata definition is returned. The identifier can be used in any GetMetadata response, however. Just as many metadata sections can contain the same Dialect attribute, multiple sections can be returned with the same identifier, such as when multiple XML Schema definitions within the same target namespace are returned. (The specification explicitly encourages multiple metadata sections in this case.)

Three kinds of metadata sections are possible: embedded metadata, metadata references, and metadata locations.

With *embedded metadata*, the actual metadata appears embedded directly inside the metadata section. The contents of the metadata section belong in this case to the specific XML dialect that the corresponding attribute identifies.

With *metadata reference*, a "MetadataReference" element of endpoint reference type encodes the endpoint reference where the actual metadata can be retrieved using a WS-MetadataExhange "Get" call.

Finally, with *metadata location*, a single "Location" element appears inside the metadata section. It contains a URL from which to retrieve the corresponding metadata using the common retrieval mechanism for the corresponding URL scheme. For example, the retrieval mechanism for an HTTP URL is an HTTP GET request.

Metadata references and locations allow service endpoints to control the amount of data returned with a GetMetadata response message. This is particularly important when an unqualified (or generic) GetMetadata request is received, potentially resulting in a large amount of actual metadata. Instead of sending back all that information, the responding endpoint can provide specific endpoints or URLs so that the original requester can retrieve individual units of metadata as it becomes necessary. Therefore, WS-MetadataExchange provides two mechanisms for controlling the amount of information returned with a GetMetadata request. First, requesters can limit the scope of the request using the dialect and identifier parameters. Second, service endpoints can use the indirection mechanisms of metadata references and location URLs to achieve a similar result.

Indirection serves a second purpose: It allows service endpoints to offload the metadata retrieval function to specialized service endpoints or applications, while maintaining the principle of making the endpoint the primary contact point for requesters who are looking for service metadata.

The structure of a GetMetadata response is summarized in the pseudo-grammar that follows.

```
<wsx:Metadata ...>
    [<wsx:MetadataSection Dialect='xs:anyURI'
                          [Identifier='xs:anyURI']? >
        [<dialectSpecificElementName>
        ...
        </dialectSpecificElementName>+
        |
        <wsx:MetadataReference ...>
            endpoint-reference
        </wsx:MetadataReference>
        |
        <wsx:Location>xs:anyURI</wsx:Location>
        ]
    </wsx:MetadataSection>]*
</wsx:Metadata>
```

Get Request

Metadata reference endpoints are required to support a single operation with the only purpose of returning a specific set of metadata definitions. The WS-MetadataExchange "Get" operation takes no parameter data and returns the actual metadata indicated by the metadata section that contained the reference. The metadata reference is a dedicated endpoint whose function (from the point of view of the service requester) is limited to returning one unit of metadata when it receives a Get request.

Metadata Exchange Example

Now you can put together the message exchanges that were just described in a set of related exchanges. The exchange begins with a "GetMetadata" request from a requester application, soliciting WS-Policy metadata; the request message contains the following data:

```
<wsx:GetMetadata>
  <wsx:Dialect>
      http://schemas.xmlsoap.org/ws/2002/12/policy
  </wsx:Dialect>
</wsx:GetMetadata>
```

The response contains a list of metadata sections with metadata references of where to retrieve the actual policies:

```
<wsx:Metadata>
   <wsx:MetadataSection Dialect=
   "http://schemas.xmlsoap.org/ws/2002/12/policy"
   Identifier=
   "http://example.com/endpoint-policies/p-sec">
      <wsa:Address>
      http://example.com/endpoint-policies-eprs-get/p-sec
      <wsa:Address>
   </wsx:MetadataSection>
   <wsx:MetadataSection>
   <wsx:MetadataSection>
   ...
</wsx:Metadata>
```

A Get request that is directed to the endpoint contained in the first metadata section contains an empty Get message (together with the appropriate Action header):

```
<wsx:Get/>
```

The returned message from this operation contains the actual policy being sought, for example:

```
<wsp:Policy>
   <wsp:ExactlyOne>
     <wsse:SecurityToken>
       <wsse:TokenType>wsse:Kerberosv5TGT</wsse:TokenType>
     </wsse:SecurityToken>
     <wsse:SecurityToken>
       <wsse:TokenType>wsse:X509v3</wsse:TokenType>
     </wsse:SecurityToken>
   </wsp:ExactlyOne>
</wsp:Policy>
```

9.1.4 Default Protocol Binding

The idea behind the dynamic retrieval of metadata from a service endpoint assumes that little or no information is known about the service endpoint prior to the metadata exchange interaction. This, of course, is not necessarily the common case, but it is certainly an important one to support. In particular, the specific protocol binding to access the endpoint might be unknown at the time the bootstrapping process is to begin. It is recommended that endpoints complying with WS-MetadataExchange support a default SOAP over HTTP protocol binding; other protocols can be supported as long as that fact is explicitly represented in the endpoint description metadata. In the absence of a statement indicating an alternative protocol, the default protocol is assumed to apply.

Note, however, that WS-MetadataExchange does not solve the problem of how to communicate to a requester an alternative binding in the bootstrap process. The solution to this problem will likely involve other specifications.

9.2 Future Directions

WS-MetadataExchange is a public specification offered under royalty-free terms. It likely will be submitted to a standards organization to undergo formal standardization. It's difficult to predict the outcome of that process, but some of the limitations of the current specification should be eliminated. Following are three of the changes that you might expect as this process proceeds forward.

- **Support for multidialect and multi-identifier requests**—The current specification allows you to request all the metadata for an endpoint or to restrict it to a single dialect or identifier. This seems like an unnecessary limitation. Allowing you to request metadata from multiple dialects would provide additional control for requesters over the returned metadata.

- **Multiprotocol access**—Currently, there is no mechanism to bootstrap metadata exchange interactions in the most generic case unless the default protocol binding is assumed to apply. In many situations, other protocols need to be used, however. Dealing with this limitation would likely require WS-Addressing support.

■ **Mechanisms for identifying support for WS-MetadataExchange in WSDL service descriptions**—It's assumed that service endpoints support WS-MetadataExchange in addition to their business interfaces. This fact needs to be clearly specified in the WSDL description of the service; a mechanism to do so will need to be defined. (Although adding a port to the service definition is straightforward, it's probably not the most convenient approach from the usability perspective.)

9.3 Summary

Explicit service description information (metadata) is a central aspect of SOAs and the Web services framework. Explicit metadata is the key to effective decoupling between service applications. Several mechanisms allow communicating metadata between service providers and requesters. Centralized registries such as UDDI rely on a third party to aggregate information about services and enable both discovery of services and retrieval of service descriptions. WS-MetadataExchange defines a WSDL interface so that service requesters can retrieve metadata directly from the service provider. This model does not support service discovery, but it's advantageous because a third-party infrastructure is not required for requesters to retrieve full information about a service provider. WS-MetadataExchange enables dynamic configuration at the requester side and allows providers to dynamically customize their policies based on the identity of the requester or specific conditions under which the interaction takes place. For this reason, WS-Metadata is a key piece for bootstrapping service interactions. Finally, the WS-MetadataExchange interface can accommodate additional metadata types beyond the ones commonly considered today (XML Schema, WSDL, and WS-Policy), such as semantic service descriptions.

Part 5

Reliable Interaction

This part begins the journey into the domain of quality-of-service characteristics of Web service interactions with a discussion of reliable interactions. The figure that follows shows where this topic falls in the Web services stack.

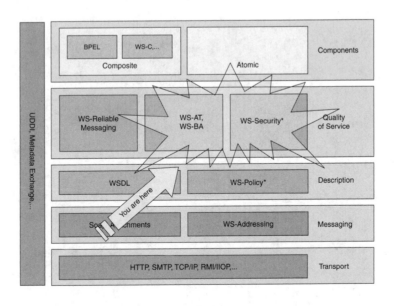

Chapter 10, "Reliable Messaging," discusses the WS-Reliable Messaging (WS-RM) specification. WS-RM defines protocols for establishing and maintaining a reliable interaction between a client and a service. It supports several different qualities of service, such as in-order and exactly-once delivery.

The second chapter in this section, Chapter 11, "Transactions," discusses a venerable topic that is key to enabling business interactions using Web services: how Web services can agree on the outcome of multiparty interactions. This chapter presents two protocols: WS-Atomic Transactions for atomic transactions with ACID properties, and WS-Business Activity for loosely coupled coordination, where intermediate steps are visible to the participants. Both protocols are built on top of the WS-Coordination specification, which provides a framework for developing distributed coordination protocols.

Chapter 10

Reliable Messaging

Since the early 1990s, the information technology (IT) community has leveraged reliable messaging as a means of mitigating the issues presented in the scenarios and the motivations covered in this chapter. The IT community has been using message queue technologies such as WebSphereMQ from IBM, SonicMQ from Sonic, and MSMQ from Microsoft, in addition to reliable publish/subscribe technologies such as Tibco Rendezvous. The Java Community Process (JCP) has developed the Java Message Service API (JMS) in an effort to unify the myriad application programming interfaces (APIs) to these proprietary environments for the Java platform. These entities have adapted many of these reliable messaging environments for use in a Web services context by enabling them to carry SOAP messages and by describing their bindings using Web Services Description Language (WSDL). However, to date, each vendor tends to exploit its own proprietary protocol for the transmission of the message between its source and its destination. It's only possible to achieve interoperability between these proprietary messaging environments by means of gateways between disparate environments, each tailored to a specific pair of environments.

With the emergence of Web services as the preferred integration solution for distributed systems, it is now realistic to think about the possibility of a unified interoperability standard for reliable messaging.

WS-Reliable Messaging has the greatest potential for becoming the standard for reliable messaging for Web services. Therefore, this book focuses on that specification.

10.1 Motivation for Reliable Messaging

L. Peter Deutsch, a noted computer scientist, has been attributed with publishing what has become known in software engineering circles as the "Eight Fallacies of Distributed Computing." He first presented them at a talk he gave to the researchers and engineers at Sun Microsystems Labs in 1991. At the time Deutsch first presented the fallacies, there were only seven. He added the eighth sometime later. The eight fallacies are as follows:

1. The network is reliable.

2. Latency is zero.

3. Bandwidth is infinite.

4. The network is secure.

5. Topology doesn't change.

6. There is one administrator.

7. Transport cost is zero.

8. The network is homogenous.

Web services are, at their essence, distributed applications. Certainly, when designing any Web service, you should carefully consider these words of wisdom. Ask yourself whether you have inadvertently relied upon any of these false assumptions in making your design decisions.

The next sections dive deeper into a few of these fallacies and discuss their relevance to Web services.

10.1.1 The Network Is Reliable

The first of these fallacies, "The network is reliable," is one trap into which many software engineering projects fall. Given that most Web services deployed today use Transmission Control Protocol (TCP), a highly reliable connection-oriented host-to-host network protocol, you might think that it's unimportant to concern yourself with the inherent unreliability of the network. However, TCP is only reliable to the extent that the sending TCP stack can be certain that a message has been delivered to the TCP stack at the receiving host. Likewise, the receiving host can only be certain that it has either received a message reliably, or it has not. Things can still go wrong from the perspective of the Web service, which resides far above the TCP/IP interface.

First, consider that the reliability of the TCP protocol is limited in its scope to the two communicating TCP stacks and everything in between. Although the receiving TCP stack assumes responsibility for ensuring that received messages are passed to the application layer, the process could terminate before the TCP stack has been able to perform its responsibilities in this regard. Messages that have been successfully received and acknowledged at the TCP layer could be lost from the perspective of the application.

Second, a sending process might terminate before the sending application knows that the receiving TCP stack has received and acknowledged its message, and the receiving application has processed it.

Either of these two failure modes can leave a Web service consumer or provider in an inconsistent state with respect to its counterpart. Although this might not present a problem for certain stateless and/or idempotent operations such as an HTTP GET, it can present quite a serious problem for others that are not idempotent.

If you are going to provide for reliable messaging in the context of Web services, you need to keep these issues in mind.

10.1.2 Latency Is Zero

Whether dealing with distributed components of an application on an intranet or over the Internet, latency between the distributed components impacts reliability. In the time it takes a message to be transmitted from sender to receiver, all manner of things can go wrong. The network could become partitioned due to a router failure or a severed or disconnected network cable. The destination host could crash. The process in which the receiving component is running could terminate.

When considering latency in terms of a round-trip request and response (or stimulus and response), latency becomes an even greater concern. If the service provider is overwhelmed with requests to process, you can often count latency in seconds, if not minutes. Processing a request can involve significant computational resources, or it might depend on another distributed component. Processing a request might even require manual intervention in some cases. The longer the latency, the greater the potential for something to go wrong, leaving the distributed application in an inconsistent state.

10.1.3 There Is One Administrator

Even in an intranet context, this fallacy often rears its ugly head. Although your IT department might assign a single group to be responsible for the network, in the context of a Web service, many administrators typically exist. In most cases, these administrators have rather parochial interests. There might be one administrator for each database, one for each of the application servers that host the Web service components, one for the demilitarized zone (DMZ) and firewall complexes, one for the server room, and so on. Administrators might not always coordinate their activities with your Web service's needs. All of this can lead to circumstances in which certain components of a Web service implementation become unavailable (during an upgrade or routine maintenance, for example), often at critical and unexpected times.

Expanding the scope of Web services to the context of the Internet, things get even more interesting and complicated. You can no more expect to coordinate activities related to the components of a Web service when the administrator(s) of those components are employed by your business partners than you can expect to win the lottery!

Therefore, you need to design your Web service so that it can recover from failures related to the unavailability of a distributed component brought down for routine maintenance or failure.

10.2 Reliable Messaging Scenarios

Considering the issues highlighted by the previous elaborated fallacies, various strategies are available for designing a more robust and reliable system.

10.2.1 Store and Forward

In many scenarios in highly distributed systems, the best you can hope to achieve is to get information closer to its intended destination. This allows for more efficient use of the network resources and decouples the initial sender and intended recipient such that they do not need to be running concurrently. In other words, the sending system does not need to be running when the receiving node receives and processes the information, and the receiving node does not need to be running when the sending node transmits the information in the first place.

E-mail is at its essence a store-and-forward system. When you send an e-mail, it typically is transmitted first to your Internet service provider (ISP), where it is stored on disk. Then the ISP's sendmail server transmits the message to a server that is closer yet to the intended recipient (for example, the sendmail server at the intended recipient's ISP). Eventually, the intended recipient logs into her ISP and retrieves all new e-mail messages that have arrived. If any of the distributed components along the e-mail's message path is unavailable, the node at which the message is currently located attempts to retransmit the message later until such time as the message transmission, or hop, is successful.

10.2.2 Batch Window

This scenario is a derivative of the store-and-forward scenario discussed in the previous section. Consider two trading partners who want to exchange purchase orders reliably. One uses a batch system to process orders, and the other uses an online system that processes them in near real time. Clearly, there's an impedance mismatch between the two partners' systems. The partner with the batch order processing system might be in no position to rip and re-place its existing batch system for any number of valid reasons, both business and technical.

An effective strategy for dealing with this impedance mismatch is to interpose a store-and-forward architecture between the two systems. You can employ this architecture at either partner or at both. The impedance mismatch is mitigated by virtue of the fact that the messages transmitted as individual messages can be collected into a batch for processing. The converse is also true. Neither side needs to be concerned with the fact that its counterpart has a different process-ing design.

10.2.3 Failure Recovery

Another scenario is that of failure recovery. Consider two trading partners that have been exchanging order information over time. One suffers a catastrophic failure of its order management system and has to recover from the previous evening's backup. That partner has lost all the orders that it has received since the backup from which it recovered was performed, and it must find some way of resynchronizing its system with that of its trading partner. Similarly, the part-ner whose system did not fail has an interest in having its trading partner fulfill all the orders that it has sent. Although the two partners could manually recon-cile their systems, a manual reconciliation does not scale to scenarios that in-volve several trading partners. Had the partners been using a protocol that reliably exchanged messages that leveraged a persistent store and a capability to redeliver messages that had previously been acknowledged, they might be able to recover from such a failure in an automated manner, saving time and money in the process.

10.2.4 Long-Running Transactions

People often use atomic transactions with two or or three-phase commit strate-gies when designing distributed systems to ensure that the distributed compo-nents of the system have a consistent view of their shared state.

However, in many scenarios, use of a transaction processing monitor is not prac-tical. You would never consider locking resources for extended periods neces-sary for completion of something as long running as a purchase order life cycle.

Further, because of security considerations, you would never think twice about letting an external party place locks on your system's resources; that party could easily mount a denial-of-service (DoS) attack that could cripple your systems.

Using a reliable messaging protocol, paired with a protocol such as WS-Business Activity, to manage the compensation of application-level faults, you can overcome these concerns while enabling a more reliable interaction. The reliable messaging protocol ensures the dependable delivery of the messages, and the application-level compensation ensures that the long-running transaction either completes successfully or suitably compensates any failure.

10.3 Architectural Concepts

Of all the proposals for reliable messaging for Web services, WS-Reliable Messaging seems to have the most promise for broad adoption and widespread deployment necessary to become a standard for interoperability. That is because its sponsors represent a majority market-share in both the reliable messaging and Web services solution space.

WS-Reliable Messaging is by far the simplest of the proposed specifications. It focuses exclusively on the reliable messaging aspect. The addressing aspect has been factored out into a separate specification called WS-Addressing, covered in detail in Chapter 5, "WS-Addressing."

Reliable messaging is enabled by virtue of something called a *Sequence*, which is effectively a shared context for a set of messages to be delivered with a common quality of service between a sending and a receiving endpoint. Each message within a *Sequence* is assigned a unique message number, starting with 1 and increasing monotonically, by one, for each subsequent message in the Sequence. The receiving endpoint acknowledges receipt of the messages within a Sequence by indicating the range of messages it has received using a *SequenceAcknowledgement*. Each SequenceAcknowledgement message carries the acknowledgement information for all the messages that have been received within a Sequence. Hence, a SequenceAcknowledgement message does not require retransmission should it fail to reach the sending endpoint of the original message, because the information is sent with a subsequent SequenceAcknowledgement message.

As with the other reliable messaging specifications proposed, WS-Reliable Messaging is defined as a set of SOAP Header extension elements that enable a range of qualities of service for a Web service, from at-most-once through exactly-once delivery assurances, preservation of message order, and duplicate detection. However, unlike the other proposals, WS-Reliable Messaging accomplishes this with a much simpler syntax and more efficient processing semantics.

10.4 Processing Model

The WS-Reliable Messaging specification defines an abstract model for the protocol and four distinct roles: Application Source and RM Source on the sending endpoint, and Application Destination and RM Destination at the receiving endpoint.

The Application Source role is typically played by the application code running on the endpoint from which messages are to be delivered reliably. It initiates the protocol by sending a message (logically) to the RM Source, which then assumes responsibility for transmitting—and possibly retransmitting—the message to the destination role at the receiving endpoint. The RM Source is also responsible for processing any SequenceAcknowledgement messages from the RM Destination and taking appropriate action.

The RM Destination role at the receiving endpoint receives messages (re)transmitted by the RM Source role at the sending endpoint. It is responsible for acknowledging receipt of the message and (logically) delivering the message to the Application Destination role, which is typically played by the application code that runs on the receiving endpoint. The RM Destination role is responsible for affecting the quality of service associated with the Delivery Assurance policy specified for the receiving endpoint.

Figure 10-1 demonstrates this model.

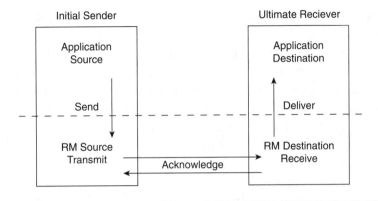

Figure 10-1   Reliable Messaging model.

This model is like that of the TCP protocol. The WS-Reliable Messaging protocol is limited in its scope to the RM Source and RM Destination roles at either endpoint. Aside from the assurances that the RM Destination observes to fulfill the specified delivery assurances (At-Most-Once, At-Least-Once, Exactly-Once, and Ordered), the Application Source role can only be certain that the message has been reliably delivered to the RM Destination role at the receiving endpoint.

If the application code at the Application Source role needs to have some sort of application-level acknowledgement that the message was actually processed, the WS-Reliable Messaging protocol is inadequate for the task. An application-specific acknowledgement message is required, such as a PurchaseOrderAck as an application-level acknowledgement/response to a submitted PurchaseOrder.

Note, however, that this separation of concerns is important. Examine the previous example in light of this separation of concerns. Consider that a PurchaseOrderAck message sent in response to a PurchaseOrder submission message might take upward of 24 hours to process in the use case, where the receiving partner processes its received PurchaseOrders in a batch window once a day. Waiting 24 hours for some indication that a PurchaseOrder has been lost in transit between the sending and receiving endpoints can have serious consequences for the business partner that makes the request. It can even lead to loss of revenue when order fulfillment is time-sensitive. Clearly, relying exclusively on the application-level acknowledgement as an indicator that the message was successfully transmitted is not an ideal situation for all use cases.

Leveraging an infrastructure-level (or, more precisely, a middleware-level) acknowledgement, decoupled from the application-level processing of the message, as the indicator of successful transmission of a message enables the sending endpoint to respond more quickly to failed transmission attempts. The failed message transmission can be retried until its receipt has been acknowledged. The receiving software can take the necessary steps to ensure that the message is eventually delivered to the application by means of a persistent store or message queue that the receiving application accesses when it is ready and able.

This model is highly effective at mitigating the issues discussed earlier in the "Motivation for Reliable Messaging" section.

The ensuing sections discuss how the WS-Reliable Messaging protocol realizes this model.

10.4.1 Sequence Lifecycle

An RM Sequence has a well-defined lifecycle. It begins with the RM Source requesting the creation of a new Sequence of the RM Destination using the CreateSequence operation. The following example demonstrates the CreateSequence message.

```
<?xml version="1.0" encoding="UTF-8"?>

<soap:Envelope
xmlns:soap="http://www.w3.org/2003/05/soap-envelope"
xmlns:wsrm="http://schemas.xmlsoap.org/ws/2005/02/rm"
xmlns:wsa="http://schemas.xmlsoap.org/ws/2004/08/addressing">
 <soap:Header>
  <wsa:MessageID>
   http://example.com/guid/0baaf88d-483b-4ecf-a6d8-a7c2eb546817
  </wsa:MessageID>
  <wsa:To>http://example.com/service/B</wsa:To>
    <wsa:Action>
      http://schemas.xmlsoap.org/ws/2005/02/rm/CreateSequence
    </wsa:Action>
  <wsa:ReplyTo>
   <wsa:Address>http://example.com/service/A</wsa:Address>
  </wsa:ReplyTo>
 </soap:Header>
```

```
<soap:Body>
  <wsrm:CreateSequence>
    <wsrm:AcksTo>
      <wsa:Address>http://example.com/service/A</wsa:Address>
    </wsrm:AcksTo>
  </wsrm:CreateSequence>
 </soap:Body>
</soap:Envelope>
```

The CreateSequence element has a single required child element, the AcksTo, which indicates the WS-Addressing endpoint to which SequenceAcknowledgement messages are to be delivered.

Upon receipt of the CreateSequence message, the RM Destination responds by creating a new Sequence, assigning it a unique identifier, and by returning a CreateSequenceResponse message, containing the Sequence's identifier, to the RM Source. The following example demonstrates a CreateSequenceResponse message.

```
<?xml version="1.0" encoding="UTF-8"?>
<soap:Envelope xmlns:soap="http://www.w3.org/2003/05/soap-envelope"
xmlns:wsrm="http://schemas.xmlsoap.org/ws/2005/02/rm"
xmlns:wsa="http://schemas.xmlsoap.org/ws/2004/08/addressing">
  <soap:Header>
    <wsa:MessageID>
   http://example.com.com/guid/0baaf88d-483b-4ecf-a6d8-
a7c2eb546818
   </wsa:MessageID>
    <wsa:To>http://example.com/service/A</wsa:To>
    <wsa:RelatesTo>
      http://example.com/guid/0baaf88d-483b-4ecf-a6d8a7c2eb546817
    </wsa:RelatesTo>
    <wsa:Action>

http://schemas.xmlsoap.org/ws/2005/02/rm/CreateSequenceResponse
    </wsa:Action>
  </soap:Header>
  <soap:Body>
    <wsrm:CreateSequenceResponse>

<wsrm:Identifier>http://example.com/RM/ABC</wsrm:Identifier>
    </wsrm:CreateSequenceResponse>
  </soap:Body>
</soap:Envelope>
```

The Sequence then transmits messages between the RM Source and the RM Destination. When all of the messages in a Sequence have been transmitted and successfully acknowledged, the Sequence is terminated. Upon receipt of the SequenceAcknowledgement that acknowledges the entire range of messages in the Sequence, the RM Source sends a TerminateSequence one-way message to the RM Destination. Upon receipt of the TerminateSequence message, the RM Destination is free to reclaim any resources that are associated with the Sequence. It can do so because it can be assured that the RM Source has received the final SequenceAcknowledgement message covering the full range of messages in the Sequence and will be sending no further messages in the Sequence.

If the RM Destination receives any subsequent messages in the Sequence, it can be assured that these messages must have been caught in the network and can be safely discarded without action. In fact, if the RM Destination receives any message belonging to a Sequence about which it has no knowledge, it can safely discard the message without taking action because it can assume that the message belongs to a Sequence that has been terminated.

If the RM Destination does not receive the TerminateSequence message, it may preserve the state associated with the Sequence until the Sequence expiry duration expires so that it can respond with a retransmission of the final SequenceAcknowledgement message if any subsequent messages for the Sequence are received.

10.4.2 Basic Syntax

The WS-Reliable Messaging specification defines four SOAP header elements: Sequence, SequenceFault, SequenceAcknowledgement, and AckRequested. In addition, a companion specification, WS-RM Policy Assertion, defines a set of domain-specific policy assertions, to be used in context of WS-Policy and WS-Policy Attachments for purposes of specifying the quality of service details related to a Sequence.

The sections that follow explore each of the syntax elements in detail.

10.4.3 Sequence Element

The core element of the WS-Reliable Messaging protocol is the Sequence element. Each message within a Sequence between sending and receiving endpoints must include a Sequence SOAP header element. The following is an example of a SOAP message containing a Sequence header that initiates a new Sequence and establishes the initial expiration date for the Sequence:

```
<soap:Envelope
  xmlns:soap="http://schemas.xmlsoap.org/soap/envelope/"
  xmlns:wsa="http://schemas.xmlsoap.org/ws/2004/08/addressing"
  xmlns:wsrm="http://schemas.xmlsoap.org/ws/2005/02/rm">
  <soap:Header>
    <rm:Sequence>
      <rm:Identifier>
        20030818-11010001-0500@example.com
      </rm:Identifier>
      <rm:MessageNumber>1</rm:MessageNumber>
    </rm:Sequence>
  </soap:Header>
  <soap:Body>
    ...
  </soap:Body>
</soap:Envelope>
```

The Sequence element has three child elements: Identifier, MessageNumber, and LastMessage. The Identifier and MessageNumber elements must be present in each Sequence element.

The Identifier element is the unique identifier of the Sequence. The same value must be present on each message in a Sequence.

The MessageNumber element carries a positive integer that represents the message's position within a Sequence.

The LastMessage element is included only on the last message in a Sequence. It signals to the receiving endpoint that this message is the last in the Sequence.

In addition, you can extend the Sequence element so that it can carry additional attributes and elements from foreign namespaces. This allows the Sequence element to be composed in several ways, some of which the authors of the WS-Reliable Messaging specification might not have anticipated.

A Sequence can be short-lived or long-running. It can have as few as one message or as many as 18,446,744,073,709,551,615 messages. Therefore, you can leverage the protocol for a wide variety of use cases. Partners who exchange relatively few messages at infrequent intervals might choose to establish a new Sequence for each burst of activity, whereas partners who have long-term relationships with frequent exchanges of messages might choose to do so under the context of a single Sequence. In either case, the protocol is always the same.

A Sequence can apply to all of the messages traveling in a particular direction (for example, from sender to receiver) in a portType/interface, to messages traveling in a particular direction within selected operations in a portType/interface, or to particular input or output messages traveling in a particular direction. Technically, a Sequence can apply to all traffic traveling in a particular direction between two endpoints, regardless of whether they have been described as a single portType/interface.

10.4.4 SequenceAcknowledgement Element

Messages within a Sequence are acknowledged by a receiving endpoint by means of the SequenceAcknowledgement SOAP header element. As previously mentioned, the SequenceAcknowledgement SOAP header element contains acknowledgement information about all of the messages in a Sequence. It does this by means of a set of one or more child AcknowledgementRange elements, each of which carries an upper and lower bound of contiguous messages that have been received within a Sequence.

Technically, the correctness of the protocol can be accomplished by virtue of the receiving endpoint sending just one acknowledgement message with a SequenceAcknowledgement element in response to the receipt of a message that has a Sequence element with the LastMessage element present.

Of course, waiting until all the messages within a Sequence have been received before sending an acknowledgement message might be impractical in many, if not most, circumstances. As you will soon see in the section titled "10.4.8 Policy Assertions," a receiving endpoint is typically configured with a maximum interval between acknowledgement messages using the AcknowledgementInterval policy assertion. A sending endpoint then expects to receive an acknowledgement message within the specified AcknowledgmentInterval after transmitting a message. Failure to receive a SequenceAcknowledgement message within the specified time interval might indicate a problem at the receiving endpoint and result in a retransmission attempt for any unacknowledged messages.

The following is an example of a SequenceAcknowledgement element that acknowledges receipt of messages 1 through 10.

```
<soap:Envelope
   xmlns:soap="http://schemas.xmlsoap.org/soap/envelope/"
   xmlns:wsrm="http://schemas.xmlsoap.org/ws/2005/02/rm">
   <soap:Header>
     ...
     <rm:SequenceAcknowledgment>
       <rm:Identifier>
         20030818-11010001-0500@example.com
       </rm:Identifier>
       <rm:AcknowledgmentRange Upper="10" Lower="1"/>
     </rm:SequenceAcknowledgment>
   </soap:Header>
   <soap:Body>
     ...
   </soap:Body>
</soap:Envelope>
```

Next is an example of a SOAP message that contains a Sequence Acknowledgement SOAP header element. This element indicates that it has not received the third message in a Sequence that has five messages (as perceived from the receiving endpoint's perspective). Note that the SequenceAcknowledgement element has two AcknowledgementRange child elements: one that acknowledges receipt of messages 1 and 2, and a second that acknowledges receipt of messages 4 and 5.

```
<soap:Envelope
  xmlns:soap="http://schemas.xmlsoap.org/soap/envelope/"
  xmlns:wsrm="http://schemas.xmlsoap.org/ws/2005/02/rm">
  <soap:Header>
    <rm:SequenceAcknowledgment>
      <rm:Identifier>
        20030818-11010001-0500@example.com
    </rm:Identifier>
        <rm:AcknowledgmentRange Upper="2" Lower="1"/>
        <rm:AcknowledgmentRange Upper="5" Lower="4"/>
      </rm:SequenceAcknowledgment>
  </soap:Header>
  <soap:Body>
    ...
  </soap:Body>
</soap:Envelope>
```

The sending endpoint that received such a SequenceAcknowledgement would determine that message 3 needed to be retransmitted until the sending endpoint received a message carrying a SequenceAcknowledgement SOAP header element indicating that the receiving endpoint had, in fact, received message 3.

```
<soap:Envelope
  xmlns:soap="http://schemas.xmlsoap.org/soap/envelope/"
  xmlns:wsrm="http://schemas.xmlsoap.org/ws/2005/02/rm">
  <soap:Header>
    ...
    <rm:SequenceAcknowledgment>
      <rm:Identifier>20030818-11010001-
        0500@example.com</rm:Identifier>
        <rm:AcknowledgmentRange Upper="5" Lower="1"/>
    </rm:SequenceAcknowledgment>
  </soap:Header>
  <soap:Body>
    ...
  </soap:Body>
</soap:Envelope>
```

10.4.5 AckRequested Element

The third SOAP header element defined by the WS-Reliable Messaging specification is the AckRequested element. A sending endpoint might include an AckRequested SOAP header element in a message as a means of asking the receiving endpoint to send an acknowledgement message immediately instead of waiting for the acknowledgement interval to expire.

The following SOAP message is an example of use of the AckRequested element.

```
<soap:Envelope
  xmlns:soap="http://schemas.xmlsoap.org/soap/envelope/"
  xmlns:wsa="http://schemas.xmlsoap.org/ws/2003/03/addressing"
  xmlns:wsrm="http://schemas.xmlsoap.org/ws/2005/02/rm"
  xmlns:wsu="http://schemas.xmlsoap.org/ws/2002/07/utility">
  <soap:Header>
    ...
    <rm:Sequence>
      <rm:Identifier>20030818-11010001-
      0500@example.com</rm:Identifier>
      <rm:MessageNumber>1</rm:MessageNumber>
    </rm:Sequence>
    <rm:AckRequested/>
  </soap:Header>
  <soap:Body>
    ...
  </soap:Body>
</soap:Envelope>
```

10.4.6 SequenceFault Element

The fourth and final SOAP header element defined in the WS-Reliable Messaging specification is SequenceFault. It carries fault detail information related to the processing of the Sequence, SequenceAcknowledgement, and AckRequested SOAP header elements. The fault information is carried as a SOAP header element because faults that are related to the processing of SOAP header elements must also be conveyed as SOAP header elements per the SOAP specification(s).

The SequenceFault element has two required child elements: Identifier, to identify the Sequence to which the fault applies, and FaultCode, to carry the qualified name (QName) of one of the fault codes defined in the WS-Reliable Messaging specification. It might also have one or more AcknowledgementRange child elements if the fault was generated in response to processing a SequenceAcknowledgement.

In addition, the specification provides for extensibility of the SequenceFault element by means of an XML Schema wildcard element.

The following is an example of a SOAP message carrying a SequenceFault SOAP header element. It indicates that the Sequence has been refused because of insufficient resources at the RM Destination to allocate a new Sequence.

```
<soap:Envelope
  xmlns:soap="http://schemas.xmlsoap.org/soap/envelope/"
  xmlns:wsrm="http://schemas.xmlsoap.org/ws/2005/02/rm"
  xmlns:wsu="http://schemas.xmlsoap.org/ws/2002/07/utility">
  <soap:Header>
    <rm:SequenceFault>
      <rm:FaultCode>rm:SequenceRefused</rm:FaultCode>
    </rm:SequenceFault>
  </soap:Header>
  <soap:Body>
    <soap:Fault>
      <faultcode>soap:Server</faultcode>
      <faultstring>
      insufficient resources for new Sequence.
      </faultstring>
    </soap:Fault>
  </soap:Body>
</soap:Envelope>
```

10.4.7 Delivery Semantics Supported

The WS-Reliable Messaging protocol is an At-Least-Once protocol. That means that each message will be delivered to the RM Destination at least once in the correct operation of the protocol. This base enables the RM Destination to offer the full spectrum of delivery assurances to the Application Destination, ranging from At-Most-Once to At-Least-Once and Exactly-Once to Ordered.

For instance, the RM Destination could maintain a limited buffer for messages received and discard duplicates and the oldest undelivered messages in the buffer as new messages are received within a Sequence after the buffer size is exceeded. That would provide At-Most-Once delivery semantics to the Application Destination.

Alternatively, the RM Destination could be implemented such that it did not check for and discard duplicate messages, thus providing At-Least-Once delivery semantics to the Application Destination.

The RM Destination could apply Exactly-Once delivery semantics by applying duplicate detection to the At-Least-Once semantics.

The RM Destination could provide "Ordered" delivery semantics by ensuring that it buffered those messages that have gaps in the Sequence until messages are received that fill those gaps before delivering the messages to the Application Destination.

Ultimately, it is the RM Destination's responsibility to fulfill the delivery assurance requirements of the Application Destination. This simplifies the protocol and increases the potential for interoperability.

10.4.8 Policy Assertions
The companion WS-RM Policy Assertion specification defines a policy assertion that is intended for use in the context of WS-Policy and WS-Policy Attachments. The policy assertion is aimed at enabling endpoints that participate in the WS-Reliable Messaging protocol either to specify their requirements or to indicate the protocol's observed behavior to a prospective partner.

10.4.9 Inactivity Timeout
This assertion property specifies (in milliseconds) a period of inactivity for a Sequence. If during this duration an endpoint has received no application or control messages, the endpoint MAY consider the Sequence to have been terminated due to inactivity.

```
<rm:InactivityTimeout Milliseconds="86400000"/>
```

10.4.10 Retransmission Interval
A ReliableMessaging source may optionally specify a base retransmission interval for a sequence. If no acknowledgement has been received for a given message within that interval, the source will retransmit the message. The retransmission interval may be modified at the discretion of the source during the lifetime of the sequence. This assertion property does not alter the formulation of messages as transmitted, only the timing of their transmission.

The sequence may optionally specify that the interval will be adjusted using the commonly known exponential backoff algorithm.

```
<rm:BaseRetransmissionInterval Milliseconds="3000"/>
<rm:ExponentialBackoff/>
```

10.4.11 Acknowledgement Interval

Acknowledgements can be sent on return messages or sent stand alone. In the case where a return message is not available with which to send an acknowledgement, a ReliableMessaging Destination may wait for the duration of the acknowledgement interval before sending a stand alone acknowledgement. If there are no unacknowledged messages, the ReliableMessaging Destination may choose not to send an acknowledgement.

This assertion property does not alter the formulation of messages or acknowledgements as transmitted. Its purpose is to communicate the timing of acknowledgements so that the source may be tuned appropriately. It does not alter the meaning of the <AckRequested> directive.

```
<rm:AcknowledgementInterval Milliseconds="1000"/>
```

10.4.12 Basic WS-Reliable Messaging Profile

Given that the policy assertion properties that comprise timing considerations can be arranged into any number of possible combinations, the authors of the WS-Reliable Messaging specification have defined a base timing profile that is intended to help promote interoperability.

The specifics of this profile are as follows:

```
<wsp:Policy>
  <rm:RMAssertion>
    <rm:BaseRetransmissionInterval Milliseconds="3000"/>
    <rm:ExponentialBackoff/>
    <rm:InactivityTimeout Milliseconds="86400000"/>
    <rm:AcknowledgementInterval Milliseconds="1000"/>
  </rm:RMAssertion>
</wsp:Policy>
```

The authors have assigned this profile the following URI designation:

`http://schemas.xmlsoap.org/ws/2005/02/rm/baseTimingProfile.xml`

Therefore, you can reference it using a WS-Policy Attachment PolicyReference.

10.5 Strengths and Weaknesses

On the plus side, WS-Reliable Messaging offers the full range of quality of service that you would expect. The protocol is quite simple, but in many respects, it is far more efficient and effective than the other proposed specifications.

WS-Reliable Messaging has been carefully architected to be fully composeable with other Web services specifications that have been or have yet to be published by IBM, Microsoft, and their partners.

Specifically, WS-Reliable Messaging can be composed with WS-Addressing to enable a wide variety of reliable message exchange patterns (MEPs). However, WS-Reliable Messaging does not require composition with WS-Addressing or any specific version of WS-Addressing. For example, consider the case in which WS-Reliable Messaging is used with the synchronous SOAP/HTTP binding, such that the SequenceAcknowledgment is carried in a SOAP message on the HTTP response message. Typically, there would be no need to address information in this use case. Yet, it enables a far more robust and reliable exchange of messages between the sending and receiving endpoints. If a SequenceAcknowledgement message fails to reach the sending endpoint that initiated the HTTP request, the acknowledgement information is carried on the HTTP response for the next message in the Sequence without requiring that the sending endpoint resend the unacknowledged message.

WS-Reliable Messaging does not require specialized logic to validate required interdependencies between header elements that cannot be expressed in XML Schema, as do some of the other two proposed specifications that this chapter has reviewed. Therefore, off-the-shelf schema validators, such as the Apache Xerces parser, can validate the SOAP header elements.

WS-Reliable Messaging has also been carefully designed to be extensible. It can add optional extension element and attribute content from a foreign namespace in a manner that does not require implementations to be upgraded but allows those that do upgrade to take advantage of the extended features.

10.6 Examples

The subsequent examples demonstrate a typical message exchange using the WS-Reliable Messaging protocol. What follows is the initial message to create the Sequence using a CreateSequence message.

```
<?xml version="1.0" encoding="UTF-8"?>
<soap:Envelope
  xmlns:soap="http://www.w3.org/2003/05/soap-envelope"
  xmlns:wsrm="http://schemas.xmlsoap.org/ws/2005/02/rm"
xmlns:wsa="http://schemas.xmlsoap.org/ws/2004/08/addressing">
<soap:Header>
  <wsa:MessageID>
   http://example.com.com/0baaf88d-483b-4ecf-a6d8-a7c2eb546817
  </wsa:MessageID>
  <wsa:To>http://example.com.com/service/B</wsa:To>
    <wsa:Action>
      http://schemas.xmlsoap.org/ws/2005/02/rm/CreateSequence
    </wsa:Action>
  <wsa:ReplyTo>
<wsa:Address>http://example.com.com/service/A</wsa:Address>
  </wsa:ReplyTo>
 </soap:Header>
 <soap:Body>
  <wsrm:CreateSequence>
    <wsrm:AcksTo>
      <wsa:Address>
        http://example.com.com/service/A
      </wsa:Address>
    </wsrm:AcksTo>
  </wsrm:CreateSequence>
 </soap:Body>
</soap:Envelope>
```

Next is a CreateSequenceResponse message.

```
<?xml version="1.0" encoding="UTF-8"?>
<soap:Envelope
xmlns:soap="http://www.w3.org/2003/05/soap-envelope"
xmlns:wsrm="http://schemas.xmlsoap.org/ws/2005/02/rm"
```

```
xmlns:wsa="http://schemas.xmlsoap.org/ws/2004/08/addressing">
  <soap:Header>
    <wsa:MessageID>
   http://example.com.com/guid/0baaf88d-483b-4ecf-a6d8-a7c2eb546818
  </wsa:MessageID>
    <wsa:To>http://example.com.com/service/A</wsa:To>
    <wsa:RelatesTo>
       http://example.com.com/guid/0baaf88d-483b-4ecf-a6d8a7c2
➥eb546817
    </wsa:RelatesTo>
    <wsa:Action>

http://schemas.xmlsoap.org/ws/2005/02/rm/CreateSequenceResponse
    </wsa:Action>
  </soap:Header>
  <soap:Body>
    <wsrm:CreateSequenceResponse>
      <wsrm:Identifier>
         http://example.com.com/RM/ABC
      </wsrm:Identifier>
    </wsrm:CreateSequenceResponse>
  </soap:Body>
</soap:Envelope>
```

After WS-Reliable Messaging creates the Sequence, messages can begin flowing for the Sequence. In the next example, the Sequence has three messages, and one of the messages is lost in transit, requiring a retransmission.

Message 1

```
<?xml version="1.0" encoding="UTF-8"?>
<soap:Envelope
xmlns:soap="http://www.w3.org/2003/05/soap-envelope"
xmlns:wsrm="http://schemas.xmlsoap.org/ws/2005/02/rm"
xmlns:wsa="http://schemas.xmlsoap.org/ws/2004/08/addressing">
  <soap:Header>
    <wsa:MessageID>
       http://example.com.com/guid/71e0654e-5ce8-477b-bb9d-34f05
➥cfcbc9e
    </wsa:MessageID>
    <wsa:To>http://example.com.com/service/B</wsa:To>
    <wsa:From>
      <wsa:Address>
         http://example.com.com/service/A
      </wsa:Address>
    </wsa:From>
    <wsa:Action>
       http://example.com.com/service/B/request
    </wsa:Action>
```

```
    <wsrm:Sequence>
      <wsrm:Identifier>
         http://example.com.com/RM/ABC
      </wsrm:Identifier>
      <wsrm:MessageNumber>1</wsrm:MessageNumber>
    </wsrm:Sequence>
  </soap:Header>
  <soap:Body>
    <!- Some  Application  Data  ->
  </soap:Body>
</soap:Envelope>
```

Message 2

```
<?xml version="1.0" encoding="UTF-8"?>
<soap:Envelope
xmlns:soap="http://www.w3.org/2003/05/soap-envelope"
xmlns:wsrm="http://schemas.xmlsoap.org/ws/2005/02/rm"
xmlns:wsa="http://schemas.xmlsoap.org/ws/2004/08/addressing">
  <soap:Header>
    <wsa:MessageID>
       http://example.com.com/guid/daa7d0b2-c8e0-476e-a9a4-d164154
➥e38de
    </wsa:MessageID>
    <wsa:To>http://example.com.com/service/B</wsa:To>
    <wsa:From>
      <wsa:Address>
         http://example.com.com/service/A
      </wsa:Address>
    </wsa:From>
    <wsa:Action>
       http://example.com.com/service/B/request
    </wsa:Action>
    <wsrm:Sequence>
      <wsrm:Identifier>
         http://example.com.com/RM/ABC
      </wsrm:Identifier>
      <wsrm:MessageNumber>2</wsrm:MessageNumber>
    </wsrm:Sequence>
  </soap:Header>
  <soap:Body>
    <!- Some  Application  Data  ->
  </soap:Body>
</soap:Envelope>
```

Message 3

```
<?xml version="1.0" encoding="UTF-8"?>
<soap:Envelope
```

```
xmlns:soap="http://www.w3.org/2003/05/soap-envelope"
xmlns:wsrm="http://schemas.xmlsoap.org/ws/2005/02/rm"
xmlns:wsa="http://schemas.xmlsoap.org/ws/2004/08/addressing">
 <soap:Header>
  <wsa:MessageID>
   http://example.com.com/guid/0baaf88d-483b-4ecf-a6d8-
➥a7c2eb546817
  </wsa:MessageID>
  <wsa:To>http://example.com.com/service/B</wsa:To>
  <wsa:From>
   <wsa:Address>
     http://example.com.com/service/A
   </wsa:Address>
  </wsa:From>
  <wsa:Action>
    http://example.com.com/service/B/request
  </wsa:Action>
  <wsrm:Sequence>
   <wsrm:Identifier>
    http://example.com.com/RM/ABC
   </wsrm:Identifier>
   <wsrm:MessageNumber>3</wsrm:MessageNumber>
   <wsrm:LastMessage/>
  </wsrm:Sequence>
 </soap:Header>
 <soap:Body>
  <!- Some Application Data ->
 </soap:Body>
</soap:Envelope>
```

The RM Destination has not received message 2 because of a transmission error, so it responds with a SequenceAcknowledgement for messages 1 and 3.

```
<?xml version="1.0" encoding="UTF-8"?>
<soap:Envelope
xmlns:soap="http://www.w3.org/2003/05/soap-envelope"
xmlns:wsrm="http://schemas.xmlsoap.org/ws/2005/02/rm"
xmlns:wsa="http://schemas.xmlsoap.org/ws/2004/08/addressing">
 <soap:Header>
  <wsa:MessageID>
   http://example.com.com/guid/0baaf88d-483b-4ecf-a6d8-
➥a7c2eb546817
  </wsa:MessageID>
  <wsa:To>http://example.com.com/service/A</wsa:To>
  <wsa:From>
   <wsa:Address>http://example.com.com/service/B</wsa:Address>
  </wsa:From>
   <wsa:Address>http://example.com.com/service/B</wsa:Address>
  </wsa:From>
```

```
<wsa:RelatesTo>
  http://example.com.com/guid/0baaf88d-483b-4ecf-a6d8-
➥a7c2eb546817
</wsa:RelatesTo>
<wsa:Action>
```

http://schemas.xmlsoap.org/ws/2005/02/rm/SequenceAcknowledgement
```
</wsa:Action>
<wsrm:SequenceAcknowledgement>
 <wsrm:Identifier>
  http://example.com.com/RM/ABC
 </wsrm:Identifier>
 <wsrm:AcknowledgementRange Upper="1" Lower="1"/>
 <wsrm:AcknowledgementRange Upper="3" Lower="3"/>
</wsrm:SequenceAcknowledgement>
</soap:Header>
<soap:Body/>
</soap:Envelope>
```

The sending endpoint discovers that the RM Destination did not receive message 2, so it resends the message and requests an acknowledgement.

```
<?xml version="1.0" encoding="UTF-8"?>
<soap:Envelope
xmlns:soap="http://www.w3.org/2003/05/soap-envelope"
xmlns:wsrm="http://schemas.xmlsoap.org/ws/2005/02/rm"
xmlns:wsa="http://schemas.xmlsoap.org/ws/2004/08/addressing">
 <soap:Header>
  <wsa:MessageID>
   http://example.com.com/guid/0baaf88d-483b-4ecf-a6d8-
➥a7c2eb546817
  </wsa:MessageID>
  <wsa:To>http://example.com.com/service/B</wsa:To>
  <wsa:From>
   <wsa:Address>http://example.com.com/service/A</wsa:Address>
  </wsa:From>
  <wsrm:Sequence>
   <wsrm:Identifier>
    http://example.com.com/RM/ABC
   </wsrm:Identifier>
   <wsrm:MessageNumber>2</wsrm:MessageNumber>
  </wsrm:Sequence>
  <wsrm:AckRequested>
   <wsrm:Identifier>
    http://example.com.com/RM/ABC
   </wsrm:Identifier>
  </wsrm:AckRequested>
```

```
    </soap:Header>
    <soap:Body>
     <!-- Some Application Data -->
    </soap:Body>
</soap:Envelope>
```

The RM Destination responds with a SequenceAcknowledgement for the complete sequence, which can then be terminated.

```
<?xml version="1.0" encoding="UTF-8"?>
<soap:Envelope
xmlns:soap="http://www.w3.org/2003/05/soap-envelope"
xmlns:wsrm="http://schemas.xmlsoap.org/ws/2005/02/rm"
xmlns:wsa="http://schemas.xmlsoap.org/ws/2004/08/addressing">
  <soap:Header>
   <wsa:MessageID>
    http://example.com.com/guid/0baaf88d-483b-4ecf-a6d8-
➥a7c2eb546817
   </wsa:MessageID>
   <wsa:To>http://example.com.com/service/A</wsa:To>
   <wsa:From>
    <wsa:Address>http://example.com.com/service/B</wsa:Address>
   </wsa:From>
   <wsa:RelatesTo>
     http://example.com.com/guid/0baaf88d-483b-4ecf-a6d8-
➥a7c2eb546817
   </wsa:RelatesTo>
   <wsa:Action>

http://schemas.xmlsoap.org/ws/2005/02/rm/SequenceAcknowledgement
   </wsa:Action>
   <wsrm:SequenceAcknowledgement>
    <wsrm:Identifier>
     http://example.com.com/RM/ABC
    </wsrm:Identifier>
    <wsrm:AcknowledgementRange Upper="3" Lower="1"/>
   </wsrm:SequenceAcknowledgement>
  </soap:Header>
  <soap:Body/>
</soap:Envelope>
```

The RM Source receives the final SequenceAcknowledgement message. Then it sends a TerminateSequence to the RM Destination to indicate that it can reclaim the resources that are associated with the Sequence.

```xml
<?xml version="1.0" encoding="UTF-8"?>
<soap:Envelope
xmlns:soap="http://www.w3.org/2003/05/soap-envelope"
xmlns:wsrm="http://schemas.xmlsoap.org/ws/2005/02/rm"
xmlns:wsa="http://schemas.xmlsoap.org/ws/2004/08/addressing">
 <soap:Header>
  <wsa:MessageID>
   http://example.com.com/guid/0baaf88d-483b-4ecf-a6d8-
➥a7c2eb546817
  </wsa:MessageID>
  <wsa:To>http://example.com.com/service/B</wsa:To>
  <wsa:Action>
     http://schemas.xmlsoap.org/ws/2005/02/rm/TerminateSequence
  </wsa:Action>
  <wsa:From>
    <wsa:Address>http://example.com.com/service/A</wsa:Address>
  </wsa:From>
 </soap:Header>
 <soap:Body>
  <wsrm:TerminateSequence>
   <wsrm:Identifier>
    http://example.com.com/RM/ABC
   </wsrm:Identifier>
  </wsrm:TerminateSequence>
 </soap:Body>
</soap:Envelope>
```

10.7 Future Directions

At the time of this writing, the authors and others who have developed implementations are performing interoperability and composeability testing on the WS-Reliable Messaging specification. After the interoperability and composeability testing are complete, the developers will republish the specification and submit it to a standards body. They haven't chosen a venue yet.

The specification is expected to be leveraged so that it provides for a standards-based interoperability protocol to bridge the various proprietary JMS provider environments.

10.8 Summary

This chapter covered the motivations for reliable messaging, including some of L. Peter Deutsch's "Eight Fallacies of Distributed Computing." Reliable messaging has served IT well as a foundation for many enterprise application integration deployments, providing the loose coupling necessary to mitigate against those fallacies. WS-Reliable Messaging promises to bring the benefits of reliable messaging to SOA and Web services, enabling enterprises to extend Web services to support reliable business-to-business (B2B) exchanges. This would replace Electronic Data Interchange (EDI) and offer the potential for a single interoperability protocol for the various proprietary Message Oriented Middleware (MOM) protocols.

Chapter 11

Transactions

This chapter covers Web service specifications that deal with transaction processing. In a Web services world, applications are constructed from the interconnection and operation of Web services. To obtain a reliable outcome, the various services that constitute the application must universally agree on an undisputed resolution. Transactions are a well-understood approach used widely in commercial systems that meet this requirement. The Web service specifications WS-Coordination [WS-Coordination], WS-Atomic Transaction [WS-Atomic Transaction], and WS-Business Activity Framework [WS-Business Activity] define the protocols required to build reliable Web service applications.

The WS-Coordination specification provides the generic foundation for coordinating outcome agreements between interoperating Web services. WS-Atomic Transaction and WS-Business Activity specifications contain definitions of atomic and business transaction protocols, respectively, that you can use with WS-Coordination. WS-Coordination is defined as an extensible framework that can support additional protocols for other coordination patterns as required.

Together, these specifications address the more general requirement to guarantee the reliable coordination of operations across Web services.

11.1 Role of Transactions in Web Services/SOA

Transactions [Bern 1997], [Gray 1993] are a fundamental concept in building reliable distributed applications. A transaction is a mechanism to ensure that all the participants in an application achieve a mutually agreed upon outcome. Traditionally, transactions have provided the following properties:

- **Atomicity**—The transaction completes successfully, and all the actions that the application performs happen, or the transaction completes unsuccessfully and none of the actions happens.

- **Consistency**—Transactions produce consistent results and preserve correct transformation of application states at completion.

- **Isolation**—Intermediate states that are produced while the transaction is executing are invisible to other transactions. Furthermore, transactions appear to execute serially, even if they are executed concurrently. You can achieve this by locking resources for the duration of the transaction so that another transaction cannot acquire them in a conflicting manner.

- **Durability**—After a transaction successfully completes, the changes are maintained unless a catastrophic failure occurs.

Transactions with these properties (often referred to as ACID) are known as *atomic transactions.*

In a Web service environment, *transactional* applications are constructed from the composition of one or more Web services, each of which might manipulate resources, adhere to the properties described earlier, and be party to an agreed overall coordinated outcome. However, in a Web services environment, the services that are the component parts of an application are typically *loosely* coupled and distributed across various independent systems spanning a network. Therefore, you might have to apply some of the properties of atomic transactions less strictly. You need more flexible forms of outcome coordination processing that have more relaxed forms of transaction to accommodate collaborations, workflow, real-time processing, and so on. Finally, there is a requirement for outcome processing that, although not necessarily requiring transactional behavior, does require the ability to identify operations that are part of the same Web service application.

WS-Coordination defines such a coordination service, and WS-Atomic Transaction and WS-Business Activity provide a starter set of the most common coordination protocols.

Figure 11-1 schematically illustrates where transactions (and the specifications described earlier) fit in the Web services model. Transactions provide a middleware service that augments the core Web services technologies of SOAP, Web Services Description Language (WSDL), and Universal Description, Discovery, and Integration (UDDI), enabling construction of a reliable computing environment.

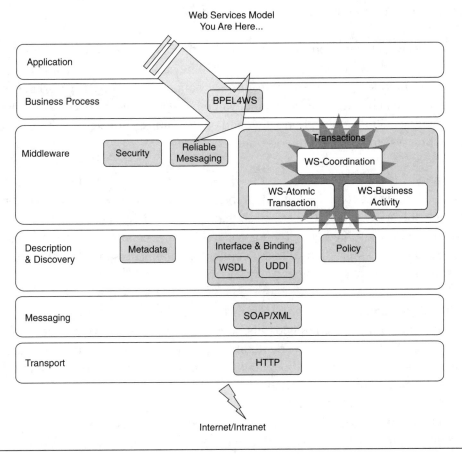

Figure 11-1   Web services and transaction.

11.2 Motivation for Transactions

11.2.1 Classic Transactions

Unfortunately, applications are prone to multiple modes of failure. When applications execute across distributed systems, they encounter greater reliability problems because such environments introduce additional sources of failure. Distributed systems generally consist of several computers connected by a network, where each system can be subject to independent failure of any of its components, such as the computers themselves, network links, operating systems, middleware, or individual applications. You must deal with failure of any component part of the application in the context of the whole application to ensure the overall correct execution of the application.

The concept of transactions is aimed at satisfying this consistency requirement through a property called *atomicity*, in which the application either completes normally, producing the intended results, or is aborted, restoring any resources that had been changed to their original values. The way this is done is typically an implementation choice, normally handled by a *transaction service* that an operating system or system middleware provides.

The application works in conjunction with system middleware that provides a transaction service to orchestrate the transaction outcome. Using the transaction service, the application indicates when the transaction begins and determines when and how it should end. The transaction service records the Web services accessed by the application so that it can perform the necessary outcome processing when the application ends.

A transaction can be completed in two ways: *committed* or *aborted* (cancelled). When a transaction is committed, all changes that are caused by operations of the business application are made durable (forced onto stable storage such as a disk). When a transaction is aborted, all changes that are made during the lifetime of the transaction are undone.

Most transaction systems in use today implement ACID transactions. They use a two-phase protocol to achieve atomicity between the Web services accessed by the application. The transaction service establishes roles, in which a *coordinator* acts on behalf of the application to orchestrate the outcome processing between the *participant* Web services (see Figure 11-2).

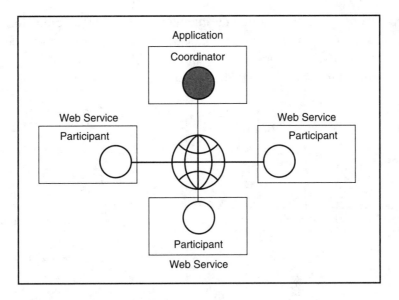

Figure 11-2   Transaction service roles.

- **Phase 1: Preparation**—During the first phase of the atomic transaction protocol, the coordinator ballots the participants for a vote on the transaction outcome. All participants indicate their particular view of the transaction outcome by responding either positively or negatively to the ballot request.

- **Phase 2: Outcome**—During the second phase of the atomic transaction protocol, the coordinator, having collected the preparation responses, informs the participants of the transaction outcome.

During the first phase, the coordinator sends the ballot request as a *Prepare* operation to the participants. The participants must make durable any state changes that occurred during the scope of the transaction. This allows the participants to either commit or abort (roll back) these changes later, after they've determined the overall transaction outcome (see Phase 1 of Figure 11-3).

Assuming that no failures occurred during the first phase, the coordinator sends the outcome as a second phase *Commit* operation to the participants. The participants can overwrite the original state of the Web service with the state made durable during the first phase (see Phase 2 of Figure 11-3).

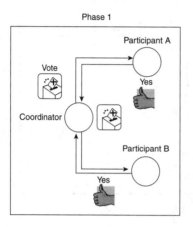
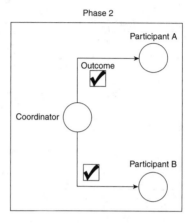

Figure 11-3   Two-phase commit protocol—success.

However, if a failure occurs during the first phase (that there is any"no" vote to the ballot request (see Figure 11-4, Phase 1), the coordinator sends the outcome as a second phase *Rollback* operation to all the participants (see Figure 11-4, Phase 2). The participants abort the work performed during the transaction and return the state of the Web service to the original state that existed prior to the transaction.

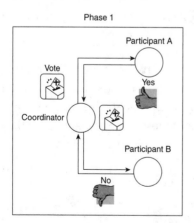
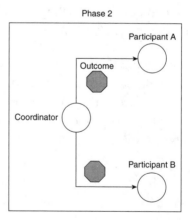

Figure 11-4   Two-phase commit protocol—failure.

To guarantee consensus, two-phase commit is necessarily a blocking protocol. After returning the Phase 1 response, each participant who returns a *Prepared* response *must* remain blocked until it has received the coordinator's Phase 2 message. Until a participant receives this message, any resources that it uses will be unavailable for use by other transactions, because to do so might violate the Isolation property of ACID behavior. Such a "classic" ACID protocol is said to be a well-formed and two-phase protocol. That is well-formed if all its operations are covered by corresponding locks and two-phased if the lock protocol acquires and releases locks in separate locking and unlocking phases such that no unlock ever precedes a lock for any of the operations.

Figure 11-5 illustrates that all the Web services that the application uses remain blocked, and the results are unavailable until the transaction is completed. If the coordinator fails before delivery of the second phase message, these resources remain blocked until the transaction recovers.

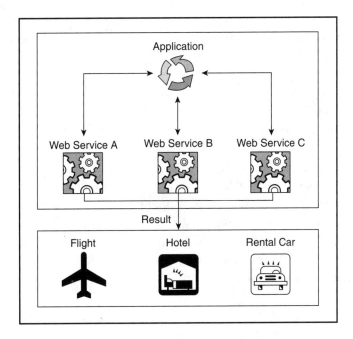

Figure 11-5   Classic transaction.

11.2.2 Business Transactions

Most business applications (workflow, business to business collaboration) need to reach a mutually agreed upon outcome. However, certain characteristics of these applications preclude the straightforward application of classic ACID transaction protocols. These characteristics include the following:

- Long duration activity[1]. Web services that a business application accesses might take longer to respond, and the overall application can remain active for an extended period of time (minutes, hours, days, weeks).

- The ability of the application to apply business logic to handle failures and continue processing when something goes wrong with a particular Web service request.

- The capability to select which Web services are included in the overall transaction outcome.

- Applications that typically span cross-enterprise business domains within which Web service implementations generally might not allow an outside control to hold their resources.

Therefore, business transactions require a mechanism to track the Web services that the application accesses, determine which Web services are included in the transaction, and provide common outcome processing across such an environment.

It is difficult, if not impossible, to use only classic transaction architectures within such environments. Long-running applications that execute using just ACID transaction properties present some real problems. The duration of the application could mean that the level of concurrency offered by a classic transaction needs to be lowered significantly, depending on approaches taken to provide isolation (such as locking).

Failures are handled differently to avoid significant amounts of work being redone because ACID transactions will abort all work done rather than selectively.

---

[1]Definition: An activity is defined as a computational unit composed of a number of tasks carried out across one or more Web services.

Some Web services might not be included within the overall outcome processing when a business application chooses to select among alternative results (such as selecting the lowest-cost provider from many solicited suppliers). Business process logic within typical business process management systems supports complex, long-running processes, where undoing the work of tasks that have already completed might be more appropriate to effect recovery. Alternatively, the business process can choose another acceptable execution path to continue forward processing. (As Figure 11-6 illustrates, the application decides the reservation only needs to include a flight and hotel operation and cancels the rental car.)

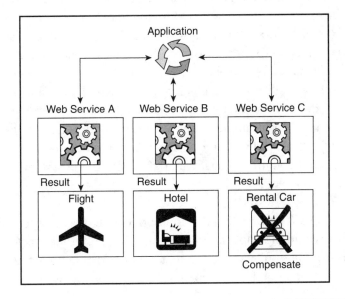

Figure 11-6   Business transaction.

In such scenarios, the properties of an ACID transaction have to be relaxed to provide what are typically referred to as *extended transactions*. An extended transaction model, for example, might relax the isolation property so that concurrent users can observe the intermediate updates of operations or in situations in which the holding of locks by operations against a service in an independent Web service is precluded (for example, to view a flight summary to check current seat availability). Figure 11-6 illustrates the Web services that the application uses, where the results of the flight, hotel, and rental car operations are made available before the transaction completes. As you shall see, protocols, such as WS-Business Activity, fall into this extended spectrum of transaction behavior, which provides a varying degree of functionality associated with each of the ACID transaction properties.

In certain classes of applications, it is known that resources acquired within a transaction can be released early, so you don't have to wait until the overall transaction finishes. If you adopt such a strategy, and if the overall transaction cancels, you might need to take certain actions to restore the system to a consistent state. Perhaps you'll need to perform compensation or countereffects on the resources that have been released early. Figure 11-6 illustrates this. Because the Web services are made available before the transaction is complete, cancellation of the rental car operation means you must perform compensation. Such recovery via compensation or fault-handling activities (which might perform forward or backward recovery) is typically application specific, might not be necessary at all, or might be more efficiently dealt with by the application. Therefore, an extended transaction model is usually more appropriate for lengthy interactions. For example, an airline reservation system might reserve a seat on a flight for an individual for a specific period of time. However, if the individual does not confirm the seat within that period, the system will reclaim it for another passenger.

Transactional support ensures that the appropriate outcome is observed across all of the tasks within the application that comprise the business activity. As indicated earlier, the results of a task might be made available before the overall business application or activity completes.

To understand business transactions more clearly, you can imagine the relatively simple scenario of arranging travel and accommodation for a conference (see Figure 11-7). Typically, an attendee requires transportation to the city where the conference is being held (via plane, train, or automobile), accommodation at a hotel (luxury, standard, or budget), and possibly other related bookings at the conference venue (a rental car or local transportation such as a shuttle, restaurant reservations, or tickets to entertainment events).

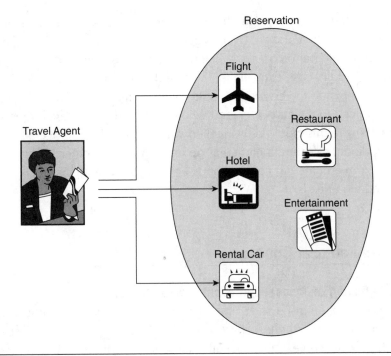

Figure 11-7   Travel arrangement scenario.

While assembling the booking, the travel agent needs to ensure that he can reserve likely options while processing the overall reservation. The business application must fulfill the travel agent's requirement to satisfy both the needs of the conference attendee and allowing Web services providers the autonomy to maintain control of its own resources (such as airlines, hotels, rental agencies, and restaurants).

The tasks that are required for the booking are interrelated within this business application, yet they are not necessarily predetermined. The tasks need to proceed independently, but all the resulting selections need to be booked together.

The travel agent offers a range of travel options that reflect a customer's preference or criteria based on such factors as cost, schedule, or availability. When the travel agent executes a task with a Web service provider, he might or might not include the task in the resulting reservation, dependent on the selection that the customer makes.

For example, the customer might either need to travel at specific times or might have more flexibility and want to consider the low-cost travel options. The travel agent would perform tasks soliciting reservations from various airlines. Based on schedule, cost, cancellation fees, and so on, the airline would perform a booking, and the customer would select a flight. The flight selected would be added to the tasks included when confirming the overall transaction. The remaining flights would be cancelled without affecting the overall reservation. In addition, selecting a particular option could affect other tasks; for example, a flight on a particular date might determine the customer's specific accommodation needs.

11.3 Architectural Concepts

11.3.1 Definition of Transaction Architectural Terms

The previous section discussed some of the basic principles of transactions and their application in example scenarios. The next section places this discussion in a Web services context, and identifies those specifications that provide the overall architectural framework for supporting transactions in the world of Web services.

Coordination

WS-Coordination defines a generic framework that allows an application to identify related operations across Web services and to enable management of any required processing when the activity ends. WS-Coordination defines protocols and services that do the following:

- Provide a context to identify Web service operations as part of a particular activity

- Allow Web services to register interest in participating in the activity outcome

- Allow the selection of a coordination protocol to be performed between the coordination service and participating Web services at completion of the activity

WS-Coordination can support any arbitrary coordination protocol. Coordination requires that one party act as the coordinator who is responsible for tracking participants involved in an activity and to execute the specified coordination protocol at activity completion. In addition, you can use WS-Coordination in scenarios other than supporting transactions. For example, an activity might do the following:

- Exploit the identifier value that is contained in the context associated with the activity to perform simple correlation across all the participating services

- Use an activity completion notification to supply a more simplified completion processing, such as to perform resource reclamation

- Define additional completion protocols, for those situations in which WS-Atomic Transaction or WS-Business Activity does not meet the application needs, such as a three-phase commit protocol

WS-Atomic Transaction and WS-Business Activity define two specific completion processing patterns to meet the common transaction processing requirements in the industry today.

Protocols for Atomic Transactions (WS-Atomic Transaction)

The protocols for atomic transactions typically handle activities that are short lived. Atomic transactions are provided through a two-phase commitment protocol. The transaction scope states that all work is either successfully completed in its entirety, or not at all. In other words, if an activity is successful, all changes resulting from operations performed during the activity are made permanent and visible. Alternatively, if the activity fails to complete successfully, none of the changes that the activity makes are made permanent and visible.

Protocols for Business Transactions (WS-BusinessActivity)

The protocols for business transactions handle long-lived activities. These differ from atomic transactions in that such activities can take much longer to complete. Also, to minimize latency of access by other potential users of the resources, the results of interim operations need to become visible to others before the overall activity has completed. In light of this, mechanisms for fault and compensation handling are introduced to reverse the effects of tasks previously completed within a business activity (such as compensation and reconciliation).

You can use the protocols in combination with each other. For example, short-running atomic transactions can be part of a long-running business activity. The actions of the embedded atomic transactions might be committed and made visible before the long-running business activity completes. Also, if a long-running business activity fails, you need to compensate for the effects of such atomic transactions. An example is multilevel transactions [Gray 1993].

11.3.2 Services and Protocols

This section covers more details about the architecture, services and protocols that are defined and implied by the WS-Coordination, WS-Atomic Transaction and WS-Business Activity Web Service specifications.

WS-Coordination Service

The WS-Coordination specification is focused on the notion of an activity. An *activity* is defined as a computation carried out as tasks on one or more Web services. An activity has a lifecycle; it is created, runs, and completes. This process can also be termed an *activity scope*. WS-Coordination specifies operations to *demarcate* the activity through the *activation service, identify* the activity by creating and passing a *context* along with a Web service operation, and record the Web services that are interested in completion processing through the *registration service.*

The following elements are associated with the coordination architecture:

- Activation service

- Context

- Registration service

- Coordination protocol

Figure 11-8 illustrates application operations, coordination contexts, and coordination operations among service requestor, service provider, coordination service, coordinator, and participant.

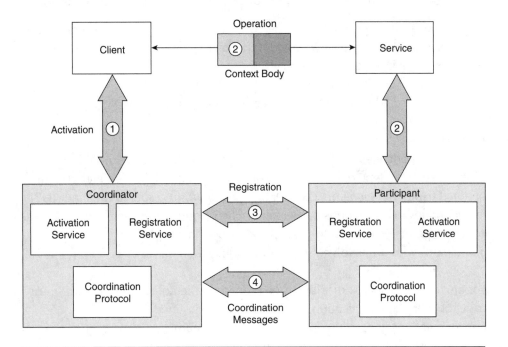

Figure 11-8   Web service transaction elements.

These elements work as follows:

1. **Activation**—The WS-Coordination activation service creates a new activity and returns a context containing an identifier that uniquely distinguishes a particular work scope. Furthermore, activation defines the coordinator who is responsible for managing the coordination protocol processing and specifies the coordination protocols that are supported (WS-Coordination, CreateCoordinationContext).

2. **Context**—The context that is returned at activation is passed along with the Web services operations and used to identify the operation as contained within the activity scope.

3. **Registration**—The Web service that is receiving an operation with context might register for inclusion in the outcome processing that is associated with the activity completion. Further, the registration selects from the coordination protocols that are supported (WS-Coordination, Register).

4. **Coordination Protocol**—A protocol service (such as WS-AtomicTransaction or WS-Business Activity) provides the logic to drive a specific completion-processing pattern.

The operations and messages for the services are defined using WSDL.

Context

Context is a container for sharing processing information between Web services. An XML type of Context is defined that specifies an identifier and an optional expiration element. The identifier is a uniform resource identifier (URI) that identifies related groups of messages. The CoordinationContext is a distinct context type that is defined to pass specific Coordination information to the participants who are involved in a transaction.

For an activity to span a distributed environment, the context information must be associated with application messages that are destined for a service. Implementations generally append context to the application message at the source to establish the execution environment at the target.

For each newly created transaction, the activation service returns a coordination context that contains the following:

- **Identifier**—A unique name to identify the CoordinationContext.

- **Expires**—An activity timeout value.

- **CoordinationType**—A defined set of coordination protocols that describe a specific completion-processing behavior.

- **Registration Service**—Address [WS-Addressing] of the registration service. The Web service registers interest and participation in a coordination protocol to determine the overall outcome of the activity.

- **Extensibility element**—Provides for optional product-specific extensions.

Activation Service

The activation service uses CreateCoordinationContext (see Figure 11-9, step 1) to do the following:

- Begin a new transaction

- Specify the coordination protocols that are available to the activity

The CreateCoordinationContextResponse returns a context that contains an identifier for the newly created transaction and the address of the registration service for the transaction (see Figure 11-9, step 2).

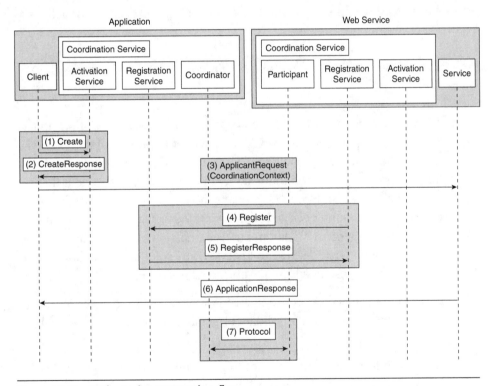

Figure 11-9   Web service transaction flow.

In addition, the activation service optionally allows the user to specify a relationship between activities. This relationship might be a superior-subordinate or parent-child nested relationship between the activities, as explained later in the Travel Agent scenario examples.

Registration Service

The registration service Register allows a Web service to register its interest in participation in the completion processing of the activity and to select the specific protocol to be used for this activity. Enrollment and selection allow the Web services involved in the activity to establish the traditional roles of coordinator and participant (see Figure 11-9, steps 4 and 5).

Transaction Protocols

The WS-Atomic Transaction and WS-Business Activity specifications define two completion-processing patterns (specifically transaction coordination protocols) that are common within the industry. These transaction coordination protocols provide the coordination service that the WS-Coordination framework defines (Figure 11-9, step 7).

Each supports the semantics of a particular kind of business-to-business (B2B) interaction:

- **Atomic Transaction (AT)**—This maps to existing ACID transaction standards. Remember that Web services are meant to promote interoperability between software applications. Historically, enabling traditional transaction systems to communicate with one another was a goal that was rarely achieved. However, mergers, acquisitions, or consolidations continue to stress the need to readily combine applications across the new business. Because traditional transaction systems currently form the backbone of enterprise-level applications, any solution must continue to accommodate these needs in a Web services environment.

    - **Intra-Enterprise**—AT is useful for intradomain environments in which a customer needs to consolidate operations across various internal applications.

    - **Inter-Enterprise**—B2B activities might require interoperability with existing transaction systems. Although such environments usually lend themselves to utilizing the more flexible facilities provided by extended transactions, if needed, existing transaction processing systems can be tied together directly using the atomic transactional protocol.

- Business Activity (BA) accommodates the requirement for a more flexible style of activity outcome processing than those that have strict ACID semantics. BA is designed specifically for loosely coupled and lengthy interactions, in which holding onto resources until completion is impossible or impractical. In this model:

  - The requirements for the properties of both atomicity and isolation are significantly relaxed. Services are requested to perform work (such as reserve a seat on a flight) in a manner in which the result of the work can be directly exposed. (For example, the seat assignment can be posted.) However, they must do so with an assumption that the work can be undone later. (The reservation can be cancelled and the seat can be reallocated.)

  - In addition, some of the work might not be included in the overall outcome. (For example, a reservation system might choose among several airlines and select the lowest available fare or most convenient flight.)

In this way, if it is subsequently decided that the work done needs to be cancelled, BA can inform the service. How services do their work and provide compensation mechanisms is generally specific to the application and is not defined by the WS-BusinessActivity specification. It's an implementation decision for the service provider. Note that the BA model has a relationship with the specific industry requirements for workflow interoperability. (For more detail, see the WS-BPEL specification [BPEL4WS]).

The WS-Atomic Transaction and WS-Business Activity coordination types provide the following transaction coordination protocols:

- WS-AT:

  - Completion
  - VolatileTwoPhaseCommit
  - DurableTwoPhaseCommit

- WS-BA:

  - BusinessAgreementWithParticipantCompletion
  - BusinessAgreementWithCoordinatorCompletion

Although AT and BA protocols match the needs of the current customer transactional use cases, they might not cover all requirements, and additional completion protocols might be required. Such an approach (as illustrated in Figure 11-10) is adaptable and allows for additional specifications to be defined and added as needed. By defining a clear separation between coordination framework and completion protocol, WS-Coordination can support a spectrum of completion processing.

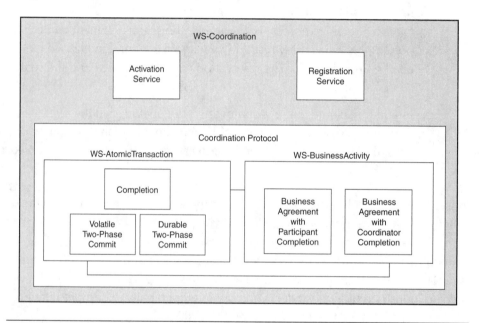

Figure 11-10   Web service coordination protocols.

One important aspect of a Web service environment that differentiates it from traditional transaction processing environments is that a synchronous request/response model is not required. WSDL allows binding to a variety of interaction styles.

The transaction protocol specifications WS-Atomic Transaction and WS-Business Activity leverage the framework provided by WS-Coordination in two ways:

- First, they allow a WS-Coordination context to be augmented with protocol-specific information to create a transaction context.

■ Second, they augment the activation and registration services with additional protocol services and associated protocol message sets.

WS-Atomic Transaction

WS-Atomic Transaction (WS-AT) is a protocol that enforces uniform outcome across all its participants. Updates are invisible outside the transaction and resources are locked for the duration of the transaction. Environments that require classic ACID transaction semantics utilize WS-ATs.

Completion Protocol

The application uses the completion protocol to direct the transaction protocol to complete an activity. The application indicates whether the desired outcome is successful (issues a Commit for the transaction) or unsuccessful (issues a Rollback for the transaction). The transaction protocol then executes and returns the outcome to the application.

To recap, when an application begins an atomic transaction, the client application establishes a coordinator that supports the WS-AtomicTransaction protocol. The client uses the WS-Coordination Service and might send a CreateCoordinationContext message to the activation service specifying the coordination type and get back an appropriate WS-Transaction context. Alternatively, the client can manufacture the appropriate context for those cases in which the client has decided not to avail itself of an activation service. The transaction context has its CoordinationType element set to the WS-Transaction AT namespace. It also contains a reference to the atomic transaction coordinator endpoint (the WS-Coordination registration service), where potential participants can be enlisted.

The client application registers for the Completion protocol so that it can later direct the outcome of the transaction. It then proceeds to interact with Web services to accomplish its business-level work. With each invocation on a Web service, the context is propagated along with any messages. This ensures that the transaction explicitly scopes each invocation.

After all the necessary application-level work has been completed, the application finishes the transaction by instructing the coordinator either to commit (see Figure 11-11, where the application finishes and the transaction is successful, and Figure 11-12, where the application finishes and the transaction is unsuccessful) or roll back the transaction (see Figure 11-13, where the application instructs the transaction to terminate).

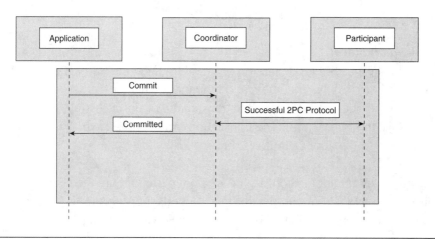

Figure 11-11   Completion protocol—successful transaction.

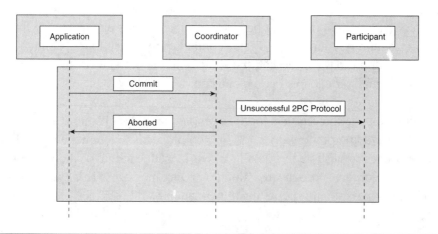

Figure 11-12   Completion protocol—transaction failure.

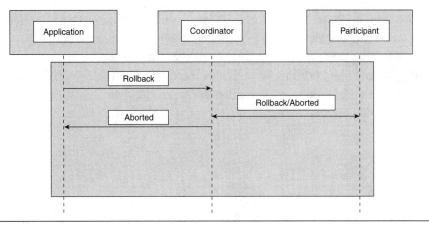

Figure 11-13   Completion protocol—application failure.

Durable Two-Phase Commit Protocol

Transaction completion uses the Durable Two-Phase Commit (2PC) protocol to perform the classic atomic transaction processing, as described earlier. Here, a two-phase commitment protocol ensures that the work is completed atomically. Note that the WS-AT specification implies no ordering of Durable 2PC participant invocations. As illustrated in Figure 11-14, during Phase 1, the coordinator sends Prepare to the transaction participants. Each participant returns Prepared, thereby successfully completing Phase 1. During Phase 2, the coordinator indicates the successful outcome, sending Commit to all the participants. All the participants return Committed to acknowledge the outcome.

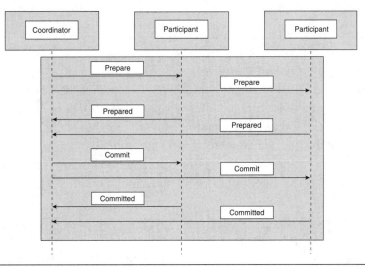

Figure 11-14   Successful two-phase commit.

As illustrated in Figure 11-15, during Phase 1, the coordinator sends Prepare
to the transaction participants. However, one or more of the participants
returns Aborted, thereby causing an unsuccessful completion of Phase 1.
During Phase 2, the coordinator indicates the unsuccessful outcome, sending
Rollback to all the remaining participants. The participants return Aborted
to acknowledge the outcome.

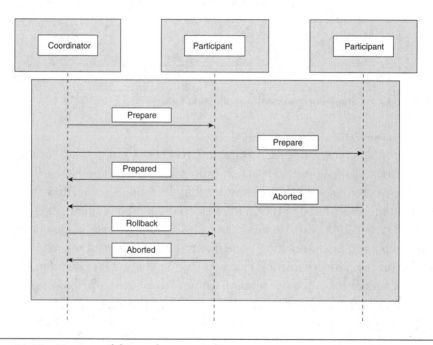

Figure 11-15   Unsuccessful two-phase commit.

Volatile Two-Phase Commit Protocol

In addition to the Durable 2PC protocol, WS-AT provides the Volatile 2PC protocol. Accessing durable storage (whatever its implementation) is often a performance bottleneck, and operating on the cached contents of the durable storage
(such as an entire database table) for the length of the transaction can often
significantly improve performance. However, you need to force that data back
to the original persistent store prior to the transaction committing.

When an atomic transaction is finishing, the coordinator executes the Volatile
2PC protocol if any participants are registered for it. The coordinator informs all
Volatile 2PC participants that the transaction is about to complete by sending

them a Prepare before any of the Durable 2PC participants. That way, the participants can perform any outstanding work and respond with a Prepared, ReadOnly, or an error message indicating Aborted. Any failures at this stage cause the transaction to roll back.

Volatile 2PC participants and other Durable 2PC participants are informed of the outcome decision at Phase 2 via the Commit or Rollback. As illustrated in Figure 11-16, during Phase 1, the coordinator sends Prepare to the volatile transaction participants. After the volatile participants return Prepared, the coordinator sends Prepare to the durable participants. During Phase 2, the coordinator indicates the successful outcome, sending Commit to both the volatile and durable participants.

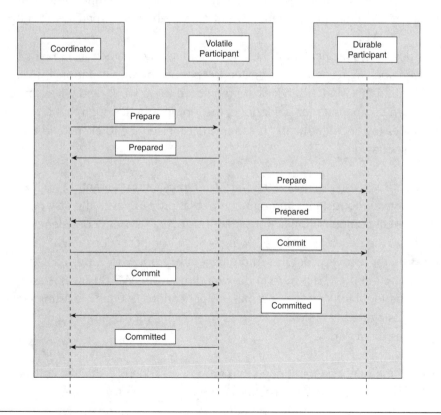

Figure 11-16   Two-phase commit—volatile/durable order.

WS-Business Activity

Most B2B applications require transactional support to guarantee consistent outcome and correct execution. Also, such applications often involve long-running computations across loosely coupled systems and components that do not share data, location, or administration. In most cases, the use of atomic transactions within such architectures is inappropriate. For example, an online bookshop might reserve books for an individual for a specific period of time. However, if the individual does not purchase the books within that period, the store puts the books back on the shelf for others to buy. Furthermore, because it is not possible for anyone to have an infinite supply of stock, some online shops might appear to users to reserve items for them but, in fact, might allow others to pre-empt that reservation. (For example, the shop might concurrently reserve the same book for multiple users.) A user might subsequently find that the item is no longer available, or he might have to reorder the item especially for him.

A BA is designed specifically for these kinds of lengthy interactions, in which exclusively locking resources over extended periods of time is impossible or impractical. In this model, services are requested to do work, and when those services can compensate for work done, they inform the BA such that if the BA later decides to cancel the work, it can instruct the service to execute its compensation behavior.

Although a BA doesn't maintain the full ACID transaction semantics, it can maintain overall consistency through compensation. However, the task of writing correct compensating actions (and thus overall system consistency) is delegated to the developers of the services. Such compensations might use backward error recovery, but they more generally employ forward recovery or a combination of both backward and forward recovery. WS-Business Activity defines a protocol for Web services-based applications to enable existing business processing and workflow systems to interoperate across implementation and business boundaries.

An application might be partitioned into scopes. A scope is a specific collection of Web service operations. Such scopes can be nested to arbitrary levels, forming parent and child relationships. A parent can select which children to include in the overall outcome protocol, thereby making nonatomic outcomes possible. The WS-Business Activity protocol defines a consensus group that allows the relaxation of atomicity based on business-level decisions. In a similar manner to nested transactions, if a child experiences an error, a parent might catch it. If this happens, the parent might be able to compensate and continue processing.

Scopes and the parent-child relationship that nesting provides are important for many reasons, including the following:

- **Fault-isolation**—A scope failing (perhaps because a service it was using fails) does not necessarily mean the enclosing scope will fail, thus undoing all the work performed so far.

- **Modularity**—Work is logically partitioned into scopes such that the tasks that span business boundaries are accommodated using well-formulated concepts exhibited by existing workflow systems. If a scope is already associated with the invocation of a service, within which a new scope is begun, the new scope is nested within it. If the service is invoked without a parent scope, the service's scope is simply top level.

When a child completes, it signals to the parent that the work it has done can be compensated later if required. The parent performs compensation if it needs to reverse the effects of the work that the child performed.

Unlike the atomic transaction protocol, in which participants inform the coordinator of their state only when specifically requested to do so, a child can specify its outcome to the parent without solicitation. This feature is helpful when an operation fails because the application's exception handler can use the notification to modify the goals and drive processing forward without having to wait until the end of the transaction. A well-designed application using the WS-Business Activity protocol should be proactive, if it is to perform well.

Underpinning all of this are three fundamental assumptions:

- All state transitions are reliably recorded, including application state and coordination metadata (the record of sent and received messages).

- All request messages are acknowledged so that problems are detected as early as possible. This avoids executing unnecessary tasks and allows earlier and less costly problem detection.

- As with atomic transactions, a response is defined as a separate operation and not as the output of the request. Message input-output implementations typically have timeouts that are too short for some business activity responses. If the response is not received after a timeout, it is resent. This is repeated until a response is received. The request receiver discards all but one of the identical requests it receives.

As with atomic transactions, the business activity model has multiple protocols: Business Agreement with Participant Completion and Business Agreement with Coordinator Completion

Business Agreement with Participant Completion

Under the Business Agreement protocol with Participant Completion, a child activity is initially created in the Active state. After a child task finishes, it must be able to compensate for the work that was performed. The child task sends a Completed message to the parent and waits to receive the final outcome of the BA from the parent. This outcome will either be a Close message, meaning that the BA has completed successfully, or a Compensate message, requesting the child task to reverse the effects of its work.

As illustrated in Figure 11-17, after all the participants return Completed, the coordinator indicates a successful outcome, sending Close to the participants. Then the participants return Closed to acknowledge the outcome.

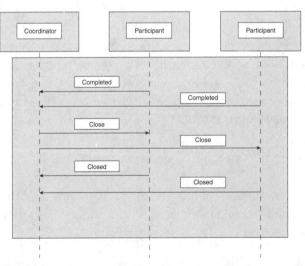

Figure 11-17   Successful business agreement with participant completion.

As illustrated in Figure 11-18, after all the participants return Completed, the coordinator indicates the unsuccessful outcome, sending Compensate to the participants. Then the participants return Compensated to acknowledge the outcome and undo the work for the transaction.

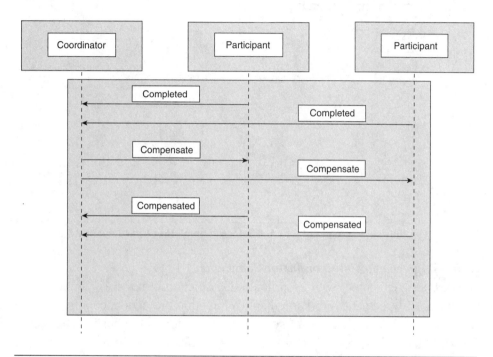

Figure 11-18   Unsuccessful business agreement with participant completion.

A child task might finish the work it was created to do and decide it no longer needs to participate in the activity. In this case, the child task can unilaterally send an Exit message to the parent that is equivalent to the participant resigning from the business transaction. (As illustrated in Figure 11-19, a participant ends involvement in the transaction by sending an Exit to the coordinator, and the coordinator acknowledges the action by returning Exited. After all the other participants return Completed, the coordinator indicates a successful outcome, sending Close to all the remaining participants. The participants then return Closed to acknowledge the outcome.)

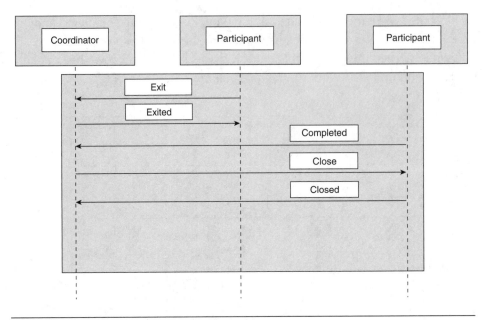

Figure 11-19   Business agreement with participant completion—participant exit.

Business Agreement with Coordinator Completion

The Business Agreement with Coordinator Completion protocol is identical to the Business Agreement with Participant Completion protocol except that the child cannot unilaterally decide to end its participation in the business activity. The child task relies on the parent to send a Complete message when it has received all requests to perform work. The child then acts as it does in the Business Agreement with Participant Completions protocol (see Figure 11-20).

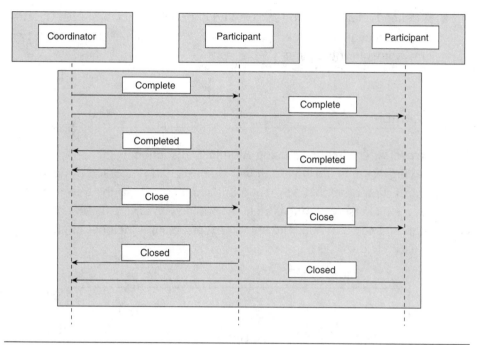

Figure 11-20   Successful business agreement with coordinator completion.

General Considerations

The scenario infers several fundamental requirements on a Web service implementation:

- The usage throughout the distributed environment of a "universally" understood Activation Service definition (that is, a context that includes both an identifier and a coordinator address).

- The ability to establish and reference a coordinator (an endpoint address that is understood throughout the network).

- (Optional) For efficiency through the reduction of network flows, the ability to construct a subordinate node that uses the Activation Service definition to control the outcome of some part of distributed activity.

- (Optional) The ability to optimize flows by including protocol messages on the regular application message flow.

■ A defined relationship for context and endpoint association (that is, an agreed mechanism for exchanging context and establishing an execution environment for the target Web service).

11.4 Example

11.4.1 Travel Agent Scenario Using Atomic Transaction

The following example illustrates a travel agent scenario modeled using the atomic transaction protocol (WS-AT). In this simple scenario, the travel agent processes a travel reservation that includes booking an airline flight, hotel accommodation, and car rental. The completed reservation includes all three bookings (see Figure 11-21).

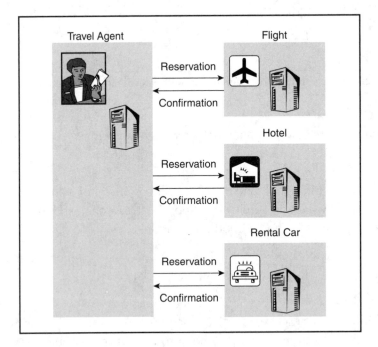

Figure 11-21   Atomic transactions—travel scenario.

Example   249

Activation

The travel agent application creates a transactional activity by using the WS-Coordination framework's Activation Service. It does this by sending a CreateCoordinationContext request to the Activation Service. The Coordination Service returns a Coordination Context that uniquely identifies the transaction and includes the address of the Registration Service.

Application Calls Web Service

The application then performs operations on Web services. The Coordination Context obtained earlier is passed along as a SOAP Header on application calls to the various Web services to identify the activity that is associated with the operation (illustrated in Figure 11-22).

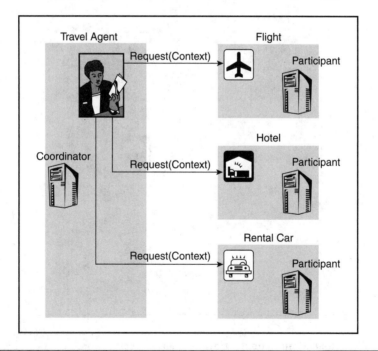

Figure 11-22   Atomic transactions—travel scenario—application message passes CoordinationContext.

Registration

The first time that a Web service processes a CoordinationContext, it issues a register to the WS-Coordination framework's Registration Service by using the Registration Service address obtained from the CoordinationContext. It passes the participant's address that is to be used for the subsequent AtomicTransaction protocol messages[2], as illustrated in Figure 11-23. The Registration Service acknowledges the registration and returns the coordinator's address. This address will be used to drive the transaction protocol or notify the coordinator in the event of a fault or recovery condition.

The Web service(s) performs the operation and returns results.

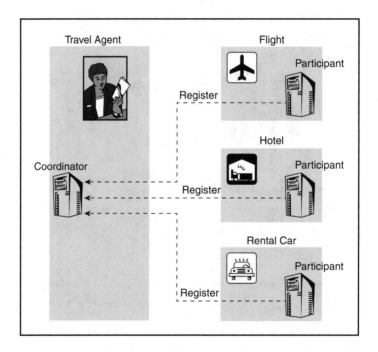

Figure 11-23   Atomic transactions—travel scenario—registration.

---

[2]Alternatively, the target can choose to create a subordinate coordinator (using a create operation specifying a coordination context of the superior coordinator). The subordinator coordinator registers with the coordinator specified on the received coordination context and the resource registers with the subordinate coordinator.

Example   251

Note that the CoordinationContext can also be included on the application response so that information can be returned in the context extension element. Certain transaction implementations exploit the ability to return implementation-specific information.

Completion/Coordination

The application completes the activity. After assuming that everything is satisfactory, the application issues a Commit (AtomicTransaction/2PC protocol) message on the coordinator.

The coordinator performs the transaction agreement protocol for which the Web service(s) registered (in this scenario, the 2PC protocol). The protocol solicits the resource status via Prepare, and then it transmits a final outcome, either a Commit or Rollback (2PC protocol) message, to each resource that registered. The Participant address that was sent during registration locates the correct Resource instance to be Committed or Aborted. The Web service votes positively for the two-phase commitment protocol and returns Prepared to the coordinator (illustrated in Figure 11-24).

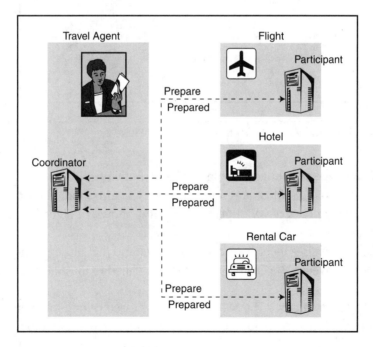

Figure 11-24   Atomic transaction—travel scenario—Phase 1.

The coordinator collects all the votes and determines that the transaction can be committed or aborted. For a successful transaction, the Coordinator sends Commit to the participant Web services. The Web service acknowledges the commitment message and returns Committed to the coordinator (as illustrated in Figure 11-25).

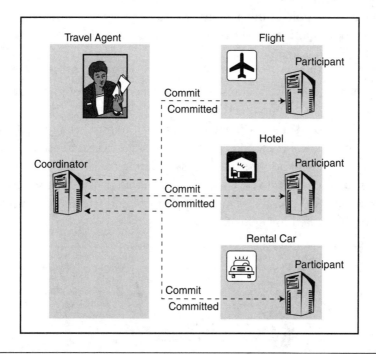

Figure 11-25   Atomic transaction—travel scenario—Phase 2.

11.4.2 Travel Agent Scenario Using Business Activity

The following example illustrates a travel agent scenario modeled using the Business Activity protocol (WS-Business Activity), shown in Figure 11-26.

This example exercises the same travel agent scenario that illustrates atomic transactions. However, the example has been modified to illustrate the following:

- **Relaxed atomicity**—The Web services accessed during the transaction can be selectively included in the overall application outcome.

Example   253

- **Relaxed isolation**—Web services complete the application requests and expose the result outside the transaction.

- **Compensation**—Web services provide additional outcome processing if the overall application fails to reverse operations that are exposed outside the transaction.

- **Simplified modeling**—Employing a parent-child relationship between the application and Web services allows a clear separation of business logic versus completion processing.

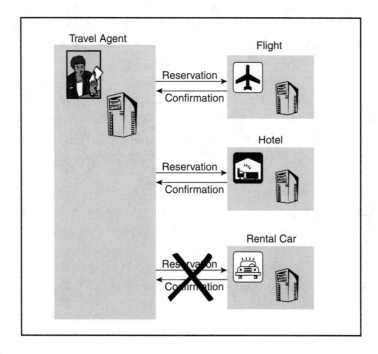

Figure 11-26   Business activity—travel scenario.

Activation

The travel agent application creates a transaction for the business activity by using the WS-Coordination framework's Activation Service. The CreateCoordinationContext request is sent from application to the Activation Service and the Coordination Service returns a CoordinationContext that uniquely identifies the Business application. As outlined for atomic transactions, the application registers using the Registration Service that is specified in the Coordination Context:

- The application defines itself as responsible for driving the Completion protocol to complete the activity.

- The Coordinator Service address is returned on the call that the application uses to invoke the Completion protocol.

The application then uses the existing transaction to create a parent-child relationship between the application and the Web service it is about to invoke. The Coordination Framework's Activation Service provides an optional extension of Create to indicate the NestedCreate that allows this.

The CreateCoordinationContext request is sent from an application to the Activation Service. The Coordination Service returns a CoordinationContext that the parent application uses to uniquely identify the child Web service. The CoordinationContext is used on subsequent calls to the Web service(s).

Application Calls Web Service
The application performs a business operation (eg, to book a hotel room) supported by a Web service.

The message sent includes a CoordinationContext SOAP Header for the business transaction that the Web service will use (see Figure 11-27).

Example   255

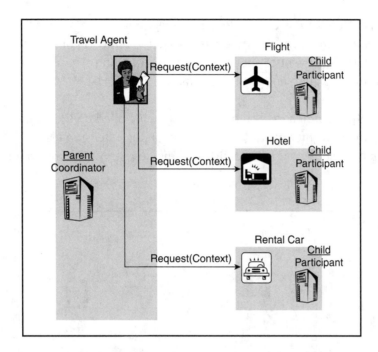

Figure 11-27   Business activity—travel scenario—application message passes coordination context.

Registration

The first time that a Web service processes a CoordinationContext, it issues a Register to the WS-Coordination framework's Registration Service. It does this by using the Registration Service address from the CoordinationContext. It passes the Participant's address to be used for subsequent BusinessActivity protocol messages.

The Registration Service acknowledges the registration and returns the Coordinator address (which drives the transaction protocol) or notifies the Coordinator in the event of a fault or recovery condition. The Web service(s) performs the operation and returns results (see Figure 11-28).

Note that the CoordinationContext can also be included on the application response to allow information to be returned in the extension element. Certain transaction implementations exploit the ability to return implementation-specific information.

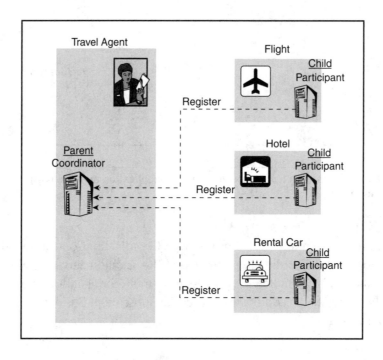

Figure 11-28   Business activity—travel scenario—registration.

Web Service Completion
The Web service(s) performs the application request and indicates that it is finished with processing by sending a Completed message to the coordinator. At this point, the Web service results might be exposed outside the transaction if other applications invoke the same Web service (see Figure 11-29).

Example   257

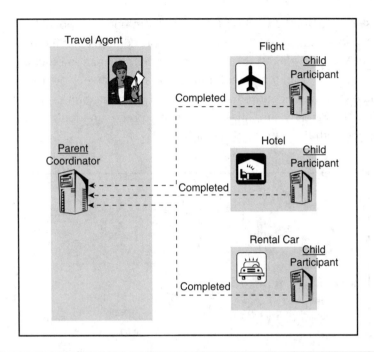

Figure 11-29   Business activity—travel scenario—Web service completion.

Coordination

Based on the Completed message, the application determines that all the Web services have been successful. Based on the customer itinerary, the travel agent decides to cancel the rental car and book the flight and hotel:

- The application rejects the transaction to the rental car Web service, which triggers the Coordination service to compensate that child transaction.

- The application accepts transactions to airline and hotel Web services, which triggers the Coordination service to close the child transactions.

The Web services respond appropriately (Compensated or Closed, as illustrated in Figure 11-30).

Using nested parent-child relationships is a recommended application pattern. Such an approach facilitates the construction of scenarios that include selective inclusion of Web service results within an overall application outcome. Removal of a child from the parent transaction processing as defined by nesting rules dictates that other children are unaffected when a sibling is excluded in this fashion. This greatly simplifies the recovery processing logic that is required when dealing with these types of scenarios.

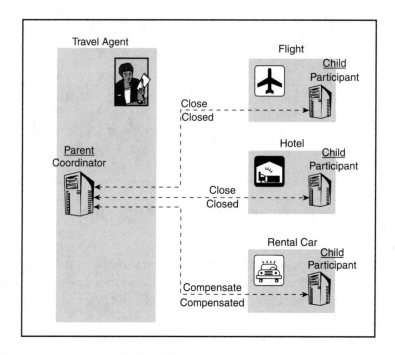

Figure 11-30   Business activity—travel scenario—transaction outcome.

Completion processing alternatives exist if a Web service exploits the additional features that the WS-BusinessActivity protocol provides. For example, the Web service in the previous example might define the reservation request to remain pending subject to explicit confirmation or cancellation from the application. In that case, the Web services would not return Completed immediately. A reservation cancellation would trigger the Web service to remove itself from the transaction via Exit (illustrated in Figure 11-31).

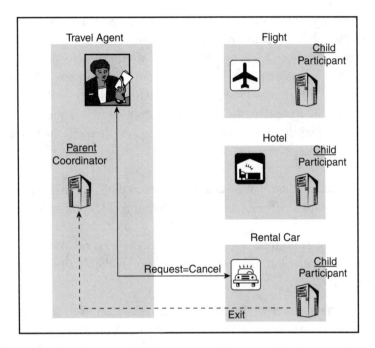

Figure 11-31   Business activity—travel scenario—Web service cancellation.

The child transaction that is executing at the Web service could also be an atomic transaction (rather than a business activity). In this case, the application aborts the child to remove it from parent transaction processing. As defined by transaction nesting rules, other children are unaffected when a sibling is removed in this fashion.

11.5 Summary

Transactions are one of the most fundamental concepts in a Web services environment to ensure reliable application processing. However, support for transactions in the Web services world does require more flexible and extensible mechanisms for controlling application outcome than those typically offered by traditional distributed and database transaction models.

The Web services transaction specifications described in this chapter provide an extensible framework for coordinating and orchestrating application outcome by defining specifications for services that provide for the creation of computational activities, their registration with an outcome coordinator, and controlling the disposition of the actions taken by the activities. The generalized framework offers the capability to specify the operational context of a request (or series of requests), controlling the duration of the activity and defining the participants that need to be engaged in an outcome decision.

In addition, specific patterns (transactions) that are typically used within the industry for coordinating the outcome of differing application styles are defined:

- **WS Atomic Transactions**—Application operations on Web services occur completely or not at all, and results are not available until the transaction is complete.

- **WS Business Activity**—Application operations on Web services exhibit a loose unit of work, in which results are shared prior to completion of the overall activity. Each participant undoes the operations it has performed within the conversation.

The Web service transaction specifications provide a flexible approach to handling outcome processing. This approach ranges from existing classic transaction patterns to more general business process.

Web service transactions augment existing application environments by providing the mechanisms that allow Web services to work together and offer a reliable computing environment. The facilities in Web service transactions address the common failures that might occur and ensure that the Web Service application achieves an agreed outcome.

Part 6

Security

This part of the book discusses the all-important topic of security. Given the reality of today's open networks, it is just impossible to conduct business transactions in a networked environment without full security capabilities. The figure that follows shows where security falls in the Web services stack.

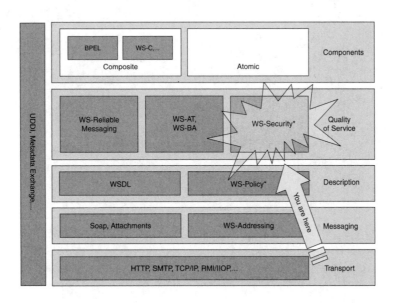

The Web services security stack is quite complete now, consisting of WS-Security, WS-Secure Conversation, WS-Trust, WS-Federation, WS-Privacy, and WS-Authorization. Chapter 12, "Security," discusses WS-Security, and introduces WS-Trust. These two specifications provide a robust framework for end-to-end secure interaction between two Web service applications.

Chapter 13, "Advanced Security," discusses WS-Trust in additional detail, and briefly presents WS-Federation, WS-Secure Conversation, WS-Privacy, and WS-Authorization. These specifications are in an earlier stage than those covered in Chapter 12. However, it is important to note that it is possible to support many useful and powerful business-to-business (B2B) and enterprise application integration (EAI) scenarios today using WS-Security, WS-Secure Conversation, and WS-Trust.

Chapter 12

Security

The previous two chapters discuss how to make Web services interactions reliable in the presence of failures. WS-ReliableMessaging and supporting middleware isolate applications from lost and duplicate messages, which might be caused by network errors. WS-Coordination, WS-Transactions, and WS-BusinessAgreement allow Web services to agree on the outcome of multiparty interactions. This chapter will show how to make Web services reliable even when the network, the Web service, or both are under possible *security attacks*. For example:

- The network traffic might be eavesdropped upon.

- An involved party might tamper with messages or attachments. For example, this party might send a message that includes portions of another message, in an effort to gain access to otherwise unauthorized information.

- An involved party might construct and send fake messages to a receiver who believes them to have come from a party other than the sender.

- An attacker might pose to the real sender and receiver parties as receiver and sender, respectively, in order to fool both of them. For example, the attacker might be able to downgrade the level of cryptography used to secure the message.

- An attacker can start a denial-of-service (DOS) attack, in which the attacker does a small amount of work that forces the attacked system to do a large amount of work. This is an important issue in design, and perhaps profiling in some cases.

Web Services Security (WS-Security) is a family of specifications that addresses these concerns. The family has many specifications, as shown in Figure 12-1.

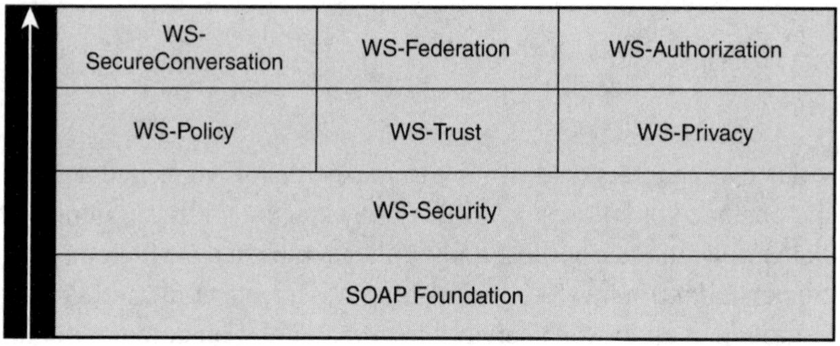

WS-SecureConversation	WS-Federation	WS-Authorization
WS-Policy	WS-Trust	WS-Privacy
WS-Security		
SOAP Foundation		

Figure 12-1   Web Services Security architecture.

Security is a complex topic that is fundamental to the adoption of Web services. This chapter discusses the most fundamental layers of WS-Security:

- **WS-Security**—SOAP Message Security 1.0 provides the foundation for security. This specification supports the following:

  - **Origin Authentication**—Identifying the origin of a message securely.

- **Integrity**—Detecting that no one has tampered with information in a message.

- **Confidentiality**—Ensuring that only the intended recipient of information is able to view it.

- **WS-Trust**—Trust is fundamental to security, and security only works because of trust relationships. Public key security works only if the certificate authorities are trusted and trustworthy. Kerberos works only if the Kerberos Key Distribution Centers and services are trusted and trustworthy. WS-Trust is a specification that enterprises and sites use to build trust relationships and interoperability. This chapter briefly discusses WS-Trust; the following chapter provides more details.

Chapter 13, "Advanced Security," discusses the other members of the WS-Security family. These specifications provide enhanced security functions, building on the foundational WS-Security specification.

Before delving into the details of WS-Security, let's look at a simple scenario that motivates the security function introduced by WS-Security. This scenario will be used in the detailed explanations in this and the following chapter.

12.1 A Motivating Example: Travel Agent Web Services

This section uses a fictional travel agency to illustrate some of these concepts. Figure 12-2 depicts the scenario described in this section. The Fabrikam456 Travel Agency offers air, hotel, and car-rental services to its customers through several different business portals. In turn, Fabrikam456 uses Web services to interact with travel suppliers such as hotel chains and airlines.

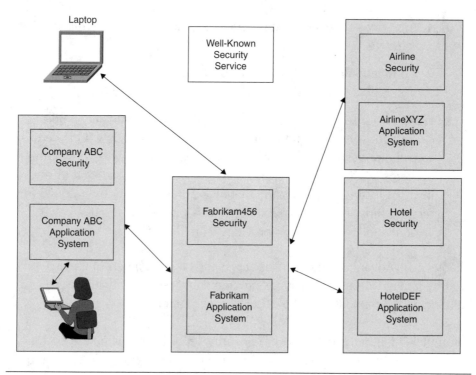

Figure 12-2   Travel agency scenario.

CompanyABC is one of Fabrikam456's clients, allowing its employees to arrange travel through Fabrikam456. In some instances, the employees are traveling and are outside CompanyABC's network. These employees have a laptop/notebook application that uses Web services to interact directly with Fabrikam456 over the Internet. At other times, the employees are on site and use a CompanyABC application, which in turn uses Web services to interact with Fabrikam456.

Fabrikam456 would like to offer an integrated set of services to its customers. The idea is this: A requester submits a single travel request, listing cities and dates. Fabrikam456 responds with an itinerary containing reservations for the hotels, airlines, and vehicles. Fabrikam456 wants the flexibility to extend these services for certain partners based on a variety of criteria (gold service, preferred customers, and so on), and to allow customers to specify certain preferences (aisle seats on planes, nonsmoking rooms, and so on). Finally, many suppliers of travel services have direct relationships with customers, such as frequent flier programs. Customers should be able to exploit these programs when booking through Fabrikam456.

12.2 Roles of Security in Web Services

Security is a complex issue. Many aspects of security pertain to enterprise information systems and their interactions with public and private networks. Although this section and the next section will show how to use the WS-Security family of specifications to secure *some* aspects of a Web services interaction, there are many other security concerns that will not be covered. For the most part, the WS-Security family of specifications addresses these additional concerns. In either case, it is very important to be familiar with the role of WS-Security in the Web services' overall context.

Several things can play a role in the security of a Web service. One must define security policy, security architecture, and standards. WS-Policy provides a framework to define policies that set the constraints and capabilities of a Web service. Many of the policies are beyond the scope of this book, however. Enterprises have operational and compliance policies about the following:

- Securing notebook computers that might contain passwords or confidential information.

- What can and cannot be disclosed to phone callers.

- In many cases, application business logic needs to be secure. This might necessitate code reviews and extensive testing.

- The network infrastructure must be configured properly, including routers, DNS servers, firewalls, and network monitoring and management systems.

- The hardware, operating system, and middleware used for running this Web service must have the latest security patches and must be free of viruses.

- Operators of the system must have adequate training in security.

- The systems and the procedures to operate them must be audited periodically.

- Trust relationships must be established with business partners, which might necessitate the definition of legal contracts and responsibilities.

- Requests to a Web service must be authenticated and authorized properly.

- Messages to and from a Web service must be protected from unauthorized access and modification.

All these policies are required to properly secure the Web service interactions. The WS-Security specifications described in this chapter cover the last three items in the list, but this is not a complete security solution; security on the other hand is not absolute. One must employ other appropriate means to cover the other aspects of security.

12.3 Motivation for Using WS-Security

Even for the last three requirements mentioned in the previous section, one can use well-established security transport-level and network-level technologies such as SSL/TLS and IPSec. SOAP supports HTTP/S. Why is WS-Security needed, yet another set of security specifications? Why are SSL/TLS and IPSec insufficient for protecting Web services transactions? Why is SOAP over HTTP/S insufficient?

WS-Security is not meant to *replace* any existing security technologies, and one should use them whenever they're available. Instead, WS-Security augments and federates existing security infrastructures and provides a unified model for application programmers and system administrators.

For example, when Web services are interacting within a controlled environment such as a corporation's intranet, WS-Security can propagate the original sender's identity in messages. In this model, WS-Security simply defines the interoperable XML Schema for security information and its placement in SOAP messages. This security model relies on things such as the physical security of the network, and it propagates security information to ensure the correct operation of applications that need it (for example, when a customer ID is used as a key to retrieve account information).

In a complex and hostile environment, WS-Security can provide a fuller range of protection end to end. In both the controlled and hostile environment cases, the same model and the same base mechanism are employed and are mostly transparent to applications.

In addition, existing security technologies can't solve two specific problems:

- Web services introduces intermediaries, which might need to inspect or modify at least some parts of passing messages. These intermediaries are not always completely trusted and should not have access to sensitive data. Thus, end-to-end security for the entire message path is required. In this example, some information might need to flow *through* Fabrikam456 to the travel suppliers, but Fabrikam456 should not see it.

- Web services integrates multiple systems with different security domains and technology, and thus the need for a mechanism to translate or exchange security information from one domain to another. Web services security must be extremely flexible, accommodating many different security models. In this example, an end user might authenticate itself to CompanyABC's security infrastructure. This authentication information must somehow propagate to Fabrikam456 and the travel suppliers, and it must be converted to a format that is meaningful and trustworthy for these environments.

SSL, IPSec, and HTTP-S do not meet these requirements. The can secure point-to-point connections such as those between the end user and CompanyABC's systems, or between CompanyABC's system and Fabrikam456. The integrity and confidentially aspects of these technologies have no end-to-end security or persistency. Although these technologies might provide in-transit integrity and confidentiality, these attributes are lost after the message is delivered.

12.4 End-to-End Security When Intermediaries Are Present

As discussed in Chapter 4, "SOAP," SOAP is architected to allow messages to go through one or more SOAP intermediary nodes before they reach their final destination. In this example, some information in the travel request flows through Fabrikam456 to the travel suppliers. Fabrikam456 augments the travel request and modifies some sections.

Intermediaries must be able to access the header and the body, possibly deleting and/or adding some header blocks, so network- or transport-layer security such as IPSec and SSL/TLS needs to be terminated at each intermediary. The intermediary might not be able to reestablish the security information from the original sender because it might not be authorized (that is, it doesn't have original sender's keys). This situation is depicted in Figure 12-3. This structure is appropriate if the intermediary is trusted.

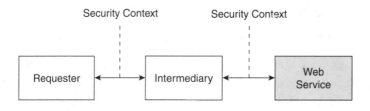

Figure 12-3   Point-to-point configuration.

However, if one does not want the intermediary to access or modify some parts of the message, or if the end services want to authenticate the requester without trusting the intermediary, then it is necessary to set up an end-to-end security context, as shown in Figure 12-4. Also, some of the information might require additional levels of protection such as:

- End-to-end integrity, for example, for the original travel request and the original sender,

- End-to-end confidentiality, for example for frequent flier numbers, account numbers, and similar information.

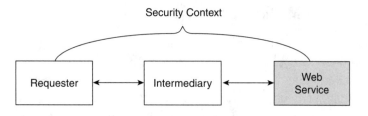

Figure 12-4   End-to-end configuration.

Establishing such end-to-end security requires a mechanism above the transport layer. This is why a message-layer security is required: this is precisely what WS-Security provides. The original message must be secure end to end, independent of the point-to-point protocols.

WS-Security: SOAP Message Security provides support for end-to-end message security. This specification introduces three key concepts:

- **Security tokens**—SOAP messages can contain security tokens with authentication information. These tokens can flow with the message through intermediaries to vouch for message claims to downstream systems.

- **Signature elements**—SOAP messages can contain digital signature information for all or part of a message. In this example, CompanyABC's application signs the message or part of the message. The downstream travel services use the signature to verify that CompanyABC's original request has not been changed, and to vouch that the message came from CompanyABC.

- **Encryption element**—SOAP messages can be encrypted, either wholly or in part. In this example, CompanyABC's application encrypts some information in the original message so that only AirlineXYZ can read it.

WS-Security defines a *SOAP Security Header* format that contains subelements for security tokens, signature elements, and encryption elements. These concepts are presented in more detail later in this chapter.

12.5 Federating Multiple Security Domains

Web services technology is often used to integrate several existing applications available on the network. These applications might be extremely diverse in terms of hardware, operating systems, middleware, and in their configurations. In addition, they might reside in different security domains that have different security policies and are dependent on different security infrastructure, such as PKI and Kerberos. This example assumes that each "site" has its own security infrastructure. The infrastructure might be very rigorous, such as Kerberos, or ad hoc, using simple user ID and password databases. It is also assumed that a well-known, in-network security provider, such as a trusted certificate authority, is available in the network.

To date, translating security information from one system in one security domain to another system in another security domain has not been easy. To solve this problem, standard syntax and semantics to express the security information, and rules to translate it, are required. Although WS-Security as it is defined today does not solve all these issues, it is certainly a firm step in that direction, thanks to its flexibility and extensibility.

WS-Security helps solve these problems by defining the following:

- A standard interoperable format (schema) for transporting security information (identity tokens, signature elements, and encryption elements and claims).

- A standard Web services interface (WS-Trust) that Web services can use to create, exchange, and validate security tokens issued by other domains, and that requesters can use to translate credentials from one domain into tokens accepted by another domain. In this example, AirlineXYZ calls back to CompanyABC's security infrastructure, through the WS-Trust's WSDL interface, to validate tokens in a message.

- A set of concrete security policy documents (extensions of WS-Policy) that allow sites and Web services to document their support for WS-Security and their requirements on callers. For example, a site might use WS-Policy to document which messages (or parts of messages) must be signed and which certificate authorities the site trusts.

12.6 A Brief History

When XML was conceived as a means to exchange business data across the Internet, it was immediately recognized that those documents had to be secured. Accordingly, in 1999, W3C and IETF jointly started the XML Signature Working Group to define a set of specifications for digitally signing XML documents. XML Signature became a W3C Recommendation in 2002. In parallel, W3C also worked on a new specification for encrypting parts of XML documents (XML Encryption). XML Encryption was also made into a W3C Recommendation in 2002.

Because SOAP is based on XML, it was natural to assume that XML Signature and XML Encryption should be used to protect SOAP messages. Thus, in April 2002, IBM, Microsoft, and VeriSign jointly published a specification of WS-Security, which later became the OASIS standard Web Services Security: SOAP Message Security 1.0 (WS-Security 2004). (This book will simply refer to it as WS-Security.) IBM and Microsoft also published a roadmap, laying out additional security specifications. Figure 12-1 was from that roadmap.

12.7 Architectural Concepts

Web services can be accessed by sending SOAP messages to service endpoints identified as WS-Addressing endpoint references; these messages request specific actions from the service provider, and often trigger SOAP-message responses (including fault indications). Within this context, the broad goal of securing Web services breaks into two subsidiary goals: providing facilities for securing the integrity and confidentiality of the messages, and ensuring that the service acts only on message requests that express the claims required by the security policies. The challenge for WS-Security is to enable secure integration of extremely diverse systems and infrastructures. Figure 12-5 shows the model WS-Security uses for coping with this challenge.

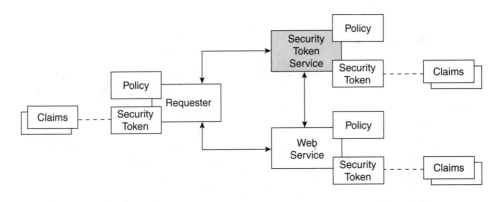

Figure 12-5   WS-Security model.

In this example, suppose someone wants to send a request to Fabrikam456. The requester might have *claims* regarding the message's security properties, such as identity and authorization claims. For example, the requester might have "logged on to" Kerberos and received a Ticket Granting Ticket that identifies the requester and specifies access privileges.

WS-Security provides a way to represent the set of claims. This is represented as a *security token*, and WS-Security defines a standard XML format for transporting security tokens. Some tokens might be issued by a trusted third party. For example, an X.509 certificate is usually issued by a certification authority (CA). In the WS-Security model, a trusted third party is called a *Security Token Service (STS)* because one of its tasks is to issue security tokens. The Security Token Service (STS) might be well-known in a public network, such as an Internet CA, or it might be an infrastructure service within an enterprise's network.

In this example, CompanyABC wraps an ad hoc user name/password logon service with an STS interface that issues security tokens. CompanyABC's STS issues the tokens in a format that WS-Security specifies, and it encrypts the token with a key known to CompanyABC and the requester (that is, CompanyABC's certificate).

The implementing Web service, on the other hand, has a set of requirements for a request to be accepted, such as "X.509-based authentication is required" and "Message must be encrypted by an AES key and have a key length of 128 bits." These requirements are described as the service's *policy*, and in particular *security policy*, which is made known to the requester through UDDI or WS-MetadataExchange. Based on the service's security policy, the requester decides which claims it must use (that is, which security tokens to propagate with the message) and what kind of protection is necessary for the request.

If the requester expects a reply (as is generally the case), it can also state its requirement of protecting the reply through a security policy associated with the requester. Similarly, the STS *itself* is a Web service. The STS has its own policy that states the security requirements on its communications.

WS-Security defines the standard format for transporting security tokens and their mapping to SOAP headers; the specification includes an XML Schema for this purpose. WS-Security also recognizes specific types of security tokens, which support common security infrastructure. Currently, WS-Security has five types of security tokens recognized as profiles in WS-Security:

- A username token (`<wsse:UsernameToken>`) is a claim on identity. It can have a password, in which case the token also represents a claim that the requester knows the password.

- An X.509 certificate (`<wsse:BinarySecurityToken>`) is a claim regarding a binding between a public key and its subject, endorsed by a trusted third party.

- A Kerberos ticket (`<wsse:BinarySecurityToken>`) is a claim that states: "I, the owner of the session key contained in this ticket, am authorized to make a request to the specified services."

- A Security Assertion Markup Language (SAML) assertion uses the generic SAML language syntax for representing security-related assertions, such as identity, attribute, and authorization-decision assertions.

- A Rights Expression Language (REL) license represents ISO/IEC 21000-5 Rights Expressions with respect to the WS-Security specification.

WS-Security also defines a processing model for signing and encrypting security tokens in SOAP messages. This supports the integrity of the tokens, prevents their forgery, and precludes unauthorized access to their information.

For example, CompanyABC might sign and encrypt user security tokens that it issues. Fabrikam456 and AirlineXYZ are assured that CompanyABC issued the token because the signature is verified, but they cannot examine its contents (username, password) because the token is encrypted (opaque). Fabrikam456 and AirlineXYZ might call back to CompanyABC through WS-Trust, passing the encrypted token to determine if it is still valid, or to request authorization decisions (such as, do CompanyABC's policies authorize international travel based on a request with this particular token?).

WS-Trust defines the interfaces to a Security Token Server. In this example, the security infrastructure systems of CompanyABC, Fabrikam456, the well-known security service, the airline and the hotel might provide WS-Trust interfaces for other sites and for network users. For example, AirlineXYZ might use CompanyABC's STS WS-Trust interface to validate a token that it receives through Fabrikam456.

12.8 Processing Model

The preceding section defined the architecture concepts. This section documents the model for processing messages with respect to the WS-Security standards. The processing model of WS-Security is built on top of the substrate provided by SOAP, XML Signature, and XML Encryption. Therefore, this section first looks at the processing models of these specifications.

12.8.1 XML Signature

XML Signature protects parts of an XML document from unauthorized modifications using a cryptographic technique called *digital signature.* The signature algorithm can be either a symmetric cryptosystem such as Triple DES and AES (Advanced Encryption Standard), or an asymmetric (public key) cryptosystem such as RSA and DSA.

The following XML fragment shows the basic syntax of XML Signature. The `<ds:Signature>` element can be the top-level XML element or can be embedded somewhere in a larger XML document. In WS-Security, this element is embedded in a SOAP (security) header block:

```
<ds:Signature>
  <ds:SignedInfo>
    <ds:CanonicalizationMethod Algorithm="..."/>
    <ds:SignatureMethod Algorithm="..."/>
    <ds:Reference URI="...">
       <ds:Transforms> ... </ds:Transforms>
       <ds:DigestMethod Algorithm="..."/>
       <ds:DigestValue> ... </ds:DigestValue>
    </ds:Reference> +
  </ds:SignedInfo>
  <ds:SignatureValue> ... </ds:SignatureValue>
  <ds:KeyInfo> ... </ds:KeyInfo>?
  <ds:Object> ... </ds:Object>*
</ds:Signature>
```

The digital signature algorithm specified in the `<ds:SignatureMethod>` element is used to sign the `<ds:SignedInfo>` element, and the signature value is placed into the `<ds:SignatureValue>` element. The `<ds:SignedInfo>` element in turn contains one or more `<ds:Reference>` elements, which refer to the data in the message that are to be signed. Because the digest values of the referenced data are included in the `<ds:SignedInfo>` element, a cryptographic binding exists between the referenced data and the `<ds:SignedInfo>` element. That is, if the reference data changes, the digest value of the data also changes, resulting in a different value in the `<ds:DigestValue>` element within the `<ds:SignedInfo>` element.

Thanks to this indirection, XML Signature allows signing multiple parts of an XML document in a single signature operation. This is particularly useful in WS-Security, when the message body and some parts of the header blocks need to be protected from unauthorized alterations. Optionally, the key used in this operation can be specified using the optional `<ds:KeyInfo>` element.

Because signature algorithms work on binary data, the data to be signed must also be represented as binary data (or an octet string). This leads to some complications because an XML document is defined in InfoSet, not as an octet string. For example, the same XML document can be represented as a different octet string by just changing the character encoding from UTF-8 to ISO-8859-1.

Other characteristics of an XML document can alter its representation as an octet string while still representing the same InfoSet; for example, the order in which attributes appear on an element or the use of certain white space characters (such a newlines). Canonical XML, defined by the W3C XML Signature Working Group, is a specification that defines an octet-string representation of an XML document which assigns a unique octet string (the canonical XML representation) to each XML InfoSet. The `<ds:CanonicalizationMethod>` element specifies the algorithm used to derive this unique representation. In WS-Security, the recommended algorithm is W3C Exclusive Canonicalization, a variation of W3C Canonical XML with namespace handling that's more suitable for SOAP messages.

12.8.2 XML Encryption

Similar to XML Signature, XML Encryption encrypts portions of an XML document. The general syntax of XML Encryption is shown here:

```
<xenc:EncryptedData (Id="")? (Type="")?>
  <xenc:EncryptionMethod/>?
  <ds:KeyInfo>
   <xenc:EncryptedKey/>?
   <ds:*/>?
  </ds:KeyInfo>?
  <xenc:CipherData>
    <xenc:CipherValue>(encrypted character data)
</xenc:CipherValue>?
    <xenc:CipherReference URI=""/>?
  </xenc:CipherData>
</xenc:EncryptedData>
```

As in XML Signature, the `<xenc:EncryptionMethod>` element specifies the encryption algorithm, and the `<ds:KeyInfo>` element specifies the encryption key or its location. Because it is a bad practice to use the recipient's long-lasting key repeatedly (such as a proof of possession key for identity claims) when encrypting a large amount of data, the encryption key is generated randomly for each message. This encryption key, sometimes called a *session key*, is then carried in the same message but it is encrypted using the recipient's long-lasting key, or some other set of keys that both the parties know. The `<xenc:EncryptedKey>` element is used for this purpose.

When some part of an XML document needs to be encrypted, it can be replaced with the `<xenc:EncryptedData>` element, with both the key information and the encrypted data. Alternatively, the key information and the encrypted data can be put into separate places using two `<enc:EncryptedData>` elements. In WS-Security, the latter method is used because the key information needs to be in the header block, whereas `<enc:EncryptedData>` must stay in the original position of the data within the SOAP envelope.

12.9 Putting the Pieces Together

We now show how WS-Security uses these techniques to secure Web service interactions.

12.9.1 The Basic Model

In its simplest form, WS-Security carries a single signed security token asserting the requester's security information without further protection. The following SOAP envelope shows this:

```
<S:Envelope xmlns:S="..."
    xmlns:wsse="http://docs.oasis-open.org/wss/2004/01/...">
  <S:Header>
        ...
      <wsse:Security>
          <wsse:UsernameToken wsu:Id="...">
              <wsse:Username>alice</wsse:Username>
          </wsse:UsernameToken>
      </wsse:Security>
        ...
```

```
    </S:Header>
    ...
    <S:Body>
        ...
    </S:Body>
</S:Envelope>
```

The WS-Security specification defines a header block called `<wsse:Security>`, which might contain one or more security tokens. A message might contain zero or more `<wsse:Security>` headers. If multiple security headers exist, each one must be targeted at a different SOAP Actor or Role. In this case, one security token, the `<wsse:UsernameToken>` element, asserts the identity of the requester.

This form is useful when the sender node and the receiver node are located in a controlled environment, or when the transport or lower layers provide sufficient protection (such as when the connection is protected by TLS or IPSec). One typical usage scenario is to propagate the end user's identity to back-end Web services. In Figure 12-6, the end user's identity is authenticated by the HTTP front-end server using HTTP Basic Authentication. The front-end server then forwards the identity information to the back-end Web service using the username token in WS-Security. Because the front-end server is located in the same security domain as the Web service, the Web service can trust the assertion regarding the end user's identity. Protection during transmission is provided by hop-by-hop SSL/TLS connections.

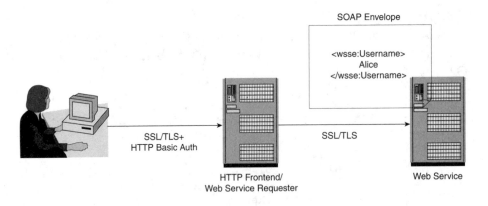

Figure 12-6   Propagating the end user's identity.

In this scenario, this might be the internal security model for CompanyABC. The company's application executes in a Web application server, which uses Web services to connect with other applications. The Web server uses an intraenterprise security system to authenticate the user ID and password. The Web services infrastructure trusts the Web server and simply accepts the security token.

WS-Security also protects messages against unauthorized access and modification during network transition. The following message structure shows WS-Security defined elements in a SOAP message whose body is protected by XML Signature for integrity and XML Encryption for confidentiality:

```
<S:Envelope xmlns:S="..."
    xmlns:wsse="http://docs.oasis-open.org/wss/2004/01/..."
    xmlns:xenc='http://www.w3.org/2001/04/xmlenc#'
    xmlns:ds='http://www.w3.org/2000/09/xmldsig#' >
    <S:Header>
            ...
        <wsse:Security>
            <wsse:BinarySecurityToken>
 ...(e.g., X.509 Certificate) ...
            </wsse:BinarySecurityToken>
            <xenc:ReferenceList>
                <xenc:DataReference URI="#bodyID"/>
            </xenc:ReferenceList>
            <ds:Signature>
              ...(for the message body) ...
            </ds:Signature>
        </wsse:Security>
            ...
    </S:Header>
    ...
    <S:Body>
        <xenc:EncryptedData ID="bodyID">
            ...
        </xenc:EncryptedData>
    </S:Body>
</S:Envelope>
```

In addition to security tokens, the WS-Security header block, `<wsse:Security>`, might also contain encryption directives (in the `<xenc:ReferenceList>` element) and signature directives (in the `<ds:Signature>` element). Typically, a security token carries an X.509 certificate that is used in conjunction with the signature. The receiving node will process these subelements in the order they appear. In this case, it processes the binary security token and extracts the

X.509 certificate within, decrypts the message body that is referenced by the `<xenc:ReferenceList>` subelement, and verifies the signature contained in the `<ds:Signature>` element. Consequently, the sender node is responsible for prepending subelements as they are processed during the message's composition.

12.9.2 Model with Intermediary

Because the `<wsse:Security>` element is a SOAP header block, it can be targeted at any SOAP receiver that might be on the message path, using the role attribute (or the actor attribute if the envelope uses SOAP 1.1). Accordingly, a SOAP message can contain multiple `<wsse:Security>` header blocks, but each block *must* be targeted to a different receiver. The order of these header blocks doesn't matter because the SOAP specification does not specify any particular order when targeting headers to intermediaries. It is possible to have one security header block with no target, which is assumed to apply to the message and all actors. An intermediary node should process header blocks targeted at the node, then remove them, and optionally add new header blocks, before transferring the message to the next node in the message path. A message can still be protected against unauthorized accesses and modifications in the presence of un-trusted intermediaries if the originator signs it with its own signature and encrypts it with the key of the ultimate receiver.

In this example, CompanyABC can sign some of the request information it forwards to Fabrikam456, which defines the request for travel. Fabrikam456 can add information to the request as it interacts with the airline and hotel. Because the original request information is signed, the airline and hotel are assured that CompanyABC originated the travel request, and can process Fabrikam456's operations within the context of the original request. CompanyABC's application might encrypt the message also (with keys known to all parties) and send private information to the airline and hotel, which Fabrikam456 will not be able to examine. This information might include account and discount information, contract numbers, and so on.

12.9.3 Trust Relationships

A security token can be self-generated (as in the case of a username token) or vouched for by a trusted third party. If the message's sender and receiver are both in the same security domain (or have a direct trust relationship), and the communication channel is protected at the transport level, self-generated security tokens can be trusted. Otherwise, security tokens must be vouched for by a third party who is trusted by both the sender and the receiver. In the WS-Security model, this trusted third party is a Security Token Service. WS-Trust defines protocols and standard WSDL interfaces to communicate with an STS.

When a security token service is involved in establishing a trust relationship, two interaction models exist. One is the *pull model*, where the receiver checks the validity of a received security token with the security token service. The other is the *push model*, where the sender first requests that a token be issued by the security token service.

Figure 12-7 shows the pull model of trust establishment. The requester makes a request to the Web service, which is associated with explicit or implied security claims. An example is an identity claim, expressed as a username token along with a password as proof of possession. The Web service then verifies that the password belongs to the claimed requester by consulting with the STS. This corresponds to a directory lookup operation in conventional IT configurations.

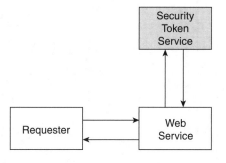

Figure 12-7   The pull model of trust relationships.

For example, this model may be used if CompanyABC employees have an application on their notebooks that allows them to interact with Fabrikam456 while traveling. The notebook application produces a security token based on user ID and password for the user in CompanyABC. The notebook application encrypts this token with CompanyABC's public key. The notebook application and CompanyABC rely on the WellKnown Security provider for certificate support. Fabrikam456 receives a Web service request for the notebook application, which contains the security token. Fabrikam456 then calls (pulls) the validation from a WS-Trust interface that CompanyABC provides.

Another example is an authorization claim, which might be implicit in the request, that the requester is authorized to call the Web service. The Web service verifies the identity of the requester by examining other security tokens, and then it consults the security token service if the requester is allowed to access the service. This corresponds to the use of an access control server in a company's intranet.

In the push model (shown in figure 12-8) the requester obtains a cryptographically signed security token from an STS in advance and then binds the token to the request. For example, the requester can log in and obtain a Kerberos Ticket Granting Ticket (TGT) from the security token service. The requester then uses a derived Ticket Granting Service ticket (TGS) to make the subsequent requests.

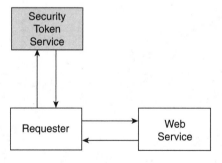

Figure 12-8   The push mode of trust relationships.

In this example, the traveler's notebook application might directly contact CompanyABC's STS and receive a security token for access to Fabrikam456. The application then forwards this token on requests to Fabrikam456. Fabrikam456 can verify the token using several means, including signature verification (the token is signed) relying on the WellKnown Security certificate authority.

When one security token can be used repeatedly, the push model is more efficient in terms of the number of communications with the security token service. The downside is that any security token might be revoked, so the receiving Web service must check its validity anyway if the policy requires it.

12.10 Interoperability

Enterprises are adopting Web services to ease application integration across heterogeneous environments within and across domain boundaries. Enterprise security architects must be confident that resources will not be exposed to unauthorized use. Technologies must be integrated with existing security infrastructure.

Web Services Security provides extensible and flexible mechanisms that suit these purposes well. However, these same benefits also make interoperability difficult. The extensibility of WS-Security introduces many options and choices. If different enterprises select different options, they might not be able to interoperate. Some guidelines are needed to limit the possibilities that infrastructures must implement and test in order to interoperate. The Web Services Interoperability (WS-I) organization defines a security profile to meet this requirement.

12.10.1 Basic Security Profile
The WS-I Basic Security Profile (BSP) provides clarifications and amplifications for a set of standards used to secure the transmission of Web services messages. The scope of the first version of the profile will include the following:

- HTTP Security

  - [HTTPS] HTTP over TLS http://www.ietf.org/rfc/rfc2818.txt.
- SOAP Message Security:

  - WSS: SOAP Message Security v1.0—The formats (schema) for security tokens, signature elements, encryption elements, their placement in SOAP headers, and references to other elements of the message.
  - WSS: UsernameToken Profile v1.0
  - WSS: X.509 Certificate Token Profile v1.0
  - WSS: SOAP With Attachments Profile (currently in draft)—This augments the basic model, with support for encrypting and signing non-XML data in SOAP attachments.

Please note that work is progressing in parallel on profiles that extend the BSP to address

- WSS: REL Token Profile (currently in draft)

- WSS: SAML Token Profile (currently in draft)

Additionally, each of these standards builds on existing standards such as XML Encryption, XML Signature, HTTP, and TLS, bringing them into scope for the profile. These standards are only in scope when used by the higher-level standards.

The framework defined in these standards is extensible and can accommodate a wide range of security models, security tokens, signature formats, and encryption technologies. The flexibility and extensibility of the framework is a challenge for interoperability, however. The BSP focuses on improving interoperability by strengthening requirements when possible (making "shoulds" into "musts"), reducing some of the flexibility (picking one right way when several alternatives are available) and extensibility. This limits the set of common functionality that vendors must implement and test for interoperability.

The guiding principles enumerated in the BSP declare that the profile should do no harm, make statements that are testable when possible, and focus on inter-operability. The profile should not try to address any issues in the profiled standards that do not affect interoperability, and enhancing interoperability should not create new security threats.

The profile includes requirement statements about two kinds of artifacts, SECURE_ENVELOPE and SECURE_MESSAGE. A SECURE_ENVELOPE is a SOAP envelope that has been subjected to integrity or confidentiality protection. A SECURE_MESSAGE expands the scope of the SECURE_ENVELOPE to include protocol elements transmitted with the SECURE_ENVELOPE that have been subjected to integrity and/or confidentiality protection.

In order to conform to the BSP, any artifact that contains a construct addressed in the profile must conform to any statements that constrain its use. Conformant receivers are not required to accept all possible conformant messages. Conformance applies to deployed instances of services. Because major portions of the profile might not apply in certain circumstances, individual URIs might be used to indicate conformance to the following parts of the profile: the core profile, username token, X.509 token, and SOAP attachments. Additional URIs will be used as additional token profiles are profiled by the BSP working group (such as SAML, REL, and Kerberos).

12.11 Future Directions

Although WS-Security defines an interoperable syntax and a set of processing rules for exchanging security information and protecting messages, applying them randomly might not make systems secure. One must consider all the relevant aspects of security and balance them against their cost. The use of username tokens makes perfect sense in one environment, but it does not provide any security in other environments.

Because flexibility was more important in the design of WS-Security, many options might lead to insecure implementations. As the industry learns more about the real world security requirements of Web services, best practices or patterns for using WS-Security securely will gradually emerge.

12.12 Summary

This chapter has discussed the basic mechanisms that can be used to make Web services interactions reliable in the presence of security attacks. A family of WS-Security specifications has been defined to deal with many of the aspects of Web services security. The most fundamental of these specifications, WS-Security: SOAP Message Security, provides a common syntax and a processing model for carrying security information in SOAP envelopes, enabling the integration of existing enterprise and internet security mechanisms. Using basic WS-Security Web service requesters and providers can ensure the integrity and confidentiality of their interactions and check and transmit identity and authorization information among others. Other specifications in the WS-Security family, which provide solutions for other security needs of Web service users, are reviewed in the next chapter.

Chapter 13

Advanced Security

As presented in Chapter 12, "Security," WS-Security provides the basis for the other security specifications, as shown in Figure 13-1. WS-Security: SOAP Message Security provides a complete, flexible, end-to-end, multiparty model for authentication, message integrity, and confidentiality. The secure messaging protocols rely on security tokens. WS-Trust introduces the concept of a *security token server,* which is a Web service that issues, renews, and validates security tokens.

Chapter 7, "Web Services Policy," discussed the WS-Policy framework. WS-SecurityPolicy defines the model Web services use to document their WS-Security support and requirements for requesters. This chapter provides additional details on WS-SecurityPolicy.

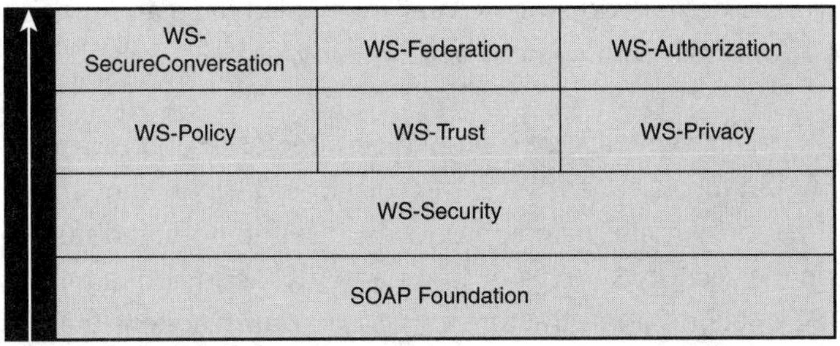

WS-SecureConversation	WS-Federation	WS-Authorization
WS-Policy	WS-Trust	WS-Privacy
WS-Security		
SOAP Foundation		

Figure 13-1   Web services security architecture.

WS-Security: SOAP Message Security is optimized for exchanging a small number of messages. A requester might engage in a prolonged "conversation" with a Web service. WS-SecureConversation builds on WS-Trust and message security to provide support for multimessage, long-lived conversations. WS-SecureConversation provides a better level of security and improved efficiency. This chapter also provides an overview of WS-Secure Conversation.

WS-Trust supports security tokens. Collaboration between enterprises often requires sharing additional information, such as customer identity information and preferences. WS-Federation extends WS-Trust to provide these functions, and is discussed later in this chapter.

The final two specifications in the security family are WS-Authorization and WS-Privacy. These specifications are in progress. This chapter describes their role and purpose.

13.1 WS-Trust

WS-Security messages contain security tokens, which a requester can obtain in many ways. The requester might have a username and password or possess an X590 certificate, which allows the requester (or application) to form a security token. These ad hoc approaches work in many cases, but more sophisticated multiparty scenarios might require a more flexible model.

Consider the example from the previous chapter. How does a traveling user, as an employee of CompanyABC, get a valid token for access to Fabrikam456 travel? He might have a logon username and password to Fabrikam456, but this would be as a private individual. The user might also have an X509 certificate, but this does not prove employment by CompanyABC.

CompanyABC might replicate their employee directories and provide them to Fabrikam456, but this is expensive. It also discloses a significant amount of private information. An alternate approach is to set up a limited trust relationship between the security systems of CompanyABC and Fabrikam456. CompanyABC's security infrastructure can issue security tokens that Fabrikam456 accepts. WS-Trust is an extensible specification to support this scenario and more complex models.

WS-Trust defines a conceptual model for using a Web service. A requester examines the WS-SecurityPolicy statements associated with a Web service. The policy statements specify the type and authority of security tokens that the Web service requires for messages it processes. If the requester does not possess acceptable tokens, it must obtain them. One way is to contact a *security token server (STS)* that the Web service's policy statements identify as acceptable.

A security token service (STS) is a Web service that has a WSDL interface and processes secure SOAP messages. An STS issues, renews, and validates security tokens. Consider again the example from the previous chapter.

1. The traveling user's application sends a *RequestSecurityToken (RST)* message to the STS interface of CompanyABC's security infrastructure. This message requests a security token that applies to Fabrikam456. The RST message itself contains a security token that authenticates the requester to CompanyABC. CompanyABC's STS might require additional signature information and encryption on the request.

2. If satisfied, CompanyABC responds with a *RequestSecurityTokenResponse* message that contains the security token that the traveling user submits to Fabrikam456. The response might contain additional information, such as the lifetime of the token and proof-of-possession data. It might also contain key information, which allows the requester to compute a key. WS-Trust supports an extensible set of models for issuing keys or information that allow a requester and an STS to derive keys.

3. The traveling user's application uses the returned token on messages it sends to Fabrikam456. The application uses any keys that are provided or derived to properly encrypt and sign information in the message and header, to comply with Fabrikam456's security policies.

4. Fabrikam456 validates that the incoming message complies with its security policies. For example, Fabrikam456 might verify that the security token has been signed by CompanyABC using an X509 certificate issued by WellKnownSecurityService.

RequestSecurityToken and RequestSecurityTokenResponse are the messages that define the interface to an STS. These are abstract, base messages. WS-Trust defines a set of *bindings* that associate concrete semantics and extensions to the messages. For each binding, WS-Trust documents a set of WS-Addressing Action URIs that define the semantics. WS-Trust also introduces a `<RequestType>` element that takes a URI value to define the semantics of the message. WS-Trust defines the following bindings:

- **Issuance**—Based on the security token in the request, a new token is issued.

- **Renewal**—Renew a token.

- **Validation**—Validate a token.

```
<wst:RequestSecurityToken>
      <wst:TokenType>...</wst:TokenType>
      <wst:RequestType>...</wst:RequestType>
      <wst:Base>...</wst:Base>
      <wst:Supporting>...</wst:Supporting>
          ...
      <wsp:AppliesTo>...</wsp:AppliesTo>
      <wst:Claims Dialect="...">...</wst:Claims>
      <wst:Entropy>
            <wst:BinarySecret>...<wst:BinarySecret>
      </wst:Entropy>
      <wst:Lifetime>
            <wsu:Created>...</wsu:Created>
            <wsu:Expires>...</wsu:Expires>
      </wst:Lifetime>
</wst:RequestSecurityToken>
```

The preceding code snippet provides an overview of the elements in a Request Security Token (RST) message. TokenType identifies the type of token requested. An STS might return many types of tokens. RequestType specifies the binding, that is, issuance, renewal, or verification. Base is the security token the requester is using to obtain the new security token. AppliesTo is the Web service, specified by a WS-Addressing endpoint reference, for which the requester wants a security token. Entropy allows the requester and the STS to exchange information for deriving keys. The WS-Trust specification provides more details on the elements of the RST and Request Security Token Response (RSTR) messages.

In addition to AppliesTo, WS-Trust allows one Web service to request a security token on behalf of another. The requester can specify the endpoint reference of the service on whose behalf it is requesting the token. Consider the traveling CompanyABC employee. The contract between CompanyABC and Fabrikam456 might require CompanyABC's STS to contact Fabrikam456's to obtain a token. CompanyABC would obtain the security token on behalf of the requesting applications.

WS-Trust also defines a model for challenges. Upon receiving a message with a security token in it, a service might send a challenge, forcing the requester to demonstrate its right to use the token. If the requester passes an X509 certificate, the service might respond with a challenge that contains some random data. The requester must sign the random data with the private key associated with the certificate, demonstrating proof of possession. The challenge model strengthens security by eliminating some attacks.

WS-Trust provides support for specifying key sizes and algorithms in the request and response messages. The specification also provides support for passing policy information in messages.

Each Web service endpoint logically implements a *trust engine* that must understand the WS-Security and WS-Trust model. The trust engine of a Web service must verify the following:

- The security token is sufficient to comply with the Web service's policy, and the message conforms to the policy (for example, the necessary elements are encrypted or signed).

- The security tokens are proven signatures.

- The issuers of the security tokens (including all related and ancestral security tokens) are trusted by this site to issue the claims they have made.

The trust engine might need to send tokens to a security token service to exchange them for other security tokens, which it can use directly in its evaluation. If the trust engine determines that the conditions are met and the requester is authorized to perform the operation, the Web service can process the Web service request within the aforementioned trust model.

There are many ways to assert trust, and two methods of assessing the presence of a trust relationship. WS-Trust describes these two methods, which depend on whether the assessment is based on information from within a message flow (*inband*) or outside it (*out-of-band*).

13.1.1 In-Band

As part of a message flow, a security token service might be asked to exchange a security token (or some proof) of one form for another. This exchange request is made either by a requester or by another party on the requester's behalf:

- If the security token service trusts the provided security token (for example, it might trust the token's issuing authority), and the request can prove possession of that security token, the exchange is processed by the security token service. This is an example of an *in-band direct trust relationship.*

- In the case of a *delegated request,* in which another party provides the request on behalf of the requester, the security token service generating the new token might not need to trust the authority that issued the original token because it trusts the security token service making the request. The basis of the trust is the relationship between the two security token services.

13.1.2 Out-of-Band

An administrator or other trusted authority can designate that all tokens of a certain type are trusted. The security token service maintains this as a trust axiom and may send it to trust engines so they can make their own trust decisions (or revoke it later). Alternatively, the security token service might provide this function as a service to trusting services.

13.2 WS-SecureConversation

WS-Security is a simple model for message security. It works fine for small numbers of messages exchanged between Web services occasionally. However, WS-Security has two drawbacks when a requester and a Web service engage in a prolonged, multiple-message exchange:

- Relying on PKI for signatures and encryption is not computationally efficient.

- Signing large amounts of data with public keys is considered "poor form" and diminishes the security of the key. The more information that's encrypted with a key, the easier it becomes to break the key.

WS-SecureConversation solves these problems by doing for WSS:SOAP Message Security what SSL/TSL did for HTTP/TCP-IP. The endpoints use PKI and WS-Security to exchange a session-specific set of keys. This allows for more efficient encryption and improved security for keys.

The key concepts in WS-SecureConversation are the *Security Context* and the *Security Context Token (SCT)*. WS-SecureConversation defines the format and schema for an SCT. WS-SecureConversation also defines an extended binding of WS-Trust, which allows Secure Token Servers to generate and return SCTs. In another model, a Web service requester can itself generate an SCT.

Messages within a conversation contain the SCT in a header included by the sending Web service. The SCT contains or implies a shared secret. The requesting Web service obtains the secret from an STS in a RSTR, and then forwards the secret (encrypted) to another service. WS-SecureConversation documents algorithms for using the shared secret to derive session keys to be used for encrypting communication exchanged within the conversation.

13.3 WS-Privacy

Web Services Privacy Framework (WS-Privacy) describes syntax and semantics for binding privacy policies to Web services and instances of data in messages. The main emphases of WS-Privacy are on enabling policies to be processed by Web service providers and requesters (in contrast to interfacing with human users), and on ensuring good usability in chains of Web service invocations within or across enterprises. WS-Privacy builds on WS-Policy and related standards. It does not define a new privacy policy language, but it offers the means to bind such existing languages to a Web service.

Web services often handle sensitive personal data, including a person's attributes, typical B2C customer data such as shipping address and credit card number, and detailed customer records in B2C and B2B scenarios. Web services might act on behalf of a requester, such as an appointment calendar service, so that essentially the data remains personal.

Personal data usually falls under a *privacy policy,* which restricts its usage to specific purposes and recipients. This privacy policy can be partially prescribed by law, be stated voluntarily by a service owner, or be set by the person concerned. A goal of Web services is widespread interoperability, and it is thus expected that services with different purposes and different owners will frequently interact. Hence, it is essential that Web services be able to adapt their interaction patterns in accordance with promised or required privacy restrictions, and that such restrictions can be communicated between different Web services.

Furthermore, many Web services can handle data from multiple sources, which might be governed by different and varying policies. An example would be a Web service requiring access to your passport number and driver's license number. Each piece of data can be gathered from a different source, and thus can have a different privacy policy. For such services, it is important to be flexible in adapting to these policies at different levels of granularity. This applies both to services that respond directly to the requesters and to those that offer processing facilities within an enterprise, such as storage or statistics services.

Because privacy polices are written in native policy languages, there must be a way of incorporating native privacy policies into wsp:Policy assertions. This is done with a new type of assertion, called a *privacy assertion*. A WS-Policy policy can incorporate this privacy assertion to indicate the privacy promises and requirements of services and data elements.

A privacy assertion is a promise that the policy's subject makes about how the privacy-sensitive data it receives will be used in the future. It can also represent a privacy requirement that the policy's subject expects the receiver of privacy-sensitive data to honor.

13.4 WS-Federation

The term *federated identity* has various meanings. To an individual user, it means the ability to associate his various application and system identities with one another. To an enterprise, federated identity provides a standardized means for directly providing services for trusted third-party users, or those that the business doesn't manage directly. An enterprise associates with others in a *federation*, such that the identities from one enterprise domain (or *identity provider*) are granted access to the services of the other enterprises (or *service providers*).

Federated Identity Management refers to the set of business agreements, technical agreements, and policies that enable companies to become partners. This lowers their overall identity management costs, improves the user experience, and mitigates security risks in Web services-based interactions.

WS-Federation builds on this specification to define mechanisms for brokering and federating trust, identity, and claims. *Federation* is the overall term for a set of distinct, heterogeneous enterprises that want to provide an easy-to-use, single sign-on identity model to their users. *Single sign-on* means that after a user signs on with one member of the federation, he can interact with other members without reauthentication. Enterprises can be corporate entities, Internet Service Providers (ISPs), or associations of individuals.

A federated environment differs from a traditional single sign-on environment in that there are no established rules limiting how enterprises transfer information about a user. However, there might be an established business policy for an enterprise's participation in the federation, much like there is today when companies decide to do business together.

WS-Federation describes how to use the existing Web services security building blocks to provide federation functionality, including trust, single sign-on (and single sign-off), and attribute management across a federation. WS-Federation is really a family of three specifications: WS-Federation, WS-Federation Passive Client, and WS-Federation Active Client.

WS-Federation itself describes how to implement a federation in a Web services world. In particular, WS-Federation focuses on the relationships between parties, and the high-level architecture that supports these relationships. The two individual documents, WS-Federation Active and WS-Federation Passive, describe how to implement individual federation solutions.

WS-Federation Active describes how to implement federation functionality in the active client environment. Active clients are those that are Web services-enabled. That is, they can issue Web service requests and react to a Web service's response. Leveraging the Web services security stack, WS-Fed Active describes how to implement the advantages of a federation relationship, including single sign-on, in an active client environment.

WS-Federation Passive describes how to implement federation functionality in a passive client environment. A passive client is one that is not Web services-enabled. The most common passive client is a plain old HTTP browser. WS-Fed Passive describes how to leverage the advantages of a federation relationship, such as single sign-on, in a passive client environment. Because this solution uses the WS-Security foundation of the infrastructure support, the same components used to provide a passive client solution might be utilized for an active client solution as well.

The logical architecture described in WS-Federation, together with the functionality described in the Web services security stack, supports both the active and passive client scenarios. The complete family of WS-Security specifications provides companies with a standards-based, interoperable, secure digital identity and trust platform for Web services-based architecture. Furthermore, these specifications promote reusability of existing IT security investments, enabling companies to work with multiple security token types and multiple scenarios, including HTTP browsers, enhanced browsers, active clients, and application-to-application connectivity.

13.5 WS-Authorization

The purpose of WS-Authorization is to describe how access policies for a Web service are specified and eventually managed. The goal is to describe how claims can be specified within security tokens, and how these claims will be interpreted at the endpoint.

WS-Authorization is designed to be flexible and extensible with respect to both authorization format and authorization language. This enables the widest range of scenarios and ensures the long-term viability of the security framework.

WSS: SOAP Message Security defines the basic mechanisms for providing secure messaging, and for carrying security tokens that represent a set of claims. WS-Authorization uses these basic mechanisms, and defines additional primitives and extensions for security token exchange to enable the issuance and dissemination of credentials regarding authorization within different trust domains.

To protect information assets, a service provider needs to ensure that the accessing requester is qualified. WS-Authorization defines extensions to WS-Trust for issuing and exchanging authorization tokens. Using these extensions, applications can engage in secure communication designed to work with the general Web services framework, including WSDL service descriptions and SOAP messages.

To achieve this, WS-Authorization reuses headers and elements defined by the WS-Trust specification to request authorization tokens and manage authorization policies. An *authorization token* is a kind of security token, and therefore it is possible to reuse the existing Web service infrastructure that deals with security tokens.

13.6 Web Services Authorization Model

In the Web service security model defined in WS-Authorization, a Web service checks whether an incoming access request with a set of claims (such as name, privilege, capability, and so on) and contextual information (such as current time and so on) is qualified to invoke the target service or to perform the requested operation. If the requester is not qualified, the Web service ignores or rejects the request. A service can indicate its required claims and related information in its policy, as described by WS-Policy and WS-PolicyAttachment specifications. How to request claims in relevance to security tokens from a security token service is described in the WS-Trust specification.

An authorization check is performed by an *authorization service,* a kind of STS (security token service) defined in WS-Trust. A requester or a Web service can invoke the authorization service with an appropriate set of claims and security tokens. The authorization service retrieves the applicable authorization policies and determines whether the access should be allowed or denied, using an authorization engine. It returns the result of the authorization, either by issuing an authorization token or by returning some messages. The authorization token proves the privileges or capabilities of the holder of the token, but it could cover broader semantics, such as a validation result (valid or invalid) of the authorization token, enumerated rights of the requester, and conditional responses (the access is allowed, provided such-and-such a condition is satisfied). The authorization token is one of the security tokens defined in WSS: SOAP Message Security and relevant specifications. Thus, the mechanism designed for issuing and exchanging security tokens in WS-Trust is reusable in WS-Authorization specification. The model that is adapted from WS-Trust is illustrated in Figure 13-2.

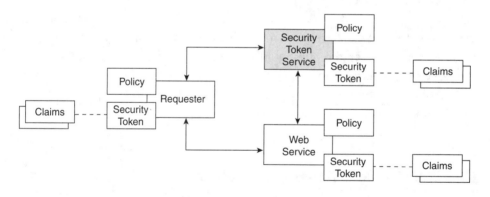

Figure 13-2   The trust model of WS-Trust.

The authorization service returns an error message if the authorization service cannot process the access request correctly. For example, some claims or the security tokens are missing and there is no applicable rule found for the requested service.

The authorization service does not assume any specific authorization engines, authorization policy specification languages, or authorization tokens. The authorization model defines interfaces between an authorization service and a requester, or an authorization service and a Web service.

The security of the Web service authorization model depends on the authorization policy managed by the authorization service.

13.7 Security and Policy

WS-SecurityPolicy defines policy assertions for the security properties of Web services. In particular, WS-SecurityPolicy defines policy assertions for use with WS-Policy that apply to WSS: SOAP Message Security, WS-Trust, and WS-SecureConversation. These assertions are primarily designed for describing policies related to the features defined in the WSS: SOAP Message Security, WS-Trust, and WS-SecureConversation specifications, but they can also be used for describing security requirements at a more abstract or transport-independent level.

The primary goal of WS-SecurityPolicy is to define an initial set of assertions that describe how messages are secured on a communication path. The intent is to allow flexibility in terms of the tokens, cryptography, and mechanisms used, including leveraging transport security, while being specific enough to ensure interoperability based on assertion matching.

One goal of the security policy model is to leverage the WS-Policy framework. Consequently, wherever possible, the security policy assertions do not use parameters or attributes. This enables element QName matching without security domain-specific knowledge (see Chapter 7, "Web Services Policy").

13.8 Assertion Model

To provide richer semantics for combinations of security constraints and requirements, and to enable element QName matching of policy assertions, the assertions are separated into simple types: those that express what parts of a message are being secured (scope), those expressing general aspects or preconditions of the security model (conditions), and those identifying the mechanism that is used to provide the security (security binding).

To indicate the scope of the constraints and requirements, assertions identify body parts that are to be protected in a specific way, such as integrity or confidentiality protection.

The general aspects of security include the characteristics of the environment in which security is being applied, such as the tokens being used, which ones are for authentication and which are supporting, the applicable algorithms to use, and so on.

The security mechanism, or binding, defines how the general aspects are used to protect the indicated parts. For example, it could specify that an asymmetric token is used with a digital signature to provide authentication and integrity, and that parts are encrypted with a symmetric key, which is then encrypted using the public key of the recipient. In its simplest form, the binding defines a strong type for the open-ended and extensible `<wsse:Security>` header.

Because these characteristics are separated into assertions, many of them can be simplified so that assertion matching is sufficient, and many aspects of security can be factored out and reused. For example, it might be common that the mechanism is constant for an endpoint, but that the parts protected vary by message action.

As previously indicated, the binding defines the mechanism for providing the security. These assertions are used to determine how the security is performed and what to expect in the `<wsse:Security>` header.

Bindings are described textually and enforced programmatically. This specification defines several bindings, but others can be defined and agreed to if participating parties support it.

A binding defines the following:

- The mechanism and class of token for the initiator
- The mechanism and class of token for recipient authentication
- Any necessary key transfer mechanisms
- Any required message elements (such as timestamps)
- The content and ordering of the `<wsse:Security>` header
- How correlation of messages is performed securely (if applicable to the message pattern)
- If there are multiple phases to the security binding

These elements, along with the assertions describing conditions and scope, provide enough information to secure messages between an initiator and a receiver.

13.9 Other Security Topics

The specifications discussed in this chapter provide a strong foundation to secure Web services interactions, supporting sophisticated, automated business-to-business interactions. Additional technologies, not explicitly covered in the specifications discussed here, provide support for specific circumstances that often arise in the course of a business transaction. This section discusses the use of public key cryptography and how to provide non-repudiation capabilities in Web services interactions.

13.9.1 Public-Key Cryptography

Public-key cryptography was introduced in the mid-1970s by Whitfield Diffie and Martin Hellman. The concept is simple and elegant, yet it has had a huge impact on the science and applications of cryptography. It's based on the idea of encryption keys, private and public, as related pairs. The *private key* remains concealed by its owner, while the *public key* is freely disseminated to various partners. Data encrypted using the public key can be decrypted only by using the associated private key, and vice versa. Because the key used to encrypt plain text is different from the key used to decrypt the corresponding cipher text, this is also known as *asymmetric cryptography*.

The premise behind public-key cryptography is that it should be computationally infeasible to obtain the private key simply by knowing the public key. Modern public-key cryptography derives from sophisticated mathematical foundations, which are based on the one-way functions existing in the abstractions of number theory. A *one-way function* is an invertible function that is easy to compute but computationally hard to invert. A *one-way trapdoor function* is a one-way function that can be inverted only if one knows a secret piece of information, known as the *trapdoor*. Encryption is the easy one-way trapdoor function; its inverse, decryption, is the hard function. The only way to make the decryption as easy as the encryption is to have the private key.

Two of these one-way functions, factoring large numbers and computing discrete logarithms, form the basis of modern public-key cryptography. Factoring large numbers is a one-way trapdoor function, whereas computing discrete logarithms is a one-way function with no trapdoors.

13.10 Non-Repudiation

Sometimes the parties in a business transaction will have a dispute. To protect the interests of these parties, some evidence of the agreement must be generated and preserved, in the event that a third party must be called in to resolve the dispute. In the case of transactions initiated via Web service messages, this evidence must consist of Proof of Message Origin, Proof of Message Receipt, and Original Message content.

Secret-key cryptography alone is not sufficient to prevent the denial of an action that has taken place, such as the initiation of an electronic transaction. One can apply data privacy in such a scenario, but the fundamental flaw of a non-repudiation scheme based on secret-key cryptography is that the secret key is dispensed to more than one party.

13.10.1 Data Integrity and Data-Origin Authentication

At a much lesser cost than encrypting the entirety of a plain text, data integrity and data-origin authentication can be ensured by a secret cryptographic scheme using a *Message Authentication Code (MAC)* function.

The basic idea is to attach to each message, m, that is sent across a network the result, $h(m)$, of a mathematical function, h, applied to m itself. If an error has occurred during the message's transmission, and the received message, a, is different than m, the message's receiver can detect the anomaly by independently computing $h(a)$ and comparing it with $h(m)$.

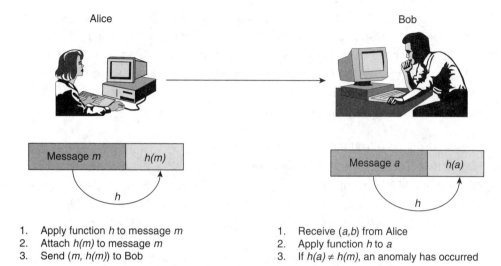

1. Apply function *h* to message *m*
2. Attach *h(m)* to message *m*
3. Send *(m, h(m))* to Bob

1. Receive *(a,b)* from Alice
2. Apply function *h* to *a*
3. If *h(a) ≠ h(m)*, an anomaly has occurred

Figure 13-3   Using MACs to detect anomalies.

The main component of a MAC function is a *hash digest function*, which is considered to be one of the fundamental primitives in modern cryptography. By definition, a hash digest function is a deterministic function that maps a message of arbitrary length to a string of fixed length, *n*. Typically, *n* is 128 or 160 bits. The result is commonly known as a *message digest*. Because the original data is often longer than its hash value, this is also referred to as the original message's *fingerprint*.

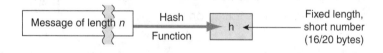

Figure 13-4   Computing message hashes.

Of course, a hash digest function is inherently non-injective. In fact, the universe of the messages that can be digested is potentially unlimited, whereas the universe of all the message digests is limited by the set of the 2^n strings with *n* bits. Therefore, multiple messages can map to the same digest. However, the fundamental premise is that, depending on the strength of the hashing algorithm, the hash value becomes a more compact representation of the original data. This means that it should be computationally infeasible to produce two messages having the same message digest, or to produce any message having a specified target message digest.

Message Digest V5 (MD5) and Secure Hash Algorithm V1 (SHA-1) are the most widely used cryptographic hash functions. MD5 yields a 128-bit (16-byte) hash value, while SHA-1 results in a 160-bit (20-byte) digest. SHA-1 appears to be a cryptographically stronger function. On the other hand, MD5 edges SHA-1 in computational performance and thus has become the de facto standard.

Hash functions alone cannot guarantee data integrity because they can't guarantee *data-origin authentication*, or the ability to authenticate the originator of a message. The problem with digest functions is that they are publicly available. If a message, m, is intercepted by an adversary after being transmitted by Alice, the adversary can change m into a different message, m', compute $h(m')$, and send Bob the pair, $(m'..h(m'))$. By simply applying the function h to the received message, m', Bob has no means to detect that an adversary has replaced m with m'.

Data-origin authentication is inherently supported by secret-key cryptography, provided that the key is shared by two entities only. When three or more parties share the same key, however, origin authenticity can no longer be provided by secret-key cryptography alone. Various secret-key authentication protocols have been developed to address this limitation.

In contrast to using a simple hash function to digest a message, a MAC function combines a hash digest function with secret-key encryption. This yields a value that can be verified only by an entity that has the secret key. This enables both data integrity and data origin authentication.

Another simple way to achieve data integrity and data origin authentication is to apply a regular hash function, h, such as SHA-1 or MD5. But rather than hashing the message, m, alone, the message is first concatenated with the key, k, and then the result of the concatenation is hashed. In other words, the sender attaches to the message *m* the tag $h(k, m)$. This solution has some theoretical weaknesses, however. A more reliable solution consists of attaching the tag $h(k, h(k, m))$.

A MAC can even be computed by using a secret-key block-cipher algorithm. For example, the last cipher text block, encrypted in CBC mode, yields the final MAC value. Therefore, the MAC so defined is a compact representation of the entire message that can be computed only by an entity that has the secret key. Known instances of this procedure employ DES and Triple-DES, resulting in DES-MAC and Triple-DES-MAC, respectively.

A MAC mechanism that uses a cryptographic hash function is also referred to as HMAC. HMAC is specified in [HMAC].

WS-Security currently does not provide a mechanism for non-repudiation. The following is one way to profile extending Web Services Security to provide Proof of Message Origin (PMO) and Proof of Message Receipt (PMR).

13.10.2 Proof of Message Origin

Proof of message origin (PMO) consists of a digital signature over original message content. Potentially, this could be a digital signature, generated by the initial sender and provided to the ultimate receiver, that envelops the entire original message. However, for Web service messages, this method is unacceptable because intermediaries might partially process the message en route from the initial sender to the ultimate receiver, altering some subset of the content. To allow for this possibility, the subset of the message content should be signed by the initial sender and targeted at the ultimate receiver, and it must *not* include the subset of the content that any intermediaries could alter. The initial sender should create a Web Service Security-conformant XML Signature that binds and provides origin authentication for the following message elements:

- The `<SOAP:Body>` element containing the application-specific message data (SOAP 1.2)

- A `<wsa:MessageID>` header block element that uniquely identifies the message (WS-Addressing)

- A `<wsa:From>` header block element that identifies the initial sender (WS-Addressing)

- A `<wsa:To>` header block element that identifies the intended ultimate receiver (WS-Addressing),

- An `<wsa:Action>` header block that identifies the intended message semantics (WS-Addressing)

- A `<wsse:KeyInfo>` element that identifies the signer's (AKA initial sender's) security token (XML Signature)

- Any additional header block elements targeted to the ultimate receiver

The initial sender's signature does not refer to the outer SOAP Header element, because that would prevent insertion and removal of individual header block elements not targeted to the ultimate receiver. The initial sender, ultimate receiver, or a third-party store the signed message content in case of a dispute.

13.10.3 Proof of Message Receipt

PMO provides the mechanism for resolving disputes related to message content. However, an ultimate receiver might still claim never to have received a message at all. PMR provides a solution to this problem.

PMR consists of a digital signature over the received message content. This could be a digital signature, generated by the ultimate receiver and provided to the initial sender, enveloping the entire original message. However, for Web service messages, this method is unacceptable. Intermediaries might partially process the message en route from the ultimate receiver to the initial sender, altering some subset of the content. To allow for this possibility, the subset of the message content signed by the ultimate receiver matches the subset of the message content signed by the initial sender and targeted at the ultimate receiver. The ultimate receiver, initial sender, or some third-party store the signed PMR in case of a dispute.

13.10.4 Delivery of Proof of Message Receipt

In some cases, messages are sent that result in immediate synchronous responses, and in other cases, responses might be delivered asynchronously. Therefore, one should provide a mechanism for delivering `<ReceiptAcknowledgement>`, either together with the response or separately.

13.11 Summary

Web services security defines basic mechanisms to secure the interaction between a service requester and a service provider. To address the richness and the complexity of Web service interactions and their need for security, a set of additional specifications that builds on WS-Security has been published or is in the process of being published.

WS-Trust defines a basic building block for creating a trusted relationship by defining a mechanism for issuing security tokens. WS-Secure Conversation uses the mechanisms defined by WS-Trust to efficiently support secure, long-lived interactions between services. WS-Federation extends WS-Trust to allow enterprises to collaborate to provide a single sign-on identification model to customers by sharing their identity information. WS-Security Policy defines assertions to represent security requirements and capabilities in the form of a WS-Policy policy. WS-Privacy and WS-Authorization are still in the process of being completed. WS-Privacy will define how to represent privacy requirements and Web service capabilities; WS-Authorization will describe how to express and manage access policies to Web services resources.

This chapter concluded with a brief review of advanced technologies and capabilities: public key cryptography and non-repudiation.

Part 7

Service Composition

This part of the book talks about how to take one or more services and compose them to form a new service. The figure that follows shows where this topic falls in the stack of Web services specifications.

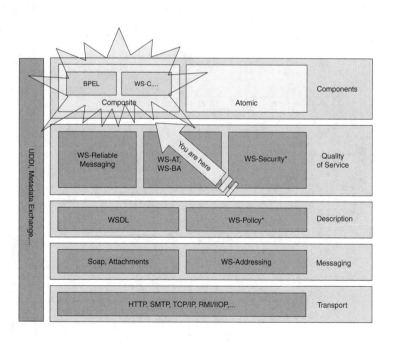

This area brings you to a new level of complexity, starting with how different services can be aggregated into more sophisticated higher-level services. Chapter 14, "Modeling Business Processes: BPEL" presents the Web Services Business Process Execution Language specification (WS-BPEL, better known as BPEL), which is being standardized at OASIS. BPEL enables service aggregations to be defined in both an abstract and an executable manner. A handful of other specifications that address different aspects or styles of composition have been proposed; however, BPEL is at this point the only one with significant following in the industry.

Chapter 14

Modeling Business Processes:
BPEL

The architecture presented thus far has illustrated how you can use Web services specifications in different combinations to create secure, reliable, transacted interactions between distributed, heterogeneous applications. Services can be offered with different views both within an organization and between organizations. Domain-specific interfaces (Web Services Description Language [WSDL 1.1] portTypes) can be standardized, such as for ticketing in the airline industry. This provides a universal plug point and shorter time to market for providers of compliant service implementations and a highly competitive and diverse set of offerings for consumers who are looking for a particular functionality. From this point on, the previously defined standards can be seen as infrastructure. These standards and specifications enable the creation of numerous services in the network and the mechanisms to discover and interact with them. To move beyond the "publish, discover, interact" model, it's required to have the ability to define logic over a set of service interactions. This not only enables you to compose a set of services, but it also enables the definition of the interaction protocol of a single service by specifying an ordering of its operations.

This is where the Web services Business Process Execution Language comes into the picture. First known as BPEL4WS but soon to be renamed as WS-BPEL, this specification is more commonly known as BPEL. It is an extensible work-flow-based language that aggregates services by choreographing service interactions. The aggregation is recursive, such that the process exposes WSDL interfaces to those that interact with it, and the corresponding services may be used in other choreographies. Designed to work in a highly dynamic environment in which services might change frequently, a BPEL process is intentionally decoupled from particular instances of the services it choreographs. BPEL layers neatly at the top of the WS specifications stack, directly using WSDL interfaces to define the functionality it offers to and requires from the services that are being composed, and for defining its interactions with them. You can access and manipulate data belonging to the choreography using XPath [XPath], and you can copy and exchange the endpoints of composed services in the form of WS-Addressing endpoint references [WS-Addressing]. With the modularity of the framework, you can add additional aspects to BPEL processes. For example, you can use WS-Policy and WS-PolicyAttachments to attach quality-of-service policies to different levels of the process and the related WSDLs, and you can use different bindings to carry out the interactions.

To understand how to use BPEL, read through the following example. A client wants to purchase service packs for a set of computers. Service packs are bundled support services, such as on-site repair, hardware warranties, and so on. Someone needs to validate the order before the client can proceed with the purchase. The validation consists of checking several things, such as whether the requested service packs are available in the client's context (geographical location, order date, and so on), whether they are compatible with the given machine(s), and whether they are compatible with the other service packs that are being requested. This example is derived from an IBM business application created by the Exploratorium Group at IBM's TJ Watson Research Center. It is further explained as a case study in Chapter 16, "Case Study: Ordering Service Packs."

You create a BPEL process to solve this problem. The BPEL process can accept the request for purchase order validation as a call to the Web service that it exposes. You then break up this request into smaller pieces, each sent to a separate specialized Web service that can validate a particular aspect. After that, you create the reply to the validation request based on the responses from the services that are called. The reply contains the results of validation for all the service packs you requested. You then return this reply to the caller. After that, the BPEL process can accept a purchase request to buy these service packs. The process then calls services to bill the client and update the client's profile to reflect the purchase.

The next two sections present the motivation for and a brief history of BPEL. Then the chapter discusses the architectural concepts of the language, illustrating how BPEL creates business processes. The chapter then moves on to the runtime aspects of BPEL, such as navigation and instance management. Finally, the chapter explores the future directions of the language.

14.1 Motivation for BPEL

The composition of objects, software components, and even business processes is well understood, and developers have created numerous proposed languages and systems over the years. However, none of these languages or systems is geared to operate in a SOA environment. SOA demands a new approach that can handle, in a first class manner, its mainstays of loosely coupled entities; on-demand interactions; frequent change of such parameters as location, availability, and quality of service; and lack of control over the platform and implementation of services that are being composed.

In such an environment, many requirements are identified for a composition model that can perform the following:

- **Flexible integration**—The composition model must be sufficiently rich to express business scenarios that partners might exchange. More importantly, it should rapidly adapt to changes in the services that it is interacting with.

- **Recursive composition**—Offering a process as a standard Web service enables third-party composition of existing services, the ability to provide different views on a composition to different parties, interworkflow interaction, and increased scalability and reuse.

- **Separation and composeability of concerns**—In keeping with the composeability of the Web services framework, the business/service-composition logic should be decoupled from the supporting mechanisms such as quality of service, messaging frameworks, and coordination protocols. Such information should be capable of being layered on or attached to different parts of the process definition if necessary.

- **Stateful conversations and lifecycle management**—A workflow should have a clearly defined lifecycle model, in which it can carry multiple stateful long-running conversations with the services that it is interacting with.

- **Recoverability**—Business processes (especially long-running ones) need to provide built-in fault handling and compensation mechanisms to deal with expected errors that might arise during execution. For example, if a credit card number is invalid, the process would ask for a new one instead of aborting entirely.

BPEL was designed to natively address these requirements. While laying out BPEL's core architectural concepts, this chapter will refer back to this list of requirements and highlight how and where BPEL addresses them.

14.1.1 A Brief History

BPEL emerged as a combination of two prior, competing XML languages for composition: the IBM Web Service Flow Language (WSFL) and Microsoft XLANG [XLANG]. Although similar in their goals, each language had a different composition approach.

In WSFL [WSFL], the flow model is a business process described as a directed graph of activities (the nodes of the graph) and control connectors (the edges of the graph). Nodes and edges of the graph are annotated with attributes, such as transition conditions, that determine the execution of the model. WSFL also provides the possibility to define a global model, in which you can specify the overall partner interactions. A global model is a simple recursive composition metamodel that allows you to describe the interactions between existing Web services and to define new Web services as a composition of existing ones.

XLANG provides a notation "for the specification of message exchange behavior among participating Web services" so that you can achieve "automation of business processes based on Web services." To achieve this objective, the major constructs of XLANG include sequential and parallel control flow definitions, long-running transactions with compensation, custom correlation of messages, exception handling, and dynamic service referral. An XLANG service description extends a WSDL service description with the behavioral aspects of the service. It allows the user to specify a set of ports in a service section of a WSDL document and extend it with a description of, for example, the sequence in which the operations that the ports provide are to be used.

In BPEL, you create the processes by using a combination of the graph-oriented style of WSFL and the algebraic style of XLANG. BPEL also allows you to recursively compose Web services into new aggregated Web services.

The first version of the BPEL4WS specification was released in 2002. Version 1.1, released in 2003, was submitted to OASIS for standardization. The group is set to produce the next version, renamed WS-BPEL version 2.0, as its first output. At the time of this writing, however, the standardization process was not yet complete, leaving WS-BPEL 2.0 in flux. As a result, this chapter uses for its reference the last stable version of the specification, BPEL4WS v1.1 [BPEL4WS]. The changes proposed so far for version 2.0 have little impact on the architectural concepts described in this chapter.

14.2 Architectural Concepts

As described in section 14.1, BPEL was created to address the requirements of composition in a service-oriented computing environment. This section describes the architectural concepts of the language in which these requirements are reflected.

This section first provides an overview of BPEL's service composition model and the elements that make up a BPEL process. Then it explains BPEL's recursive type-based composition model and describes process instance lifecycle. The rest of this section handles advanced capabilities, including event handling, dealing with exceptional behavior, and using Web services policies to attach quality of service to a BPEL process.

14.2.1 Overview of the Process Composition Model

The major building blocks of BPEL business processes are nested `scopes` that contain relationships to external partners, declarations for process data, handlers for various purposes and, most importantly, the activities to be executed. The outermost `scope` is the process definition.

Data in BPEL is written to and read from lexically scoped, typed variables. The values of these variables are either messages exchanged between the process and its partners, or intermediate data that is private to the process. In keeping with the Web services framework, BPEL variables are typed using WSDL message types, XML Schema [XML Schema] simple types, or XML schema elements. XPath is the default language for manipulating and querying variables.

Data can be read or written by activities that exchange messages between the process and its partners or by specific activities that manipulate process-data (so-called `assign` activities). Conditional expressions also read data. BPEL contains several expression types that are used for different purposes, such as defining conditions (Boolean expressions), expressing time intervals and dates (duration and date expressions), and accessing values of variables in the `assign` activity (general expressions).

The activities in a BPEL process are either structured or basic. Structured activities contain other activities and define the business logic between them. Basic activities are, for example, the inbound or outbound Web service interactions or the specific activities for data manipulation.

Activities that deal with Web services are `receive`, `reply`, `pick`, `invoke`, and `event handlers`. These activities allow a process to exchange messages with the services that it composes. They are discussed in detail in section 14.2.3, "Recursive, Type-Based Composition."

The `assign` activity atomically copies data from one location to another, using a list of copy statements that copy one value each. The common usages of an `assign` activity include constructing values by copying them from XPath expressions into a part of a variable, copying data from the part of one variable into a part of another, and copying endpoint references so that they can be exchanged between the process and its partners. This last case is the enabler of dynamic partner assignment in BPEL.

Structured activities combine multiple activities to provide higher-level business logic. These include `sequence`, `switch`, `while`, and `flow` activities. The `sequence` activity is a simple aggregation of activities executed in the order in which they are specified. The `switch` activity provides a multibranch decision construct, and the `while` activity provides a loop construct. Both `switch` and `while` have semantics from corresponding programming language constructs, such as Java. You can execute activities in parallel by nesting them in a `flow` activity. If you have to constrain the degree of parallelism, you can use conditional control links to specify a partial (acyclic) order on the set of activities nested in a `flow`.

Figure 14-1 illustrates how to create a business process for the service pack validation (SPK) example using several of these constructs. You can see the `receive` activity and its reply further downstream, in addition to several invocations that invoke the specialized validators. Surrounding these and imposing control, you see a sequence activity that imposes order on the validation and the purchasing, several nested while loops, and a scope that surrounds the purchasing section at the end.

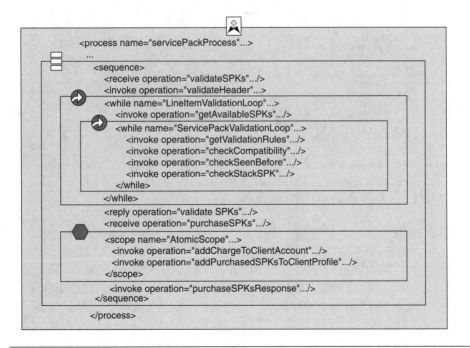

Figure 14-1   Structured activities.

A *transition condition* is associated with each control link and evaluated at completion of the link's source activity. This condition has a default value of true, but you can use any Boolean expression that relates to the values of data fields and other states of the process. On the other hand, a *join condition* is associated with an activity that is a target of links. It is a Boolean expression in terms of the link values. It is evaluated after you know all incoming link values and it must evaluate to `true` to run the activity. A joint condition's default value is an `or`. These concepts are illustrated in Figure 14-2, in which four activities are joined with control links.

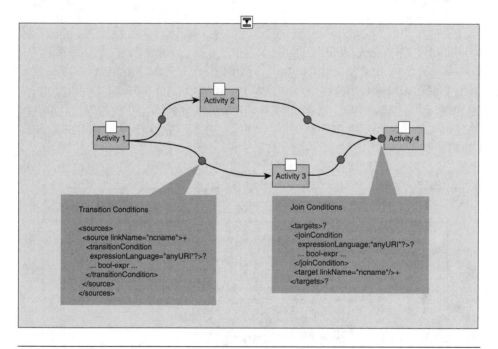

Figure 14-2   Links, transition conditions, and join conditions.

In addition to Web service interactions and nested structured activities, you can use a couple more basic activities to specify different types of behavior. These activities are called `empty`, `wait`, `terminate`, `throw`, and `compensate`. The empty activity is BPEL's rendering of a no-op. You can use it as a placeholder for other activities that you add later. The `wait` activity provides a means to interrupt the execution for a specified time interval or until a specified time has been reached, and the terminate activity stops the execution of the process immediately. Finally, the `throw` and `compensate` activities are used in conjunction with handlers for error detection and recovery, which will be discussed later.

A BPEL process might contain handlers to recognize unexpected problems and deal with them. These handlers can include operations that reverse effects from other activities that have been completed successfully before an error situation occurred.

The constructs that BPEL provides present a rich toolbox with which to create both simple and sophisticated business processes. In the sections that follow, you see how to create and use BPEL processes.

14.2.2 Abstract and Executable Processes

BPEL supports two fundamental usage patterns. One pattern is for describing business protocols called *abstract processes*, and the other is for describing *executable processes*. Business protocols or message exchange protocols describe the externally visible interactions between business partners without necessarily exposing the internal business logic of the individual partners. In contrast, executable processes contain the partner's business logic behind the external protocol.

An enterprise might present abstract processes of the existing business processes that it offers to its partners so they can know how to interact with it. The abstraction enables the enterprise to keep its private mechanisms internal while still providing the partners with the information they need. You can think of an abstract process as a projection of an executable process.

On the other hand, for a certain domain just an abstract process can be made publicly available. Service providers that want to supply the specified functionality then derive executable processes that comply with it.

BPEL provides the same language constructs to define both abstract and executable processes. Both processes have a few additional constructs that are an extension of the base language and can be used only in that variant. For example, abstract processes might have "opaque" variable assignment, to signify that a value is set but that how or what that value is remains up to the internal implementation.

14.2.3 Recursive, Type-Based Composition

A BPEL process refers to the parties that it is interacting with as *partners*. It interacts with each partner along a set of `partnerLinks`. *Partner links* are instances of typed connectors that specify the portTypes that the process offers to and requires from the partner at the other end of the link. You can think of a `partnerLink` as a channel along which a peer-to-peer conversation with a partner takes place.

The composition model is recursive: The portTypes that the process offers form (one or more) Web services with a WSDL interface. The bindings and ports for those portTypes might be specified at deployment time, depending on where the service is deployed.

To illustrate, the client and the service pack validator in the running example of this chapter can both be Web services with a callback on the purchase operation. The validator offers the "purchaseServicePacs" operation to the client, and the client offers the "purchaseServicePacsResp" operation to the validator. Therefore, the validator BPEL contains a `partnerLink` connecting the two respective portTypes, as illustrated in Figure 14-3.

Composing Services

BPEL's composition model is type based, meaning that services are composed at the portType and not at the port/instance level. A BPEL process provides control semantics around `receive`, `reply`, and `invoke` activities. Each of these activities specifies the `partnerLink-portType` operation and the variables that it relates to.

An input-only operation that a BPEL process provides corresponds to a `receive` activity in the process that explicitly marks the place in the business process logic where the inbound request message is accepted. For request-response operations, a corresponding `reply` activity is the place where the response message is handed back to the Web services client. If a process provides multiple operations, then multiple `receive` activities indicate that you must take all entry points into the process. Alternatively, a `pick` activity can refer to multiple operations to indicate that, at most, one entry point is taken. Later, you'll learn more about concurrent entry points that event handler activities define. Outbound calls to Web services that entities offer outside of the process are expressed as invoke activities.

To summarize, the `invoke` activities always refer to the operations that the partners offer. Therefore, in Figure 14-3, you see that the client has an `invoke` that refers to the validator's "purchaseServicePacs" operation. On the other hand, `receive/pick/onMessage` and their (optional) corresponding `reply` activities refer to the operations that the process offers to its partners. These are the operations included in the WSDL portType(s) of the process. Again, you can see this in Figure 14-3, where the `receive` that consumes the purchase request in the validator's BPEL refers to its own "purchaseServicePacs" operation.

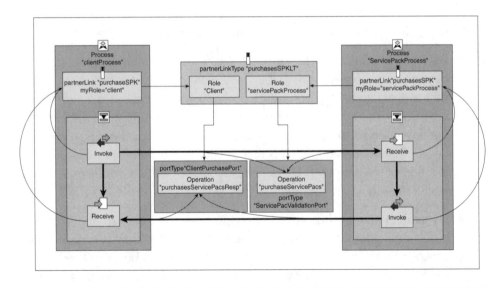

Figure 14-3   Partner links.

Binding to Concrete Endpoints of Partner Services
BPEL decouples the business logic from the available service endpoints, allowing processes to be more adaptive and more portable. When a process must execute, however, you must be able to bind each `partnerLink` along which a

partner is invoked to a concrete endpoint. Four binding schemes and their combinations are possible:

- **Static design time binding**—A process might be bound to known endpoints as part of the process logic. This is the least flexible form of binding. This binding proves useful when the endpoints are meant to be parts of the business logic. (That is, this process is made only for bank such-and-such.) Every deployment and every instance of this process will use the specified endpoint(s). For this form of deployment, an `assign` activity explicitly puts an endpoint into a variable. A subsequent `<assign>` activity then copies the value of that variable into the process's reference to a specific `partnerLink`.

- **Static deployment time binding**—In this instantiation, the process model does not refer to explicit endpoints, but a set of endpoints is defined at deployment time to the workflow management system into which the process is deployed. This form is useful if all instances of a particular deployment of a process must use the same endpoints.

- **Dynamic binding using lookups**—In this form of binding, criteria are defined on a `partnerLink` that a viable endpoint must have. These criteria are evaluated either at runtime or deployment time to search for providers whose deployed services match. Such criteria might include quality-of-service policies (cost, security, speed), transactional capabilities, or functional requirements that are not in the WSDL portType. The location of the endpoints is the responsibility of the environment in which the process is deployed or executed.

- **Dynamic binding using passed-in endpoints**—The last form of dynamic binding includes the process copying in an endpoint from a variable that was previously assigned not by the process, as in (1), but by either a response to an invocation (result of an `invoke` activity) or a request from a partner (input to a `receive` activity). The latter is illustrated in Figure 14-4. The process uses the `assign` activity as in (1) to copy that value into its reference to the `partnerLink` in question.

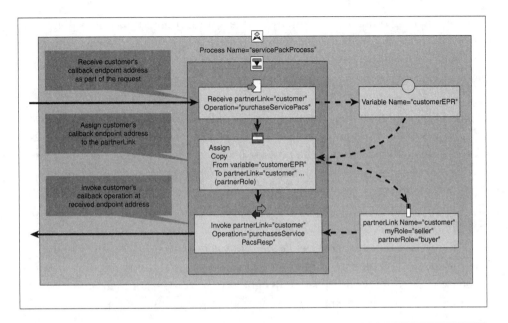

Figure 14-4   Dynamic binding of partner links.

A Conversational Approach

It was stated earlier that a `receive` or a `receive/reply` activity pair maps to one WSDL operation exposed to the partners, with the conceptual implementation of that operation being the part of the process that is executed as a result of the `receive`. In the case of a request-response operation, that is logically the block between the `receive` and its corresponding `reply`. For example, in Figure 14-1, you can see the implementation of the "validateSPKs" operation that the process offers between the first `receive` and the first `reply`, both of which refer to that operation.

Having different activities for incoming and outgoing messages and breaking up a request-response operation by using `receive/reply` enables BPEL to support a conversational pattern of composition and interaction with the partners. In BPEL, the activities between the `receive` and the `reply` might include other `receive`s, even from the same partner along the same `partnerLink`, and other `invoke`s. It's like natively being able to call a method within a method.

Depending on the process design, the process, thus, might be a controlling entity, a player on an equal footing with its partners, or a mix of the two. The result is the capability to model a wide range of relationships between a process and its partners, from peer-to-peer to master/slave.

A key architectural enabler is the bidirectionality of `partnerLinks`. A conversation occurs along each `partnerLink` for each process instance. That conversation is potentially two sided. The process instance invokes the partner, and the partner invokes the process instance. The lifetime of a conversation is the lifetime of the entire process instance, and you can see the different conversations of an instance through the specification of which `partnerLink` each interaction activity refers to. In BPEL, only one endpoint is active at any one time at each end of the `partnerLink` (one being the process instance and the other being the instance of the partner). Although that can change at different points in time because of such things as dynamic assignment, it changes for the entire instance and not only for the lifetime of one operation invocation.

Process Views

Offering possibly different portTypes along each `partnerLink`, the process can expose to each partner only the functionality that is relevant to it. One BPEL process might be exposed as one or more Web services, each service being a view on the entire process. This provides the separation of concerns of a process's provided functions.

For example, consider a process whose functions include sending requested payments to utility companies and providing auditors with a summary of payment activity. Using BPEL, such a process could publish only the payment portType to the utility companies and only the auditing portType to the auditors. This way, the utility companies do not need to know or care about the auditing capability, and the auditor cannot call the payment functions that are not meant for him.

Likewise, the partner might not need to know about the process's interactions with other entities. In addition to providing for each partner an abstract WSDL view of the parts of the process that the partner is involved with, you can go a step further with BPEL and accompany that WSDL view with the definition of an abstract process showing the parts of the process that the partner is concerned with. Such an abstract process might be simply a projection of the interaction activities that are concerned with that partner. Of course, this is not always necessary. Other options include exposing the whole executable process, exposing an abstract variant that shows interactions with multiple partners and is visible to all, or completely hiding the process based on the circumstances and the goals that the process was created to fulfill.

14.2.4 Process Instance Lifecycle

Business processes that are defined in BPEL represent stateful Web services, and as such, they might have long-running conversations with other Web services. Whenever you start a new BPEL process, a new instance of that process is created, which might communicate with other business partners. Web service definitions in WSDL are always stateless, so the messages that are exchanged in long-running conversations must be correlated to the correct business process instance. BPEL offers the concepts that allow correlating application data to process instances.

After you define and deploy a process, you can create multiple instances of it. All the instances can run concurrently and completely independently of each other. This section considers how such instances are created, destroyed, and identified at runtime.

The creation and destruction of BPEL process instances is by design implicit. In some workflow systems, each process has an explicit start and end activity. In BPEL, however, this restriction is not needed and multiple activities in a process model can kick off a process instance. You must tag these activities with the capability of instance creation by setting the createInstance attribute to `yes`. These activities must be able to receive messages (`receive`, `pick`) and come near the beginning of the process so they can be navigated to as soon as the instance is created. An instance can be created if a partner invokes an operation of the process that corresponds to one of these activities. The condition is that no active instance that already existed could consume the incoming message (see section 14.2.4.1 that follows next). After an instance is created, the "createInstance" attribute on any other activities than the one that created it loses its creation potency.

An instance terminates when its last activity completes, a terminate activity executes, or the instance experiences a fault from which it cannot recover. Figure 14-5 summarizes instance creation and termination in a BPEL process.

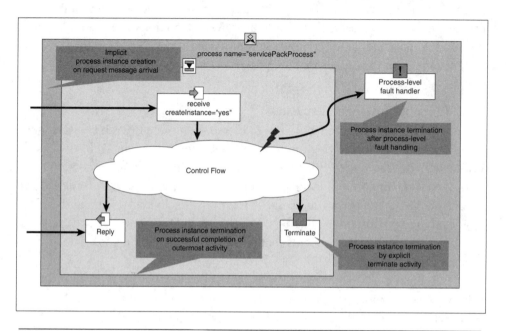

Figure 14-5   Process instance lifecycle.

Correlation

After you create an instance encompassing multiple receives, you have to figure out how to route subsequent messages to the correct created instance. In traditional middleware systems, you do this using opaque tokens that the middleware generates and maintains. BPEL, however, defines an (optional) *correlation* mechanism to enable you to do just that using parts of the application data. Two items make up these mechanisms: *properties* and *correlation sets*.

Typed properties that are named and mapped (aliased) to parts of several of the WSDL messages that the process uses are defined in WSDL. For example, to use a person's name as correlation identifier, you would define a property called "name" of type "xsd:string" that is aliased to the "name" field in the clientInformation part of a "validateServicePacks" WSDL message and the "lastName" part of a "purchaseOrder" WSDL message. These messages could be inputs to two different operations.

BPEL correlation sets are groups of these properties that identify which process instance an incoming message should be routed to. Zero or more correlation sets might subsequently be attached to the interaction activities (`receive/reply/invoke`) with a flag on whether the activity will initiate the set's data. With `invoke`, you must also specify whether you are initiating it based on the outgoing request message or the incoming response message. Initiating a correlation set corresponds to setting the values of the properties for a particular instance. You can then use values in incoming messages to look up the instance that the message is directed to by matching against the values of correlation sets of active instances.

For example, consider that the `receive` activity on the "validateSPKs" operation shown in Figure 14-1 creates an instance of a process and initiates a correlation set containing the "name" property. Assume that a message "A" comes in for the process and matches that `receive` activity. An instance is created, and the alias is used to find the "name" in the incoming message and copy it into the value of that property. Subsequent referrals to that property will have that value. More importantly, the correlation set with that value for the name property will be registered as a key to that particular instance.

Now consider that the other `receive` on the "purchaseServicePacs" operation further downstream refers to the same correlation set. A message comes in for that `receive` activity with the same name. The workflow engine looks up the name field and finds that the message must go to the same process instance as the one that message "A" had created earlier.

Correlation is a powerful concept. It enables you to maintain conversations between process instances and their partners using clearly defined and aliased portions of the application data. You can use multiple correlation sets to point to the same process instance, using different groups of properties. This enables a process instance to use different sets of identifiers for each partner or for different parts of a conversation.

If you use opaque middleware tokens for routing, correlation still enables validation of the business logic in ensuring that certain pieces of data have the same value in each instantiation of a process. One example is validating that the same account number is used in all of a person's interactions with an instance of an ordering process.

14.2.5 Event Handling

A BPEL process provides one or more Web service interfaces. In addition to the interfaces that are implemented by `receive` or `pick` activities in the regular flow, BPEL provides a means to deal with asynchronous events, which are handled concurrently to the execution of the process. These constructs are associated with the process as a whole or with a `scope`, and they are called *event handlers.*

You can use event handlers in BPEL for message events and timer-driven alarm events. For the outside world, *message events* are regular one-way or request-response Web service operations that the business process implements. Alarm events occur whenever a specified time is reached or a specified time interval expires. Both types of event handlers can contain any BPEL activity.

As an example, you can use event handlers to monitor the progress of a business process. For this purpose, the event handler is modeled as a request-response operation, in which the request specifies a query expression, and the response contains process instance status data that corresponds to the query.

14.2.6 Dealing with Exceptional Behavior

Because BPEL processes are composed out of Web services, they have to deal with faults that are a result of Web services invocations. Likewise, because BPEL processes implement regular Web services, they might return exceptional situations as faults to the invokers of these Web services. Finally, abnormal behavior might be recognized within the business logic, either raised explicitly or recognized by the BPEL runtime infrastructure.

Business processes can be long running. As a consequence, you cannot always execute them as a single atomic operation. Results of intermediate process steps are made persistent and may be visible to others. When a fault occurs in such a long-running business process, you have to undo work that is partially or successfully completed.

Within a BPEL process, the construct that is associated with handling fault situations and reversing intermediate results is the *scope*, which you can consider as an encapsulation of a recoverable and reversible unit of work. You deal with faults by using *fault handlers*. Undoing work is the responsibility of *compensation handlers*. Both handlers are either implicit or are explicitly provided by the process modeler.

In addition to these concepts that are local to a business process, abnormal behavior sometimes occurs between multiple business processes. Again, you either can achieve an all-or-nothing behavior, or you need explicit means to reverse results of work that have already been persisted. In the environment of distributed, multiplatform, multivendor business transactions, all-or-nothing behavior is described by the WS-AtomicTransaction [WS-Atomic Transactions] specification, and exception handling in long-running business transactions is described by the WS-BusinessActivity [WS-Business Activity] specification.

Fault Handling

The primary purpose of a fault handler is to catch faults and reverse partial and unsuccessful work. In a BPEL process, faults can originate from different sources. A fault can be the result of a Web service invocation, or it can be thrown explicitly from within the business logic. Furthermore, the BPEL specification lists numerous situations in which the BPEL infrastructure must detect and signal faults, such as when a BPEL variable is used before a value has been assigned to it.

For faults that are returned from a Web service invocation, the Web service interface defines a fault message that allows data to be passed along with the fault. Within the process, you can also raise faults without associated fault data. BPEL fault handlers can deal with both and can examine the fault data.

When a fault handler catches a fault, the regular processing within a `scope` stops, and exception processing begins. Therefore, in a BPEL process, fault handling is considered a mode switch from doing regular work to repairing an exceptional situation.

Compensation

The BPEL specification mandates a particular transaction model for executing business processes: In many business processes you cannot complete all work within a single atomic transaction, because processes are long-running business transactions in which many committed ACID transactions create persistent effects before a process is completed. Application-specific compensation steps undo these effects when necessary.

In a BPEL `scope`, the compensation handler reverses completed activities. You can invoke the compensation handler after successful completion of its associated `scope`, using the compensate activity. You can perform the invocation of a compensation handler either from a fault handler or from the compensation handler of the enclosing `scope`.

In its first version, the BPEL compensation handler cannot change data within the business process. The activity that is enclosed in a compensation handler typically consists of one or more Web service invocations that undo effects of other previously called Web services.

Compensation and Business Agreement Protocols

The Web Services Business Activity specification (WS-BusinessActivity) describes a model in which the compensation actions are coordinated across several business applications. When you apply this model to BPEL processes, long-running work is distributed over scopes within multiple BPEL processes and executed as nested scopes. In addition, WS-BA conceptually describes the states, state transitions, and stimuli underlying BPEL scope-based *local* transaction management.

14.2.7 Extensibility and the Role of Web Services Policies

Sometimes you need to define additional capabilities that BPEL's constructs do not provide. One approach uses BPEL's extensibility. It involves defining private extensions and providing support for them in specialized engines. The problem is that these processes can no longer be shared with others. Portability is compromised. When portability is not a goal, you can certainly take this approach. You can create domain-specific BPEL extensions for certain specialized areas. The relevant industry sectors can then standardize these extensions.

More important, however, is the ability to recognize when these capabilities are orthogonal to the business logic. Examples include quality-of-service requirements and capabilities. People often rush to add functionality to the base language when the requirements they have are better met by the other pieces of the Web services stack. This is when you apply the modularity of the Web services stack. In these situations, you can attach Web services policies to different parts of the BPEL process, the corresponding WSDLs, or both. You can attach policies to the partner construct to denote requirements that must apply along all the interactions with the specified partner. You can apply them to the `partnerLink` or even to each interaction activity. On the other hand, you can attach policies to the WSDL portTypes or ports that correspond to the process. These specify the capabilities that the process offers to its partners.

Earlier chapters presented some of the policy languages provided by Web services, such as WS-Security and WS-ReliableMessaging.

The attachment of policies to the business process enables the separation of concerns that is desirable to keep the business logic intact and first order. Therefore, when you consider adding proprietary constructs to BPEL, you should first think of whether the functionality that the constructs are trying to add is better achieved through the use of Web services policies that are orthogonal to, yet can be integrated with, the business logic.

14.3 BPEL Processing Model

The previous sections explained the different aspects that make up a process. This section delves into the runtime aspects of BPEL processes.

14.3.1 Deployment

A BPEL process exposes zero or one portType along each `partnerLink` ("`myRole`"). After the portTypes are deployed, they must be made available for invocations from the partners. With WSDL specifying that one portType corresponds to one port with the address of the available service, engines that deploy BPEL processes are expected to create such ports. The BPEL specification does not specify a deployment approach or syntax for a deployment descriptor.

The engine or workflow system to which a process is deployed is responsible for creating instances based on the instance creation activities and maintaining conversations between each of these instances and their partners, usually using correlation sets. The approach or interfaces that bind to partners at deployment time or specify locators for their binding to happen at runtime, such as in 14.2.3.2, are omitted from the BPEL specification. The workflow systems must present and support such approaches.

14.3.2 Interacting with the Process

After you deploy a process, partners interact with it by invoking the operations it offers them. The first of such invocations, targeted at an instance that creates `receive` or `pick` activity, creates an instance of the process and registers the values of correlation properties that are initialized at that point in time. The interaction activities of a process specify which variables to read outgoing messages from and which variables to write incoming messages to.

The messages in invocations of a process's operations are eventually consumed by a running `receive` activity, `pick` activity, or `event handler`. After an activity starts running, it waits for a message to arrive that it can consume, saves it in a specified variable, and completes. To disambiguate which activity might consume an incoming message, only one `receive/pick/onMessage` with the same `partnerLink`, portType, operation, and correlation set can be running at the same time. If the operation is request-response, a subsequent `reply` activity must exist further downstream in the process. After the `reply` activity executes, a response is sent to the invoker, and the call is complete.

The environment checks incoming messages for correlation information and determines whether they match an existing instance, or whether it has to create a new instance, or do neither. You can also use correlation to validate business data. For example, if you use a middleware-generated opaque token to identify process instances but the process that it refers to uses correlation sets, you can view the correlation information as a business-level check of the validity of an incoming message.

The invocations that a process instance sends to its partners are blocking. An `invoke` activity that corresponds to a request-response WSDL operation begins by sending a request and ends after it has received the response. The `invoke` activity specifies which data variable to read the request message from and which optional variable to write the response into. By the time an `invoke` activity must run, it must know the endpoint of the `partner link` to send the message to. As noted in section 14.2.3.2, multiple schemes are available for binding `partnerLinks` to actual deployed endpoints.

The result of an invocation might include an endpoint reference that you can copy using an `assign` activity to one of the process's `partnerLinks`. In this case, the process will use the new endpoint reference for all further interactions along that `partnerLink`. You can use an `invoke` activity to lookup an endpoint of a partner in a registry; that lookup is followed by an `assign` activity to copy the endpoint reference into a partner link.

14.3.3 Navigating the Process Model

Control flow in BPEL, as noted earlier, is defined using a combination of structured activities and control links. You can only define control links inside of a `<flow>` activity, at arbitrary levels of nesting. An activity must wait to proceed until it knows all the link values of its incoming links. The topmost activity of a process has no incoming link, thus it is started once you create an instance of the process.

To understand the processing model of the activity lifecycle, consider the states that a BPEL activity must go through. At first, all activities are in a default state. After an activity gets control from its parent (structured) activity and all its incoming links have fired, it evaluates its join condition to see whether it can run. If the join condition is `true`, the activity starts running. If it is a structured activity, its execution consists of running its child activities according to the prescribed semantics. After the activity completes successfully, it fires all its links with the values that result from the evaluation of their respective `transitionConditions`. For example, a `sequence` that has two activities begins by activating its first activity. After that first activity runs to completion, the `sequence` activates its second activity. After the second activity completes, the `sequence` is finished. Note that already completed activities might need to run again because of being contained in `while` loops.

Sometimes an activity gets disabled, either because it faulted while it was running or because it is within a part of the process that no longer runs. The former includes activities whose join condition evaluates to `false`. The latter includes activities in an untaken branch of a `switch` or in a scope that faulted. In such situations, the activity's outgoing links fire with negative values.

Dead Path Elimination

A BPEL `flow` activity contains a directed acyclic graph where the nodes are other activities and the edges are the links that define a partial execution order of the activities. When multiple links have the same target activity, multiple parallel execution paths are joined before this target activity is considered to run. A join condition determines whether the target activity is actually eligible for execution. When join conditions evaluate to `false`, you have two options: raising a fault or continuing to navigate through the flow. You can use both in BPEL. The actual behavior is determined by the `suppressJoinFailure` attribute of the process or an individual activity.

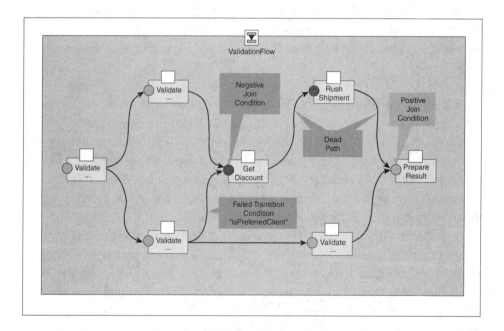

Figure 14-6   Flow graph and dead-path elimination.

Study the figure. If you suppress join failures by setting the corresponding attribute, the navigation of the flow continues with *dead-path elimination* (cf. [Ley 2000] for more details). The activity with the false join condition (see "Get Discount") is skipped, and the status of all outgoing links is set to `false`. For each of these links, this step is repeated for subsequent activities (see "Rush Shipment") until a join condition is reached that can be evaluated to `not false`. In the figure, this occurs at "Prepare Result" which can run successfully.

14.3.4 Scopes and Handlers

Scopes are the only structured activities that have activities both nested within them as well as attached to them in the form of handlers. Scopes also define data. BPEL variables are always referred to by name, and that name refers to the variable in the nearest enclosing scope.

After a scope starts running, it gives control to its enclosed activity and enables all its event and fault handlers. After a scope completes, it deactivates those handlers. If a scope completes successfully, it enables its compensation handler.

Activities in an event handler routine run concurrently as many times as the handler is triggered. The scope that the handler is defined on remains active.

Fault Handling and Compensation

If a fault occurs within a scope, the scope stops execution, disables its enclosed activities, and negatively fires all unevaluated links whose sources are in the scope but targets are outside of it. If the scope has a handler for the fault, the activities in the fault handler routine execute. Otherwise, the fault is thrown up the scope hierarchy until a handler is found to remedy the situation. If the fault reaches the process root and doesn't find a handler, it terminates the entire process.

Each fault handler of a scope can initiate the reversal of previous activity results by invoking compensation handlers for its nested scopes. This applies only to nested scopes that successfully terminated on their normal execution path.

Figure 14-7 illustrates the interplay between fault and compensation handlers. Here, an activity in the main process scope throws a fault after the successful completion of scopes 1 and 2. The fault is caught by the process-level fault handler, which calls the compensation handler of scope 1, which in turn calls the compensation handler of scope 2. After the compensation and any additional processing in the process-level fault handler are completed, the process instance terminates.

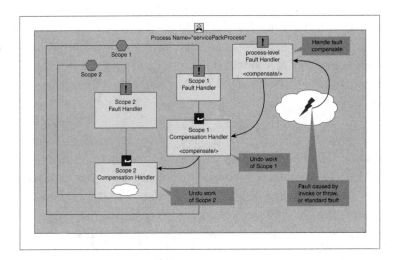

Figure 14-7   Fault handling and compensation.

The compensation handler for a scope can operate only on a snapshot of the data that was taken at the time the scope terminated normally, and not on live data of the running process instance. However, the activities in a compensation handler might invoke operations that undo external effects of the activities executed in the normal path of the scope. If no compensation handler is defined for a scope, an implicit compensation handler invokes the compensation handlers of nested scopes in reverse order of their former completion.

14.4 Future Directions

BPEL is currently undergoing standardization at the OASIS organization, with many companies and groups contributing to this effort. Although the specification was not yet a standard at the time of this writing, the changes going into effect for what will likely be called WS-BPEL 2.0 stray only minimally from the details in this chapter and keep with the core guiding principles laid out.

Web service composition, however, has many open areas for research and industrial efforts. A few of these areas that are already seeing some activity include checking compliance of executable processes with their abstract counterparts, global models, extensibility, and the definition of new standards.

The use of abstract processes beyond the ability to formally define a business process is currently being studied. Its usage to check for compliance of a running Web service is one possible approach. It was noted earlier that you can derive an abstract process from an executable or vice versa by filling in missing parts. The tricky part comes from proving compliance between an executable and an abstract process. You can make this easier by providing harsh restrictions, such as only allowing a compliant executable to replace "empty" activities and provide the needed information for any variable's assignments that are labeled opaque. Although this drastically simplifies the problem, it is simply too restrictive to provide a general solution. Discussions and research are currently underway on what it means for such compliance to exist for processes in which the differences from the abstract one are more involved.

Another future direction is the ability to wire together different processes or even Web services to form something that is similar to WSFL's global models. Although `partnerLinks` provide some information on what is required from a compliant partner, they do not have enough information to derive a complete picture of wirings and relationships when you consider scenarios in which multiple processes are wired together. For example, `partnerLinks` are not enough to describe the setup in which two separate business processes should use the same bank process. The capability to define such global models, however, is at a level of abstraction above that of BPEL and would be expected to be defined in a compatible yet separate specification.

The addition of functionality to processes, as noted earlier, might be done either through proprietary language extensions or using policies. Current extensibility areas that are being studied include the inlining of other languages, such as Java. This has been the case for the definition of the BPELJ proposal [BPELJ]. Others include the capability to include human-facing activities. Finally, there have been proposals for extensions for quality-of-service capabilities. However, those are better represented as policy attachments because they clutter the business logic.

As additional standards and specifications are proposed for the Web services framework, keep in mind their modularity and their combined usage. With layering and modularity as core Web services principles, BPEL processes are expected to take advantage of new capabilities from such future standards by layering on top of the business logic that the BPEL process provides.

14.5 Summary

Workflow languages have been around for many years, but customers are no longer willing to be locked into static environments with proprietary tools and languages. Integrated into the Web services stack and natively built for the dynamic, networked SOA environment, BPEL provides a solution to this problem.

In short, BPEL provides the full power of established workflow concepts coupled with recursive composition and dynamic binding to partners, while exploiting the rest of the Web services architecture. BPEL's place in the Web services stack allows it to inherit the expressiveness and power of both the underlying and the orthogonal standards for use in your business processes. Underlying standards provide interoperability through standardized interfaces and messaging protocols. Orthogonal (existing or upcoming) standards allow you to add features or quality-of-service aspects to your processes without changing the process model.

This chapter explained the motivation for and the architectural foundation of BPEL and its role in the SOA world. The concrete realizations of these concepts, illustrated with examples, provided the link between the architectural foundation and the concrete language elements. This chapter discussed the possible future directions for BPEL, which is finally undergoing its final phases of standardization.

Part 8

Case Studies

This part presents two case studies that tie together all the topics discussed so far. Chapter 15, "Case Study: Car Parts Supply Chain," is a business-to-business (B2B) scenario that involves a car manufacturer, a car dealer, and a parts manufacturer. Chapter 16, "Case Study: Ordering Service Parts," is based on a real business problem in IBM that is being addressed today using the Web services platform. This represents an enterprise integration scenario, which is where Web services are being deployed today.

These case studies show you how to compose the Web services platform components to solve real world problems.

Chapter 15

Case Study: Car Parts Supply Chain

This chapter discusses a business-to-business (B2B) e-commerce example illustrating a hypothetical supply chain relationship among a car dealer, the manufacturer, and a part supplier. This example is based on the one contained in [WS Architecture 2003]. The example shows how the Web services protocol stack enables secure, reliable, and transactional interactions in a B2B scenario. In this example, the dealer and supplier access Web services exposed by a car manufacturer, which enables them to efficiently maintain the supply of car parts that consumers need. The interactions also involve accessing internal applications, some of them exposed as Web services. Quality of service protocols are enabled in each of these interactions as required.

15.1 Scenario Description

In this scenario, a car dealer has secure access to a manufacturer's Web site so that he can order auto parts. The dealer can access the car manufacturer applications using a Web browser to place orders and to check the status of existing orders. The interaction requires the requester's authentication with both the dealer and car manufacturer systems. After the dealer achieves authentication, he can access a Web service on the manufacturer's site to retrieve order data and to place new orders.

The manufacturer, in turn, maintains a relationship with a parts supplier who is chartered with maintaining an appropriate supply of certain parts from the manufacturer's inventory. With this purpose, the manufacturer and the supplier have entered into an agreement by which the supplier can check inventory levels and place orders on behalf of the manufacturer when levels fall below certain thresholds. To do this, the manufacturer provides direct access to its internal systems (the inventory systems in this case) through a secure Web service.

Finally, the supplier's internal systems are Web service enabled to allow open integration among different platforms. To place an order (this time on behalf of this particular car manufacturer), the ordering application contacts the warehouse system, which is also exposed as a Web service, and transmits the order as an XML message. The warehouse application then divides the order between two provisioning systems used to fulfill orders.

15.2 Architecture

The interactions among the parties are shown in the next three figures. Figure 15-1 illustrates the dealer-to-manufacturer relationship. Employees of the car dealer log on to the dealer's intranet using their browser, and then are authenticated with the system. From the car dealer page, they are able to access the manufacturer ordering site. When this happens, credentials for the dealer employee are communicated following a WS-Federation protocol to the manufacturer, which directly authenticates and grants access to its ordering systems to the dealer's employee.

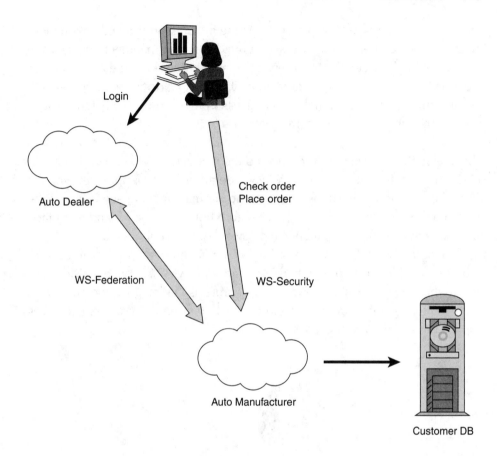

Figure 15-1   Dealer-to-manufacturer interaction.

At this point, the Web services–enabled browser can interact with the Web service that the car manufacturer provides for placing orders. The dealer's Web service retrieves and updates information from the customer database at the manufacturer. It ensures integrity of the messages exchanged by using WS-Security to sign messages sent by both parties. In Figure 15-1, wide arrows show Web services–based interactions. These include the WS-Federation taking place between authentication systems at the dealer and manufacturer sites and the interaction between the Web service–enabled browser at the dealer and the ordering Web service at the manufacturer. Thin black arrows represent other interactions, such as traditional Web requests from a browser or database access to the manufacturer's customer database.

The interaction between the supplier and the manufacturer is shown in Figure 15-2. Once again, one can see how WS-Federation allows employees who are using the supplier applications to access the car manufacturer services by logging into the supplier systems. This is because both the supplier and manufacturer have federated their authentication systems. Based on their supplier agreement, the supplier can access the status of inventories at the manufacturer and order additional supplies when levels are low. A Web service provides access to the inventory systems. WS-Security protects the integrity and confidentiality of messages that are exchanged between the supplier Web service access application and the inventory service.

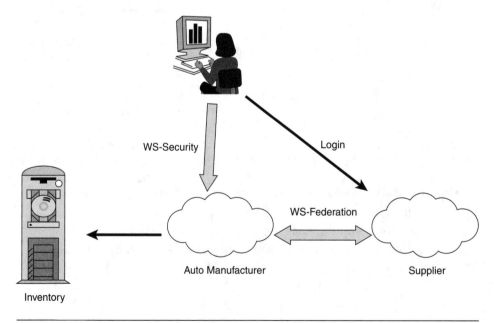

Figure 15-2   Supplier to manufacturer interaction.

Accessing the inventory system, the supplier employees detect low levels
of a certain part. They place an order on behalf of the manufacturer into the
supplier's ordering system. This interaction is shown in Figure 15-3. The
request goes to the internal warehouse system, transmitted reliably using
WS-ReliableMessaging to ensure exactly-once delivery of orders. This guarantees that orders are not lost because of network failure or because of the temporal unavailability of any of the systems involved. The warehouse system works
with two warehouse subsystems at the two production sites that the supplier
maintains.

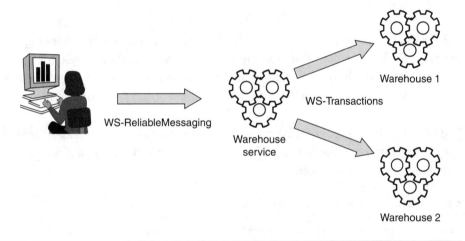

Figure 15-3   Supplier warehouse services.

The company policy requires the two sites to divide the order in a certain way,
so coordinated requests are sent to the warehouse systems at the two sites. To
ensure that the complete order is fulfilled, the complete interaction is
conducted transactionally using WS-AtomicTransactions. If one of the plants
cannot provide the requested amount, both internal warehouse requests are
cancelled, and the ordering application is informed of the error condition. The
employee can then check inventories at the plants and, if needed, override the
company policy to receive the supplies from whatever source is available.

15.3 Web Service Descriptions

This section explains how the description of the Web services involved in this scenario should be written. To focus on the fundamental aspects of the description, Web Services Description Language (WSDL) 1.1 service definitions are shown but the details of schema and policy definitions are omitted (the latter because the definition of policy assertion dialects is in an early stage). Note also that, for simplicity and readability, XML namespace declarations are omitted in this and in the next section's examples, and we limit the use of namespace prefixes to element names. Thus, the examples are meant to be illustrative rather than executable.

This example has five services: the ordering service and inventory checking at the car manufacturer, and the ordering services at the warehouse systems at the supplier (the one where orders are sent, and one in each of the two production plants). All three warehouse Web services implement the same port type.

The port type of the ordering Web service at the manufacturer provides three operations: retrieving the list of outstanding orders, checking the status of an order, and placing a new order:

```
<definitions targetNamespace="...">
<!-- WSDL definitions in this document     -->
<!-- referenced using "mfr" prefix         -->

   <types>
     <xsd:schema>
     <!-- XSD definitions for this service   -->
     <!-- referenced using "mfx" prefix      -->
       <xsd:import namespace=
                   "http://www.car-
manufacturer.com/xsd/customer"/>
     </xsd:schema>
   </types>

   <message name="customerID">
     <part name="customer" element="mfx:custID"/>
   </message>
   <message name="orderID">
     <part name="order" element="mfx:orderID"/>
   </message>
   <message name="orderInfo">
     <part name="order" element="mfx:orderInfo"/>
```

```
</message>
<message name="orderList">
  <part name="ID" element="mfx:orderList"/>
</message>

<portType name="partOrderPortType">
  <operation name="requestOrderList">
     <input message="mfr:customerID"/>
     <output message="mfr:orderList"/>
  </operation>
  <operation name="requestOrderStatus">
     <input message="mfr:orderID"/>
     <output message="mfr:orderInfo"/>
  </operation>
  <operation name="newOrder">
     <input message="mfr:orderInfo"/>
     <output message="mfr:orderID"/>
     <fault name="notAccepted" message="mfr:orderFault"/>
  </operation>
</portType>

<binding name="partOrderBinding"
          type="mfr:partOrderPortType">
  <wsp:PolicyReference URI=
          "http://www.car-manufacturer.com/policies/DSig"/>
  <soap:binding style="document"
    transport="http://schemas.xmlsoap.org/soap/http"/>
</binding>

<service name="partOrderService">
   <port name="partOderPort" binding="mfr:partOrderBinding">
      <soap:address location=
         "http://www.car-manufacturer/partOrder-svc"/>
   </port>
</service>

</definitions>
```

Note that these three operations use four WSDL message definitions. Two—customerID and orderID—are used for customer and order identification. The orderInfo message encodes all information necessary to place an order and is used to transmit order information and status, also. A list of orders is encoded as an orderList message, which relies on a schema element definition containing a variable number of orderInfo elements. Note also that the binding that the service provides is a SOAP document/literal-style binding.

The manufacturer offers a second service, this time to its parts supplier. This
service offers a single operation for retrieving the list of parts and the inventory
levels for each of them. Access to this service requires both the digital signing
and encryption of the bodies of the messages that are exchanged. This is expressed in the next block of code by the two policy attachment elements in the
port type binding.

```
<definitions targetNamespace="...">
<!-- WSDL definitions in this document    -->
<!-- referenced using "mfr" prefix        -->

  <types>
    <xsd:schema>
     <!-- XSD definitions for this service -->
     <!-- referenced using "mfx" prefix    -->

      <xsd:import namespace=
                 "http://www.car-manufacturer.com/xsd/inventory"/>
    </xsd:schema>
  </types>

  <message name="supplierID">
    <part name="suppplier" element="mfx:supplierID"/>
  </message>
  <message name="inventoryList">
    <part name="ID" element="mfx:inventoryList"/>
  </message>

<portType name="inventoryPortType">
   <operation name="requestInventoryList">
      <input message="mfr:supplierID"/>
      <output message="mfr:inventoryList"/>
   </operation>
</portType>

<binding name="inventoryBinding"
          type="mfr:inventoryPortType">
   <wsp:PolicyReference URI=
        "http://www.car-manufacturer.com/policies/DSig"/>
   <wsp:PolicyReference URI=
        "http://www.car-manufacturer.com/policies/Encrypt"/>
   <soap:binding style="document"

transport="http://schemas.xmlsoap.org/soap/http"/>
</binding>

<service name="inventoryService">
   <port name="partOderPort" binding="mfr:inventoryBinding">
      <soap:address location=
        "http://www.car-manufacturer/inventory-svc"/>
```

```
    </port>
</service>

</definitions>
```

Finally, all the internal warehouse systems at the supplier implement the same warehouse order port type. The port type offers a one-way "warehouseOrder" operation, which is shown in the definition that follows for the central warehouse service. For completeness and to support the message examples included in the next section, we also provide XML Schema element definitions for the service.

```
<definitions targetNamespace="..." >
<!-- WSDL definitions in this document    -->
<!-- referenced using "spl" prefix        -->

<types>
    <xsd:schema targetNamespace="...">
    <!-- XSD definitions in this document    -->
    <!-- referenced using "spx" prefix        -->

        <xsd:element="warehouseOrder">
            <xsd:complexType>
                <xsd:complexContent>
                    <xsd:sequence>
                        <xsd:element name="Date" type="xsd:date"/>
                        <xsd:element name="Originator"
                                        type="xsd:anyURI"/>
                        <xsd:element name="CustomerId"
                                        type="xsd:string"/>
                        <xsd:element name="ItemNo"
                                        type="xsd:unsignedLong"/>
                        <xsd:element name="Qty"
                                        type="xsd:unsignedLong"/>
                    </xsd:sequence>
                </xsd:complexContent>
            <xsd:complexType>
        <xsd:element>
    </xsd:schema>
</types>

<message name="warehouseOrder">
    <part element="spx:warehouseOrder"/>
</message>

<portType name="warehouseOrderingPortType">
    <operation name="placeOrder">
        <input message="spl:warehouseOrder"/>
    </operation>
```

```
</portType>

<binding name="reliableWarehouseBinding"
         type="spl:warehouseOrderingPortType">
   <soap:binding style="document"
         transport="http://schemas.xmlsoap.org/soap/http"/>
   <wsp:PolicyReference URI=
      "http://www.supplier.com/policies/ReliableMsgPolicy"/>
</binding>

<service name="warehouseOrderService">
   <port name="warehouseorderPort"
         binding="spl:reliableWarehouseBinding">
      <soap:address location=
            "http://www.car-manufacturer/inventory-svc"/>
   </port>
</service>

</definitions>
```

The receiving warehouse responds to the requesting application that sent the order message with a confirmation or an error message, which is sent back asynchronously. (We do not include here the definition of the port type where these messages are received.) The bindings for all warehouse services have attached policies to indicate that certain QoS protocols must be followed. As shown in the preceding service definition, the initial order is transmitted to the central warehouse service over a reliable connection using WS-Reliable Messaging. The binding attaches a policy that requires the use of the WS-Reliable Messaging protocol when the service is accessed.

15.4 Messages and Protocols

This section provides an overview of how the interactions that are carried out in this example and the specific QoS protocols that are required in each case appear on the wire as SOAP messages. First, note that all SOAP messages that are exchanged in this example are encoded according to the document-literal model. Also, in every case, the WS-Addressing specification dictates a certain set of mandatory headers to be used. Each specific QoS protocol that is used requires particular headers to be encoded. Because the basic elements are common in all the messages that are exchanged, we will show one full example and then indicate the modifications introduced in each specific exchange.

The initial interaction between the Web services–enabled browser at the dealer and the order service at the manufacturer uses digital signatures to protect message integrity. The interaction between the supplier and the manufacturer inventory service, on the other hand, requires that the messages also be encrypted. The request message used in this interaction incorporates both a digital signature and an encryption section in its WS-Security SOAP header. A sample message is shown next. Again, note that we have omitted namespace declarations; we have also removed most of the digital data corresponding to the digital signature and encrypted body for readability.

```
<S:Envelope>
   <S:Header>
      <wsa:To>
          http://www.car-manufacturer.com/inventory-svc
      </wsa:To>
      <wsa:Action>
http://www.car-manufacturer.com/svcs/
inventoryPortType/requestInventoryListRequest
      </wsa:Action>
      <wsa:ReplyTo>
         <wsa:Address>
http://schemas.xmlsoap.org/ws/2004/03/
addressing/role/anonymous
         </wsa:Address>
      </wsa:ReplyTo>
      <wsse:Security>
         <wsse:UsernameToken Id="Username">
            <wsse:Username>
            CN=Joe, OU=ordering-system,O=supplier.com, C=US
            </wsse:Username>
         </wsse:UsernameToken>
         <xenc:EncryptedKey Id="SecretKey">
            <xenc:EncryptionMethod Algorithm=
            "http://www.w3.org/2001/04/xmlenc#rsa-1_5"/>
            <dsig:KeyInfo>
               <wsse:SecurityTokenReference>
                  <wsse:Reference URI="#Username"/>
               </wsse:SecurityTokenReference>
            </dsig:KeyInfo>
         <xenc:CipherData>
            <xenc:CipherValue>
            HGRO3csrbtFLtMP3iC+s0r/...
            </xenc:CipherValue>
         </xenc:CipherData>
         </xenc:EncryptedKey>
         <xenc:ReferenceList>
            <xenc:DataReference URI="#BodyContent" />
```

```
        </xenc:ReferenceList>
      </wsse:Security>
    </S:Header>
  <S:Body>
    <xenc:EncryptedData Id="BodyContent">
      <xenc:EncryptionMethod Algorithm=
"http://www.w3.org/2001/04/xmlenc#tripledes-cbc"/>
      <dsig:KeyInfo>
        <wsse:SecurityTokenReference>
          <wsse:Reference URI="#SecretKey" />
        </wsse:SecurityTokenReference>
      </dsig:KeyInfo>
      <xenc:CipherData>
        <xenc:CipherValue>
        FOLXfmjBbaiRtn4I86CVMlrXMgm7OwC0Sf...
        </xenc:CipherValue>
      </xenc:CipherData>
    </xenc:EncryptedData>
  </S:Body>
</S:Envelope>
```

Observe how the body is encrypted inside an EncryptedData element. Note also the presence of the mandatory WS-Addressing headers—To, Action, and ReplyTo (because this is a request response interaction)—and how the anonymous URI is used in the Address field of the ReplyTo header to indicate that the response needs to be sent back synchronously over the open HTTP connection.

The message exchanges inside the supplier's enterprise network are not secured; however, different protocols ensure reliable processing of the order. First, the order message sent by the ordering application to the central warehouse Web service is exchanged using the reliable messaging protocol. A reliable messaging sequence header is used in this case, and the body is not encrypted.

```
<S:Envelope>
  <S:Header>
    <wsa:To>
        http://www.supplier.com/warehouse/orders-svc
    </wsa:To>
    <wsa:Action>
        http://www.supplier.com/warehouse/svcs/
warehouseOrderingPortType/placeOrderRequest
    </wsa:Action>
    <wsa:ReplyTo>
      <wsa:Address>
        http://www.supplier.com/requests/callback
```

```
            </wsa:Address>
        </wsa:ReplyTo>
        <rm:Sequence S:mustUnderstand="1">
            <util:Identifier>
http://www.supplier.com.com/warehouse#0936987027956930
            </util:Identifier>
            <rm:MessageNumber>1</rm:MessageNumber>
        </rm:Sequence>
        <rm:AckRequested>
            <util:Identifier>
http://www.supplier.com.com/warehouse#0936987027956930
            </rm:Identifier>
            <rm:MessageNumber>1</rm:MessageNumber>
        </rm:AckRequested>
    </S:Header>
    <S:Body>
        <spx:warehouseOrder>
            <spx:Date>2005-10-01</spl:Date>
            <spx:Originator>
                http://www.supplier.com/sales-id=67
            </spl:Originator>
            <spx:CustomerId>751-CarM</spl:CustomerId>
            <spx:ItemNo>72519-GFa</spl:ItemNo>
            <spx:Qty>50</spl:Qty>
        </spx:warehouseOrder>
    </S:Body>
</S:Envelope>
```

Observe that this ReplyTo address does not contain the anonymous URI (indicating, for instance, that one must not send the response over the current connection). Because the confirmation message is sent asynchronously, the ReplyTo endpoint reference must contain an actual address to send the response. The use of the reliable messaging protocol results in two additional headers in this message: the mandatory Sequence header identifying this as the first message in the reliable message sequence, and the AckRequested header requesting that an acknowledgement be returned to the originator of the message.

Finally, the orders that the central warehouse sends to the supplier production plants are executed as an atomic transaction, because they involve coordinated updates in the systems at the two plants. The central warehouse application initiates an atomic transaction, and the coordination service at the central warehouse initiates an exchange with the coordinators at the two plant warehouses. A coordination context in the messages exchanged supports the atomic protocol in this case. Following is one sample application message that the warehouse central service sends to the warehouse service in Plant 1, which carries the co-ordination context header message that the WS-AtomicTransaction protocol uses. A more complete example of the message's exchange in an interaction of this kind is provided in Chapter 16, "Case Study: Ordering Service Packs."

```
<S:Envelope>
    <S:Header>
        <wsa:To>
            http://www.supplier.com/warehouse-1/orders-svc
        </wsa:To>
        <wsa:Action>
            http://www.supplier.com/warehouse/svcs/
warehouseOrderingPortType/placeOrderRequest
        </wsa:Action>
        <wsa:ReplyTo>
            <wsa:Address>
                http://www.suplier.com/warehouse/callback
            </wsa:Address>
        </wsa:ReplyTo>
        <wsc:CoordinationContext>
            <util:Identifier>

http://www.supplier.com/00000000000FF4A64A2CA0902122F00
            </util:Identifier>
            <wsc:CoordinationType>
                http://schemas.xmlsoap.org/ws/2003/09/wsat
            </wsc:CoordinationType>
            <wsc:RegistrationService>
                <wsa:Address>

http://www.supplier.com/warehouse/registrationCoordinator
                </wsa:Address>
                <wsa:ReferenceProperties>
                    <spl-tx:TransactionId>
http://www.supplier.com/00000000000FF4A64A2CA0902122F00
                    </spl-tx:TransactionId>
                </wsa:ReferenceProperties>
            </wsc:RegistrationService>
        </wsc:CoordinationContext>
    </S:Header>
    <S:Body>
        <spl:warehouseOrder>
            <spl:Date>01102005</spl:Date>
            <spl:Originator>
```

```
http://www.supplier.com/warehouse-central
            </spl:Originator>
            <spl:CustomerId>751-CarM</spl:CustomerId>
            <spl:ItemNo>72519-GFa</spl:ItemNo>
            <spl:Qty>25</spl:Qty>
        </spl:warehouseOrder>
    </S:Body>
 </S:Envelope>
```

15.5 Summary

This chapter illustrated the use of SOAP, WSDL, WS-Addressing, WS-Policy, WS-Security, WS-ReliableMessaging, and WS-AtomicTransaction to address a B2B integration scenario. The example does not include a discussion of what implementation platform or technology any of the parties use. That's because Web services works at a level above that and provides a clean architecture for building integrated B2B applications.

Chapter 16

Case Study:
Ordering Service Packs

This chapter discusses a business scenario to illustrate how to apply the various Web services specifications to create effective solutions to real-world problems.

16.1 Scenario Description

When customers buy hardware, they have the option of selecting additional service packages, called service packs. *Service packs* are bundled support services, such as on-site repair, hardware warranties, and so on. One can purchase service packs when buying the hardware or later, within certain conditions. The set of service packs that a customer can buy must be validated by the manufacturer to ensure certain criteria are met, including the following:

- The service packs are compatible with products that the customer has purchased.

- The service packs are consistent with each other. Sometimes interdependencies might exist between service packs.

- The service packs selected are available within the country in which the customer is located: Certain service packs are available only in certain countries.

- The purchase is within the time period allowed for acquiring additional service packs.

In a large organization consisting of several divisions that offer many hardware products, the systems that perform each of the verifications might be hosted in various locations and operate under different environments.

16.2 Architecture

As it is often the case in intra-enterprise integration scenarios, most of the applications that provide each of the validation steps already exist and have been implemented using various technologies and on different platforms. This situation makes a perfect example for a Web services integration solution. The basic service-oriented architecture approach is to identify the core constituent services and then develop compositions and integrations of those services into additional services and the full solution.

In this case, because each of the steps of the verification and purchase processes is self-contained, typically implemented by separate applications, it is natural to model each one as a service. It is possible to model the actual ordering process as a self-standing service with two main operations: one for validating the service packs that were selected, and a second one to purchase the service pack. Both operations could be implemented as BPEL processes, although this example does not provide a BPEL implementation of the service. The overall architecture of the integrated systems is shown in Figure 16-1.

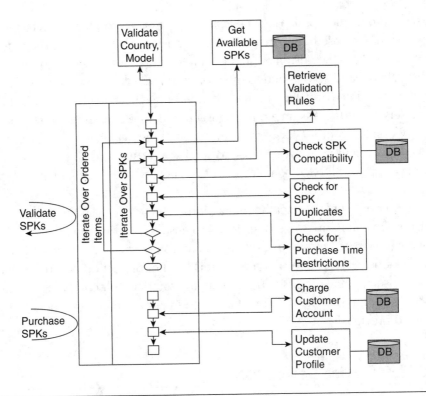

Figure 16-1   Service pack application as a service composition.

Each input request might contain multiple orders. The validate operation is a straightforward process that first iterates over the list of ordered items. and, for each item, over the service packs included with the order. For each service pack, a set of tests is executed by invoking the services that the existing applications expose for that purpose. The different tests mentioned in the previous section are sequentially performed for each service pack. As the figure shows, some tests are run against the line item as a whole (validate country and machine model), whereas others are run against individual service packs for each order.

The second operation of this service is a purchase operation that charges the cost of each purchased item (machine plus service packs) to the customer account and updates the customer profile with the purchase, a necessary step to ensure delivery and service and to monitor customer purchasing activity. These two steps are directly related and must be performed atomically as a unit. To do so, the service code starts an atomic transaction before accessing the two back-end services; the coordinator of the transaction at the aggregator service interacts with coordinators at each back-end service to ensure the all or none semantics and to roll back completed work as necessary in case of failure.

WS-Security protocols protect the interaction with the client. In the case of the validation operation, messages are signed to ensure integrity; when purchasing the service pack, the messages exchanged are also encrypted. The interaction with back-end services does not require this level of protection because it takes place in a secure environment. The atomic transaction protocol that is specified in WS-AtomicTransactions supports the execution of the purchase operation, as explained previously.

16.3 Web Service Descriptions

The aggregation service that provides the validation and purchase operations has the following service description. For simplicity and readability, Schema definitions have not been included and namespace declarations have been skipped; as in the previous chapter, the examples are meant to be illustrative rather than executable.

```
<definitions targetNamespace="...">
        <!-- WSDL definitions in this document -->
        <!-- referenced using "tns" prefix -->

        <types>
            <!-- XSD definitions for this service -->
            <!-- referenced using "xsd1" prefix -->

            <xsd:schema>
                <xsd:import
namespace="http://www.purchase.com/xsd/svp-svc">
            </xsd:schema>
        </types>
```

```
        <message name="purchaseResponse">
            <part name="purchaseResponse"
element="xsd1:PurchaseStatus"/>
        </message>
        <message name="purchaseRequest">
            <part name="purchaseRequest"
element="xsd1:PurchaseRequest"/>
        </message>
        <message name="ServicePacValidationInput">
            <part name="spvDataInput"
element="xsd1:ServicePacValidationData"/>
        </message>
        <message name="ServicePacValidationOutput">
            <part name="spvDataOutput"
element="xsd1:ServicePacValidationData"/>
        </message>

        <portType name="spvPortType">
            <operation name="purchaseServicePacs">
                <input name="purchaseInput"
message="tns:purchaseRequest"/>
                <output name="purchaseOutput"
                        message="tns:purchaseResponse"/>
            </operation>
            <operation name="validateServicePac">
                <input name="Input"
message="tns:ServicePacValidationInput"/>
        <output name="Output"
                message="tns:ServicePacValidationOutput"/>
            </operation>
        </portType>

        name="spvBinding"
            type="tns:spvPortType">
            <wsp:PolicyReference URI=
"http://www.purchase.com/policies/DSig">
        <soap:binding style="document"
transport="http://schemas.xmlsoap.org/soap/http"/>
            <operation name="purchaseServicePacs">
                <wsp:PolicyReference URI=
"http://www.purchase.com/policies/Encrypt">
        <soap:operation soapAction=
"http://www.purchase.com/spvPortType/purchaseServicePacsRequest"/>
            </operation>
            <operation name="validateServicePac">
                <soap:operation soapAction=
"http://www.purchase.com/spvPortType/validateServicePacRequest"/>
            </operation>
</binding>
```

```
    <service name="spv-svc">
        <port name="spv-svc-port" binding="tns:spvBinding">
            <soap:address
location="http://www.purchase.com/spv "/>
        </port>
    </service>
</definitions>
```

Note that the service binding indicates that all operations that the service offers require messages to be signed; the purchase operation also requires encryption. A policy requiring digital signature of messages is attached to the binding element, and a policy requiring encryption is attached to the purchase operation. As in the previous chapter, this example doesn't provide explicit policies because policy dialects are still in the process of being developed.

Among the back-end services that are integrated in this example, the focus here is on the services that the purchase operation uses. A simplified definition of the profile update service follows.

```
<definitions targetNamespace="...">
<!-- WSDL definitions in this document    -->
<!-- referenced using "tns" prefix        -->
    <types>
    <!-- XSD definitions for this service   -->
    <!-- referenced using "xsd1" prefix     -->
        <xsd:schema>
            <xsd:import namespace=
            "http://www.purchase.com/xsd/customer-profile"/>
            </xsd:schema>
    </types>
    <message name="addSPVsRqst">
        <part name="newSPVs" element="xsd1:newClientSPVs"/>
    </message>
    <message name="SPVAdditionStatus">
        <part name="ret" element="tns:status"/>
    </message>
        <portType name="SPVProfileUpdatePT">
            <operation name="updateProfile">
                <input message="tns:addSPVsRqst"/>
                <output message="tns:SPVAdditionStatus"/>
            </operation>
        </portType>
    <binding name="ProfileBinding" type="tns:SPVProfileUpdatePT">
        <wsp:PolicyReference URI=
        "http://purchase.com/policies/ATMandatory">
        <soap:binding style="document" transport=
```

```
             "http://schemas.xmlsoap.org/soap/http"/>
           <operation name="updateProfile">
             <soap:operation soapAction=
   "http://www.purchase.com/SPVProfileUpdatePT/updateProfileRequest"/>
           </operation>
       </binding>
       <service name="spv-customer-profile">
           <port name="spv-svc-port" binding="tns:ProfileBinding">
             <soap:address
                   location="http://www.purchase.com/profile "/>
           </port>
       </service>
   </definitions>
```

In this case, no security policies have been attached based on the fact that the
interaction takes place behind the enterprise firewall. However, a policy has
been attached to the binding, mandating the use of the atomic transaction protocol. The policy states that a new transaction context must be passed on when
the service is invoked. The definition of the purchase service contains a similar
binding to support the execution of the application code under an atomic transaction that the invoker service initiates.

```
<definitions name="Account"
targetNamespace="...">
<!-- WSDL definitions in this document     -->
<!-- referenced using "tns" prefix         -->
    <types>
    <!-- XSD definitions for this service   -->
    <!-- referenced using "xsd1" prefix      -->
        <xsd:schema>
        <xsd:import namespace=
             "http://www.purchase.com/xsd/account"/>
        </xsd:schema>
    </types>
    <message name="CreditAccountRequest">
       <part name="CreditAccountReq"
             element="xsd1:CreditAccountRequest"/>
    </message>
    <message name="AccountResponse">
       <part name="accountResp" element="xsd1:AccountMsg"/>
    </message>
    <message name="ChargeAccountRequest">
      <part name="chargeAccountReq"
             element="xsd1:ChargeAccountRequest"/>"
    </message>
    <message name="InsufficientAccountsFault">
       <part name="fault" element="xsd1:AccountFaultInfo"/>
```

```
      </message>
      <portType name="AccountPortType">
         <operation name="CreditAccount">
            <input name="CreditAccount"
                    message="tns:CreditAccountRequest"/>
            <output name="CreditAccountResponse"
                     message="tns:AccountResponse"/>
         </operation>
         <operation name="ChargeAccount">
            <input name="ChargeAccount"
                    message="tns:ChargeAccountRequest"/>
            <output name="ChargeAccount"
                     message="tns:AccountResponse"/>
            <fault message="tns:InsufficientAccountsFault"
                    name="f2"/>
         </operation>
      </portType>
      <binding name="AccountBinding" type="tns:AccountPortType">
         <wsp:PolicyReference URI=
              "http://purchase.com/policies/ATMandatory">
         <soap:binding style="document"
           transport="http://schemas.xmlsoap.org/soap/http"/>
      </binding>
      <service name="accounting">
         <port binding="AccountBinding">
            <soap:address
              location="http://www.purchase.com/account"/>
         </port>
      </service>
</definitions>
```

16.4 Messages and Protocols

This section concentrates on the messages exchanged as part of the atomic transaction executed by the aggregator service implementation when a customer invokes the purchase operation. This section does not discuss how the security protocols that are used in the interaction with the end user are supported by SOAP headers. Instead, refer to Chapter 15, "Case Study: Car Parts Supply Chain," where a similar usage of WS-Security is discussed in detail.

As explained previously, the implementation of the purchase operation invokes the "account charge" and the "update customer profile" operations atomically. The aggregation service initiates a new transaction, which results in a series of protocol messages exchanged between the transaction coordinators, in addition to the expected business message exchanges that the WSDL port types describe. Some of the messages received at the account service during this exchange are shown next. The initial invocation of the charge account operation contains a coordination context identifying the transaction and the registration service to use.

```
<S:Envelope>
  <S:Header>
     <wsa:To>http://www.purchase.com/account-svc</wsa:To>
     <wsa:Action>
http://www.purchase.com/services/AccountPortType/ChargeAccount
     </wsa:Action>
     <wsa:ReplyTo>
        <wsa:Address>
http://schemas.xmlsoap.org/ws/2004/03/addressing/role/anonymous
        </wsa:Address>
     </wsa:ReplyTo>
     <wsa:MessageID>uid:19884704:ff4a653d59:-7fba</wsa:MessageID>
     <wsc:CoordinationContext>
        <util:Identifier>
http://www.purchase.com/purchase/0000000000000000FF4A64A2CA
➥0902122F00
        </util:Identifier>
        <wsc:CoordinationType>
        http://schemas.xmlsoap.org/ws/2003/09/wsat
        </wsc:CoordinationType>
        <wsc:RegistrationService>
          <wsa:Address>

http://www.purchase.com/purchase/registrationCoordinator
          </wsa:Address>
          <wsa:ReferenceProperties>
             <pch-tx:TransactionId>
http://www.purchase.com/purchase/0000000000000000FF4A64A2CA
➥0902122F00
             </pch-tx:TransactionId>
          </wsa:ReferenceProperties>
        </wsc:RegistrationService>
     </wsc:CoordinationContext>
  </S:Header>
  <S:Body>
    <ChargeAccountRequest>
       <account>AX2345</account>
       <amount>800.0</amount>
    </ChargeAccountRequest>
  </S:Body>
</S:Envelope>
```

The coordination context header triggers the registration of the coordinator at the account service with the registration service passed inside the coordination context. The registration service responds with a RegisterResponse protocol message, as follows:

```
<S:Envelope>
   <S:Header>
      <wsa:RelatesTo RelationshipType="n1:Reply">
         uid:6c154704:ff4a65a8bb:-8000
      </wsa:RelatesTo>
      <wsa:To>
http://schemas.xmlsoap.org/ws/2004/03/addressing/role/anonymous
      </wsa:To>
<wsa:Action>urn:WSCoordination/registrationResponse</wsa:Action>
   </S:Header>
   <S:Body>
      <wsc:RegisterResponse>
         <wsc:CoordinatorProtocolService>
            <wsa:Address xsi:type="xsd:anyURI">
            http://www.purchase.com/purchase/coordinator
            </wsa:Address>
            <wsa:ReferenceProperties>
               <pch-tx:TransactionId>
http://www.purchase.com/purchase/0000000000000000FF4A64A2CA
➥0902122F00
               </pch:TransactionId>
               <pch-tx:ParticipantId>1</pch:ParticipantId>
            </wsa:ReferenceProperties>
         </wsc:CoordinatorProtocolService>
      </wsc:RegisterResponse>
   </S:Body>
</S:Envelope>
```

If both the account charge and the update profile operations are able to successfully complete their execution, they will return with appropriate application messages to the invoking service, and the coordinator of the transaction will drive it to completion with another set of protocol messages, terminating in a commit message sent to the two participating services. The final example shows a SOAP envelope containing the commit message sent to the account service.

```
<S:Envelope>
  <S:Header>
    <wsa:MessageID>uid:19884704:ff4a653d59:-7fb6</wsa:MessageID>
<wsa:To>http://www.purchase.com/purchase/participant</wsa:To>
    <wsa:Action>
       http://schemas.xmlsoap.org/ws/2003/09/wsat#Commit
    </wsa:Action>
    <pch-tx:TransactionId>
http://www.purchase.com/0000000000000000FF4A64A2CA0902122F00
    </pch-tx:TransactionId>
    <pch-tx:ProtocolId>
       http://schemas.xmlsoap.org/ws/2003/09/wsat#Durable2PC
    </pch-tx:ProtocolId>
  </S:Header>
  <S:Body>
    <wsat:Commit/>
  </S:Body>
</S:Envelope>
```

16.5 Summary

Service-oriented architecture (SOA) and the stack of Web services protocols provides a component-oriented paradigm for integrating new and existing applications. The impact of Web services in intra-enterprise computing is for that reason as relevant, if not more, as in B2B scenarios. The SOAP messaging protocols provide on the wire interoperability, and WSDL provides standardized representation of service capabilities. Finally, the WS-Transaction, WS-Security, and other QoS specifications support the level of interaction that everyday business interactions require.

Part 9

Conclusion

You have reached the end of your excursion into Web services. We conclude in this part with two final chapters.

Chapter 17, "Futures," has a certain speculative nature. It briefly sketches technology areas that should be added to the WS-* stack of standards at some point in the future. It covers the semantics of Web service interactions and additional aggregation mechanisms for Web services.

Chapter 18, "Conclusion," discusses the process by which the Web services platform is being defined and standardized, why it will succeed, and what the risk factors are. Furthermore, this chapter explains some of the work in progress to build other functionality on top of the core Web services platform presented in this book. In particular, it covers technologies that are essential to enable Grid computing and to manage Web services.

Chapter 17

Futures

The Web services platform discussed in this book provides an infrastructure for automated business interactions in which functional and non-functional requirements are highly demanding. To advance the degree of automation in business interactions, additional technology must be specified and standardized as part of this platform, or based upon it. This chapter outlines four topics that are likely to be important in the near future.

17.1 Semantics

A lot of work (subsumed by the term *semantic Web* [FHL03]) is currently ongoing, with the objective of adding more meaning to Web content. Semantic Web technology supports the definition of the semantics of documents, such that intelligent search will extend or even substitute today's keyword matching and information retrieval techniques of locating relevant Web content. Machine-processable representations of the semantics of structured data will support automatic transformation and matching of different formats for the same piece of information.

Combining this technology with Web service technology promises to become useful for SOA in general, and Web services in particular. For example, it might be possible to automatically detect that two Web services provide the same functionality although their port types, operations, and messages are named differently. Semantic Web technology will determine that the messages of the two port types are in fact carrying the same information, and are aggregated the same way into operations. Additional semantic annotations that describe each of the two Web services are the basis of reasoning about the functionality of the operations. The combination of semantic Web technology and Web service technology is called *Semantic Web service* technology [SWSI], where brackets are implicitly set like "Semantic (Web service)" and not like "(Semantic Web) service."

One of the underpinnings of the semantic Web is the notion of *ontology*, which is a representation of the concepts (or entities) of an application domain and all of the relationships between the concepts. Annotating artifacts of the Web, or of Web services, with knowledge in terms of ontologies makes these artifacts processable via semantic Web technologies.

Semantic Web service technology considers other forms of knowledge for describing the meaning of Web services. For example, when the ordering of operations of a Web service is important, annotating it with a BPEL process model can make its use less error prone. In Figure 17-3, port type A is annotated by process model P. Based on the process model, operation o1 is the only operation available at the beginning of an interaction with an implementation of port type A. After o1 has been used, you can expect that operation o2 will send a message. After that, operations o3 and o4 will be available for use. Operation o3 is available only under certain conditions, such as if a variable named x has a value greater than 42.

17.2 Wiring

As illustrated earlier in the book, aggregations of Web services play a central role in business interactions. Chapter 11, "Transactions," discussed aggregations of Web services based on agreement protocols, and Chapter 14, "Modeling Business Processes: BPEL," discussed aggregations of Web services based on business process models. Many more aggregation mechanisms are possible (see [KL03] for a corresponding discussion), but one particular mechanism deserves special attention because it is fundamental.

When multiple Web services are used within a business interaction, there are often mutual dependencies between these services. As shown in Figure 17-1, in order for an interaction to succeed, the invocation of operation o1 of port type A is expected to respond by using operation o2 of port type B. To be more precise, operations o1 and o2 are *inbound operations* (see Chapter 6, "Web Services Description Language") that consume messages, and port type A will somehow have an operation o3 defined to send out a message (an *outbound operation*) that is the response produced as an effect of using operation o1. This message will be provided as input of operation o2. The fact that operation o3 produces a message sent to operation o2 is graphically depicted by a link, L, in Figure 17-1. Such a link is called a *plug-link* in [WSFL]. Plug-links wire pairs of *dual* operations. That is, the operation at the start point of the plug-link begins an interaction by sending a message, and the operation at the end point of the plug-link consumes the initial messages sent.

Figure 17-1   Wiring dual operations.

Thus, there is a dependency between the two operations wired by a plug-link. At a more coarse-grained level, a partner link type in BPEL is similar to such a plug-link. A partner link type specifies that there is a mutual dependency between the two port types specified with each role of the partner link type. The provider of an implementation of the port type of one role of the partner link type requires a provider of an implementation of the port type of the other role of the partner link type for an appropriate and correct interaction (i.e. a message exchange).

A plug-link wires operations, not port types as partner link types do. This finer granularity allows annotating a plug-link to specify additional functionality. For example, a plug-link might be associated with a transformation specification that is used at runtime to map the message produced by the source operation of the plug-link into the message format expected by the target of the plug-link. This facilitates the wiring of operations in which the message formats do not even match.

Another example of information associated with a plug-link is a *locator*. This is a specification about how to find an implementation of a port type providing an implementation of the operation at the endpoint of the plug-link. Various kinds of locators might be defined, such as a query on a directory like UDDI. At runtime, when the source operation of a plug-link is used, the platform will evaluate the locator associated with the plug-link to determine an implementation of the target to which the message is to be sent.

Typically, the operations of more than one port type will be wired by plug-links. Not all operations of the port types used will be wired by plug-links, but nevertheless the collection of wired port types represents a useful aggregate for others. Thus, this aggregate can be rendered as another port type. This is achieved via *export-links* [WSFL].

In Figure 17-2, port types A, B, C are aggregated and wired via plug-links. The aggregation G (called a *global model* [WSFL]) is represented to the outside as another port type P with operation o and o'. An implementation of P is accomplished by delegating its operations to operations of the aggregate. For example, operation o is in fact implemented by operation o1 of port type A, and operation o' is implemented by operation o7 of port type C. This kind of delegation is specified by an *export link*, the source of which is the implementing operation and the target of which is the implemented operation. At runtime, when the operation o of a port with port type P is used, the platform will forward the message to operation o1 of a port with port type A. Note that the internal wiring behind P might be hidden from the outside, and port type P might be used within other wirings (that is, the aggregation model is recursive).

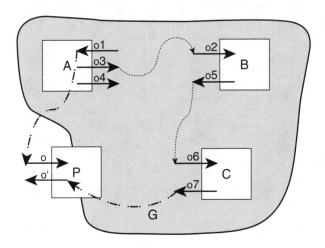

Figure 17-2   Recursive aggregation via a global model.

Note that it is absolutely fine that a global model does not export any of the operations of its encompassed port types. To a certain degree, the encompassed port types are sufficient. They are self-contained, properly supporting a complete interaction between a set of partners. In many situations, having no need to further wire operations in an aggregation (via plug-links or export-links) indicates a complete, self-contained business interaction between partners.

17.3 Ordering Constraints

When the port types that are wired together are associated with process models that constrain the order in which operations of the port types can be used,
the validity of the wiring can be checked. In Figure 17-3, the wiring shown is
valid. That is, the interaction between the two port types, A and B, is consistent. B sends out a message via operation o5, which is consumed by operation
o1. After consumption of the message, A sends out a message via operation o2
at some time. This message is consumed by B via operation o6, which is fine
because o6 is ready for use after o5 sends the message. Under certain conditions (y=0 in the example), B sends a message via operation o7. This is fine
because after o2 has been used to send a message, o4 is always ready for use.

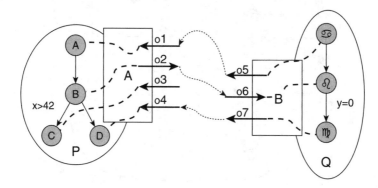

Figure 17-3   Process models as constraints and matchmaking.

Note that a plug-link from o7 to o3 (instead of o4) would be problematic, because o3 will not always be available (only in case x>42 in this example). That
is, in some scenarios, o7 might send a message for consumption by o3, but A
would not receive this message because it is in a state that makes it impossible
to receive the message. Thus, plug-links allow checking the validity of an intended interaction.

Assume two port types are given, each of which is associated with a process
model, but no wiring between them has been specified. An interesting question
is whether or not these two port types are *compatible*. Is it possible to define
plug-links in such a way that a valid interaction between the two port types can

take place? An algorithm solving this problem could be used to find partners that exchange messages in a compatible way. This goes far beyond simply matching signatures of port types by adding order of interactions between partners to the scope of matchmaking.

17.4 Contracting

Even after Web services are found that provide all operations required and support interactions in the order expected, additional kinds of matchmaking might be necessary based on the operational quality of services expected. For example, certain operations have to participate in transactions, some messages exchanged must be transported reliably, and other messages must be encrypted. The corresponding properties can be associated with port types, operations, or messages via policies (see Chapter 7, "Web Services Policy") and these policies are used to perform the corresponding matchmaking.

In many situations, additional requirements must be met. For example, when a requester is interested in a long-term relationship with a provider, you need to consider average response time of the performing operations, the availability of the service, and so on. These kinds of requirements are specified as service-level objectives. This might include the negotiation and specification of payments to be made by the requestor when all service objectives are met, as well as penalties to be paid by a provider if certain objectives are not met. All of this information is part of a contract that covers the interaction between the requester and the provider. Such a contract can even be negotiated automatically ([Dan 2004], [WS-Ag]).

Contracting is also a key prerequisite for the timely and flexible provision and consumption of services as part of the business processes of an organization, either within or across organizational boundaries [Rappa 2004]. It will very likely have a significant impact in the coming years. The possibility of a business process crossing an organizational boundary clearly raises the need to review the relation between service provisioning and service consumption as a business relationship, with all the complexity such a relationship entails: matchmaking, information exchange, negotiation, contract generation and signing, dynamic creation of different service configurations and their instantiation, service provision/consumption, monitoring of contract execution, relationship termination, evaluation, and of course, arbitration in case of dispute.

17.5 Summary

This chapter showed you some upcoming technologies that are likely to advance automation of business interactions on top of the Web service infrastructure. Semantic Web technology will support automatic understanding of the functions provided by a Web service. Wiring technology will facilitate recursive aggregation of Web services when ordering of interactions (like in BPEL) is not relevant. Annotating Web services with ordering constraints will allow discovery of interaction partners in case multiple messages must be exchanged and the order of exchange does matter. Contracting technology will support automatic negotiations of service-level objectives and associated payments, providing a key ingredient for creating businesses based on interactions on top of the Web service infrastructure.

Chapter 18

Conclusion

This book has given you a thorough understanding of the structure and composition of the Web services platform. It has discussed the fundamental concepts of service orientation and how they are rendered in the Web services platform. This final chapter briefly reviews the platform and discusses a variety of technical and non-technical issues, including Web services standardization, competing specifications and their ramifications. It also provides some perspective on Web services future specifications and the overall outlook of the Web services platform.

18.1 A Summary of the Web Services Platform

The Web services platform (as SOA) is designed to support real-world automated business interactions in which functional and non-functional requirements are much more demanding than in simple Web access to enterprise applications. What are these requirements? In summary, they are:

- The need for interoperable messaging between enterprises and middleware systems with business-level quality of service (secure, reliable, and transactional).

- A framework for describing and discovering services.

- A mechanism for reusing and composing services.

The set of specifications introduced in Chapter 3, "Web Services," and explained in detail in the rest of this book is simply a rendition of these three requirements.

Web services, in spite of their perceived complexity and the number of specifications and standards (or proposed standards), consists at its core of a minimal set of specifications that realize the service-oriented architecture (SOA) computing model. More importantly, the Web services platform and specifications support incremental consumption of capability. It is possible to start with a very small set of capabilities, and then incrementally adopt more of the functions. These are important points to realize. An application scenario can simply start with WSDL to describe services' interfaces, and use SOAP/HTTPS for message interoperability. Increased sophistication in the scenario might require adding partners to the collaboration, motivating the need for WS-Security to implement multiparty authentication, privacy, and integrating these partners using BPEL4WS to coordinate their services. Then, WS-ReliableMessaging can augment the solution to eliminate the need for lost and duplicate message processing from applications. WS-Coordination and WS-BusinessAgreement can complement the BPEL4WS processes to simplify the completion and compensation processing in the business process design. Finally, at each of these incremental stages, WS-Policy and WS-PolicyAttachment provide support for augmenting WSDL with the information necessary to document services expectations and capabilities.

The perceived complexity results from the fact that a much more complex problem is being solved than in prior Web-related standards efforts. Web services supports complex and complete business scenarios, which results in a seemingly complex aggregate set of specifications. Complexity is also due to the proliferation of competing specifications in certain areas. Still, the set of specifications presented in this book is the minimal core set upon which non-trivial business applications can be built in an interoperable, reusable manner. Other proposed specifications extend these ideas into more specific domains, from systems management to resource sharing strategies and industry-specific solutions.

18.2 Standardization

Most of the specifications that comprise the Web services platform discussed in this book were created jointly by a small group of software vendors. Several of the lowest-level specifications are now either *de jure* standards or on the way to becoming such (SOAP, WSDL, WS-Security, WS-Addressing, WS-BPEL).

However, as of this writing, many of the others are not yet undergoing the standardization process. One major reason for the relatively slow rate of submission to standards bodies is the importance of creating a sufficient level of shared technical understanding among author companies, to ensure that the new specification is technically sound and has a reasonably good chance of becoming an industrywide standard. Unlike previous standards approaches, the companies authoring these specifications go through several rounds of interoperability testing and composition of standards on customer business scenarios before submitting to a standards body. Unimplemented and untested specifications have been submitted in the past, leading to poor interoperability or irrelevancy.

If a good specification design process seriously intends to result in a successful standard, it needs to cover the following steps:

- Development of an initial concept, followed by iterative improvement, until the authors feel sufficuently comfortable with its quality to release it for wider public review.

- Release of the proposed specifications to the public, and gathering of feedback from a wide number of interested customers and vendors.

- Testing of initial implementations for multivendor interoperability that will validate the technical soundness of the proposed specification.

- Publication of an updated document, with royalty-free license terms and submission to a *de jure* standards body as appropriate.

18.2.1 Concerns About the Standardization Process

There has been much industry unease and debate about the delay in getting these specifications to *de jure* standards bodies such as the W3C and OASIS, which has resulted form the process outlined in the previous section. The following are some of the positives and negatives of the preceding approach.

The main advantage is that by the time it completes, it's likely that the resulting specifications can be successfully implemented, can be integrated with other specifications, solve real business problems, and will actually work. In fact, it is not uncommon for other standards organizations (notably the IETF and OMG) to only standardize specifications after they have been proven in practice. The W3C standardization process also has a specified implementation and validation stage.

Another positive of this process is that it allows for vetting "false start" specifications. An example of such a specification is DIME. [DIME] It was proposed as a higher-performing alternate to SOAP with Attachments [SwA], but was later retracted. It introduced new security concerns, and a much better solution was invented (in the form of MTOM [MTOM] and XOP [XOP]). Because DIME was still in a draft proposal stage, it was retracted more quickly and easily than if it had been submitted to a standards body and a technical committee had been formed to standardize that area.

Publication of specifications, vendor interoperability testing, and early developer kits make technology available to users at an early stage. They provide a forum for feedback about existing business scenarios and new ones that the specification makes available. It also stimulates the definition of additional, complementary technology.

It is also important to recognize that Web services are a single integrated platform supporting incremental adoption. In order for a family of specifications to work together to form such an integrated platform, it is essential for the specification developers to have common underlying objectives and principles. Unfortunately, the principles of simplicity, composeability, and interoperability that govern the Web services platform are all qualitative measures. It's difficult to achieve a consensus with such a large number of contributors and interests.

Finally, it is unrealistic to think that complex specifications, such as those for workflow (WS-BPEL) and transactions (WS-AtomicTransaction and WS-BusinessAgreement), can be developed by a large committee of people, without a strong starting point, in any reasonable length of time. Looking back at the history of the Internet, it is easy to identify many technologies that have been developed by key individuals instead of committees (for example, MIME and HTTP). It is also easy to identify committee-designed specifications that have had very little traction and adoption (for example, OSI and WfMC).

Although a standard needs wide input and participation to succeed, it is important to recognize the value of simple, lightweight specifications that focus on solving the immediate and critical problems well, rather than addressing a conflicting requirement's space identified by a large group of technical experts.

In the end, the biggest advantage of this slow (and sometimes frustrating) process might be its success. The two specifications that anchor Web services today are SOAP 1.1 and WSDL 1.1. Both specifications represent *de facto*, rather than *de jure*, standards and were developed jointly by a small group of vendors. Standardization in *de jure* standards organizations takes a lot of time. If the specifications developed by the aforementioned process result in workable solutions to immediate problems, they're viable technologies to be used until the formal standards are completed.

The authors of this book are confident that in spite of a the industry angst it may have caused, this approach to standardization will prove to be very effective in producing a working, integrated, componentized, and composeable Web services platform.

18.3 Competing Specifications

No discussion of the Web services platform would be complete without acknowledging the presence of many competing specifications. This section will summarize some of the competing spaces and their prognoses over time. The objective is not to provide a detailed technical analysis or comparison, but rather to point out competing specifications and indicate their relationships to other specifications of the Web services stack.

ebXML [ebXML] is a suite of standards for conducting electronic business using XML over the Internet. It includes support for XML messaging, transaction, interface definitions, service registries, and security. ebXML has the support of UN/CEFACT [CEFACT] and has been submitted to ISO [ISO]. Some industry domain-specific standards have also endorsed ebXML, but many of these bodies have also endorsed the Web service platform discussed in this book. ebXML moves forward in OASIS, as do many of the specifications discussed in this book, including WS-Security and WSBPEL.

The *Liberty Alliance* [LIB] defines a suite of specifications for federated identity management and security. Unlike the authors of most of the specifications discussed in this book, many of the companies in the Liberty Alliance are consumers of information processing technology (American Express and NTT DoCoMo, among others). IBM joined the alliance in October 2004. Liberty focuses on support for companies that want to federate user registries to support single sign-on for end users interacting with multiple Web sites. In addition to single sign-on, Liberty also provides support for sharing property information (preferences) across corporate boundaries. Liberty also defines some base technology (messaging, interface definition) to support the federation of identity systems. Liberty competes with the WS-Security specifications, especially WS-Trust and Federation.

OASIS has workgroups focusing on specifications that compete with some of the functions in the Web services platform documented in this book:

- Web Services Composite Application Framework (WS-CAF) [WSCAF] defines a model and service for composing multiple Web services in composite, transactional solutions. WS-CAF is similar to capabilities provided by WS-Coordination, WS-AtomicTransactions, and WS-BusinessAgreement.

- WS-Reliability [WSREL] is very similar to the reliable messaging protocol discussed in this book.

Web Service Choreography Description Language (WSCDL) 1.0 [WSCDL] is a specification that is in a similar area to BPEL. The focus is different, with more emphasis on a global model that composes a set of services and less emphasis on supporting the definition of specific Web services based business processes. BPEL, on the other hand, focuses almost exclusively on providing an XML language for completely defining concrete implementation business processes.

Competition between standards, specifications, and ideas is not uncommon. To some extent, this is healthy for the industry, allowing competing ideas and approaches to emerge and prove themselves. This has happened in many other areas in the IT industry, such as communication protocols (TCP/IP, ISO OSI, SNA), database models (SQL/Relational, Object/ODMG), and languages (Java, C++, Smalltalk). However, the industry is seeing incremental movement toward consolidation and integration of the Web service standards. Expect a dominant platform to emerge, supported by all of the major vendors. This platform will complement the human-centric HTML/HTTP Internet functions with support for application to application interactions and integration.

18.4 Perspectives

This section discusses some perspectives on the future of the Web services platform. Will the platform succeed? What are the risk factors?

18.4.1 Why Will It Succeed?

If this platform is successful, it will be possible to hold secure, reliable, transacted interactions between Web services running on any platform, using open standards that are supported by all vendors. Different vendors will offer wildly different programming models for this platform, but when messages finally reach the wire and flow between services, they will interoperate successfully. The final objective is at least the level of interoperability of today's Web: clients and servers can be on different platforms without having to pay attention to the platform.

Why will the Web services effort succeed? Because of four factors:

- The unprecedented level of vendor support gathered so far, which has resulted in early availability of multiple interoperable implementations.

- The consistent focus (in spite of all the noise of competing standards) on solving the core technical problems, rather than attempting to address every possible requirement. The core of specifications reviewed here provides the core function that other domain specific specifications might extend in the future.

- The composeability of the specification set, which avoids a monolithic solution and permits flexible use and adaptation of the core specifications.

- A pragmatic specification development process in which technical and interoperability issues are resolved before standardization begins.

18.4.2 Risks

Some significant risks threaten to keep this platform from achieving the lofty goal of ubiquitous interoperability. Without that, Web services isn't very valuable. Thus, the biggest risk is an unbridgeable rift between key industry players that might end up creating two or more islands of interoperability.

The IBM & Microsoft collaborative Web services effort started with Microsoft's publication of SOAP 0.9 in the fall of 1999. Since that time, there have been several deep divisions that could have easily derailed the Web services platform. However, calmer heads have prevailed, and so far the industry has been able to stay together at the lowest levels of the stack: SOAP, WS-Addressing, WSDL, UDDI, and WS-Security, as well as at the highest level with BPEL.

That leaves reliable messaging and transactions as the two key areas of contention. The IBM & Microsoft proposals have a significant advantage here, in that they build on and compose cleanly with the other Web services specifications. Thus, with some evolution of WS-Reliable Messaging, WS-Atomic Transaction, and WS-Business Activity, it will be possible to achieve consensus in the industry.

Another commonly articulated risk is that of IBM and/or Microsoft choosing to exercise their large patent portfolios against specifications and implementations, and demand royalties. However, both companies have unequivocally stated their intention to offer these specifications under royalty-free terms.

18.5 Building on the Core Platform

Many specifications are evolving and building on the core Web services platform. An area of much recent interest is support for pub-sub (*publish-subscribe*). Currently, the Web service model is based on binding and directed messaging, in which service A sends a message to service B. In the publish-subscribe model some services define events that they emit while others subscribe to receive specific events. WS-Eventing [WS-Eventing] provides basic support for pub-sub over the Web services protocols. The WS-Notification family of specifications provides enhanced support for topics, topic trees, filtering, and event brokers. These capabilities more accurately mirror the capabilities provided by existing pub-sub systems such as MQSeries and JMS. The looser, more dynamic coupling that the pub-sub enables will complement SOA's find and bind model.

It is tempting to think of Web services being stateless. This is a bit misleading. Almost all Web services manage some state data. A purchase order service, for example, manages the data in purchase orders. IBM and several other companies define the Web Service Resource Framework (WS-RF) [WSRF] to better support the linking of state data with Web services. WS-RF builds on WS-Addressing, which introduces the concept of an endpoint reference (EPR). In its simplest form, an EPR references a specific Web service through a network address. The EPR might also contain reference properties and reference parameters that refine the reference. The reference properties and parameters might, for instance, identify a specific purchase order on which the Web service should operate. The reference parameters and properties are opaque to calling services, since only the service's implementation is assumed to understand them.

WS-Resource Framework allows the association of an XML Schema complex type with a WSDL portType. The complex type defines the logical shape or structure of the information that the WSDL portType supports. For example, the WSDL service might manage purchase orders, and the associated XML complex type defines the logical structure of the purchase order.

Authors sometimes refer to the associated complex type using the term *implied resource pattern*. Examining a portType often leads a programmer to infer the existence of the data structure. The portType that manages purchase orders might have an operation supporting adding a line item to a purchase order (PO). This leads the observer to believe that purchase orders contains line items, which is a reasonable deduction. There might be no single in or out message on any of the portTypes operations that clearly defines the XML schema for a PO. The implied resource pattern allows the portType author to formally document a logical model of the data that the service manages.

The XML complex type associated to a portType logically defines the shape (or type) of the instances of data that the service manages. The WS-Addressing EPR logically *references* or *points to* instances of this schema type.

Several specifications build on the basic concept of an implied resource. WS-ResourceProperties [WS-ResourceProperties] defines an abstract interface for getting and setting elements from the resource documents. For example, if there is an implied purchase order, WS-ResourceProperties would allow a caller to get or set elements in specific purchase orders. Another specification integrates with WS-Notification to support subscribing to events when specific elements of resources change.

In addition to the implied resource model, WS-ResourceFramework and WS-Addressing also support conversation state. A Web service can maintain state that is independent of long-lived data such as purchase orders, but that is shared across multiple invocations of operations. This supports a model similar to that of Stateful Session Beans in Enterprise Java Beans, or the conversational transaction model in systems such as IBM's Customer Information Control System (CICS) [CICS] and Information Management System (IMS) [IMS].

Management and administration is as important as the enabling of application integration and service interoperability. This motivates a recently evolving set of standards for management using Web services and management of Web services. Management using Web services builds on the basic elements of the Web services platform to support interoperable system and application management solutions. WSDL defines the interfaces to management applications and agents. SOAP, HTTP, and the WS-* specifications provide communication and interoperability between management applications, and between applications and agents. Finally, BPEL4WS provides a language for implementing complex systems management *process*, such as installing or upgrading software on multiple systems. Management using Web services will be an increasingly common model.

Because Web services support multiparty business solutions, it is important that participants be able to monitor participant business processes and services. Management of Web services defines standard, common portTypes for monitoring and managing services. As time progresses, more and more services will support both a *business interface* that defines what it does (manage purchase orders) and a *control interface* that supports systems management (get request status, get average response time, cancel operation).

Web Service Distributed Management (WSDM) [WSDM], a technical committee in OASIS, is defining a model for management using Web services and management of Web services. WSDM focuses on the base management interfaces. Other standards bodies, such as DMTF [DMTF], are defining concrete XML schema and portTypes for specific resources such as *computer system* or *operating system.*

The resource modeling and management of Web services is not without standards competition in the form of alternate proposals, WS-Management and WS-Transfer. Some standards convergence will need to occur in this space as well!

Web services also form the basis for interesting solutions to *graphical user interface* composition. A *portal* is a Web site that aggregates multiple applications' interfaces into role- and task-specific work spaces. The applications appear as interacting tiles or *portlets* that are aggregated into a page. These portlets support user interactions with Web services. WS-RemotePortlets supports a model in which the view (rendering) for a portlet occurs at a remote site. Instead of the portal using WSDL/SOAP to call a remote site and retrieve model information, which the portal then renders, WSRP [WSRP] allows the portal to call a remote site and receive HTML (or some other markup language) that it aggregates into a page. In essence, WSRP supports remote procedure call for views instead of for the view controller.

Web services thus has as a model for remote procedure call and messaging be-tween applications, and, with WSRP, also a way of federating UIs. Web services would be incomplete without support for a data-centric model. The Database Access and Integration Services WG [DAIS] in the Global Grid Forum [GGF] defines a set of interfaces for federating and querying data sources using Web services. OGSA/DAI defines a specification to describe data formats, how to create, retrieve, update, and delete (CRUD) data; and how to replicate and transfer data.

18.6 Summary

The Web services platform described here is nothing but the core of a new Web-based distributed computing platform together with some value-added services that are being built on top of it. The work is by no means complete: there are many other aspects of a distributed computing platform that this book did not address.

Appendix A

References

[BaS04] M. T. Schmidt, K. Bhaskaran. "WebSphere Business Integration: An Architectural Overview," IBM Systems Journal 43(2), 2004.

[Bern 1997] P. A. Bernstein and E. Newcomer. *Principles of Transaction Processing.* Morgan Kaufmann Publishers, 1997.

[BPEL4WS] Business Process Execution Language for Web Services, version 1.1. http://www.oasis-open.org/committees/tc-home.php/wg_abbrev=wspel.

[BPELJ] BPELJ: BPEL for Java Technology http://www-106.ibm.com/developerworks/webservices/library/ws-bpelj/.

[CEFACT] United Nations Centre for Trade Facilitation and Electronic Business. http://www.unece.org/cefact/.

[Czaj 2004] K. Czajkowski, D. Ferguson, I. Foster, J. Frey, F. Leymann, M. Nally, T. Storey, S. Tuecke, S.Weerawaranna. "Modeling Stateful Resources with Web Services." Globus Alliance & IBM, 2004.

[CICS] CICS Family Overview. http://www-306.ibm.com/software/htp/cics/.

[DAIS] Data Access and Integration Working Group. http://www.cs.man.ac.uk/grid-db/.

[Dan 2004] A. Dan, D. Davis, R. Kearney, A. Keller, R. King, D. Kuebler, H. Ludwig, M. Polan, M. Spreitzer and A. Yousse. "Web Services on Demand: WSLA-Driven Automated Management." IBM Systems Journal 43(1), 2004.

[DIME] Direct Internet Message Encapsulation (DIME).
http://www.gotdotnet.com/team/xml_wsspecs/dime/draft-nielsen-dime-01.txt.

[DMTF] Distributed Management Task Force. http://www.dmtf.org/home.

[ebXML] Electronic Business XML Initiative. http://www.ebxml.org/.

[Emm 2000] W. Emmerich. *Engineering Distributed Objects.* John Wiley &
Sons, 2000.

[FHL03] D. Fensel, J. Hendler, H. Lieberman, W. Wahlster. *Spinning the
Semantic Web.* MIT Press, 2003.

[F00] R. T. Fielding. "Representational State Transfer." 2000.
http://www.ics.uci.edu/~fielding/pubs/dissertation/rest_arch_style.htm.

[Fost 2004] I. Foster, C. Kesselmann. *The Grid 2.* Morgan Kaufmann, 2004.

[GGF] The Global Grid Forum, http://www.ggf.org/.

[Gray 1993] J. Gray and A. Reuter. *Transaction Processing: Concepts and
Techniques.* Morgan Kaufmann Publishers, 1993.

[HMAC] HMAC: Keyed-Hashing for Message Authentication.
http://www.ietf.org/rfc/rfc2104.txt.

[Hohpe 2004] G. Hohpe, B. Woolfe. *Enterprise Integration Patterns.* Addison-
Wesley, 2004.

[HTTP] Hypertext Transfer Protocol – HTTP/1.1. http://www.ietf.org/rfc/
rfc2616.txt.

[IMS] IMS Family Overview. http://www-306.ibm.com/software/data/ims/.

[ISO] International Organization for Standardization. http://www.iso.org/iso/
en/ISOOnline.frontpage.

[J2EE] Java 2 Platform Enterprise Edition Specification v1.4. Sun
Microsystems Inc., 2002.

[KL03] R. Khalaf, F. Leymann. "On Web Services Aggregation," Proc.
VLDB-TeS'03. Berlin, Germany. September, 2003.

[Ley 2003] F. Leymann. "Web Services: Distributed Applications Without
Limits," Proc. BTW'03. Leipzig, Germany. February, 2003.

[Ley 2004] F. Leymann. "The Influence of Web Services on Software,"
Proc. Annual Meeting of the German Computer Society. Ulm, Germany.
September, 2004.

[Ley 1997] F. Leymann and D. Roller. "Workflow Based Applications."
IBM Systems Journal 36(1), 1997.

[Ley 2000] F. Leymann and D. Roller. *Production Workflow: Concepts and Techniques*. Prentice Hall, 2000.

[Ley 1995] F. Leymann. "Supporting Business Transactions via Partial Background Recovery in Workflow Management Systems," Proc. BTW '95. Dresden, Germany. March, 1995.

[LIB] The Liberty Alliance Project. http://www.projectliberty.org/.

[MIME] Multipurpose Internet Mail Extensions. http://www.ietf.org/rfc/rfc2045.txt.

[MTOM] SOAP Message Transmission Optimization Mechanism. http://www.w3c.org/TR/2004/CR-soap12-mtom-20040826/.

[OWL] OWL. http://www.w3.org/2004/OWL/.

[Rappa 2004] M.A. Rappa. "The Utility Business Model and the Future Of Computing Services." IBM Systems Journal 43(1), 2004.

[RN] RosettaNet. http://www.rosettanet.org/.

[RNWS] RosettaNet and Web Services. http://www.rosettanet.org/RosettaNet/Doc/0/IP0QL046K55KFBSJ60M9TQCPB3/RosettaNet+Web+ServicesFINAL+.pdf.

[RelaxNG] http://www.relaxng.org/.

[Schmi 2004] M.T. Schmidt, K. Bhaskaran. "WebSphere Business Integration: An Architectural Overview." IBM Systems Journal 43(2), 2004.

[Security Roadmap] IBM, Microsoft. "Security in a Web Services World: A Proposed Architecture and Roadmap." April 2002. http://www-106.ibm.com/developerworks/library/ws-secmap/.

[SCC14N] Schema Centric XML Canonicalization specification. http://www.uddi.org/pubs/SchemaCentricCanonicalization-20020710.htm.

[SOAP 1.1] Simple Object Access Protocol (SOAP) Version 1.1. http://www.w3.org/TR/2000/NOTE-SOAP-20000508/.

[SOAP 1.2 Part 0] SOAP Version 1.2 Part 0: Primer. http://www.w3.org/TR/2003/REC-soap12-part0-20030624/.

[SOAP 1.2 Part 1] SOAP Version 1.2 Part 1: Messaging Framework. http://www.w3.org/TR/2003/REC-soap12-part1-20030624/.

[SOAP 1.2 Part 2] SOAP Version 1.2 Part 2: Adjuncts. http://www.w3.org/TR/2003/REC-soap12-part2-20030624/.

[SwA] SOAP Messages with Attachments. http://www.w3.org/TR/2000/NOTE-SOAP-attachments-20001211.

[SWSI] Semantic Web Services Initiative. http://www.swsi.org.

[UDDIV2API] UDDI V2.04 API standard. http://uddi.org/pubs/
ProgrammersAPI-V2.04-Published-20020719.htm.

[UDDIV2DS] UDDI V2.03 Data Structure standard.
http://uddi.org/pubs/DataStructure-V2.03-Published-20020719.htm.

[UDDIWSDLBP] UDDI/WSDL Best Practice. http://www.oasis-open.org/
committees/uddi-spec/doc/bp/uddi-spec-tc-bp-using-wsdl-v108-
20021110.htm.

[UDDI301] UDDI V3.0.1 specification. http://uddi.org/pubs/
uddi-v3.0.1-20031014.htm.

[UDDIV3Features] UDDI Version 3 Features List. http://uddi.org/pubs/
uddi_v3_features.htm.

[UDDIWSDLTN] UDDI/WSDL Technical Note. http://www.oasis-open.org/
committees/uddi-spec/doc/tn/uddi-spec-tc-tn-wsdl-v202-20040631.htm.

[URI] Uniform Resource Identifiers (URI): Generic Syntax, RFC 2396.
http://www.ietf.org/rfc/rfc2396.txt.

[Voll 2004] K. Vollmer, M. Gilpin, J. Hoppermann. "ESB Usage Will Grow
As Standards Mature." Forrester Research, 2004.

[W3C Binary XML] Report from the W3C Workshop on Binary Interchange
of XML Information Item Sets. http://www.w3.org/2003/08/
binary-interchange-workshop/Report.html.

[Wied 1992] G. Wiederhold, P. Wegner, S. Ceri. "Towards
Megaprogramming: A Paradigm for Component-Based Programming."
Comm. ACM 35(22) 1992, 89–99.

[WS-Addressing] Web Services Addressing (WS-Addressing). W3C Member
Submission, August 10, 2004. http://www.w3.org/Submission/
ws-addressing/.

[WS-Ag] Web Services Agreement Specification, http://www.gridforum.org/
Meetings/GGF11/ Documents/draft-ggf-graap-agreement.pdf.

[WS Architecture 2003] IBM, Microsoft. "Secure, Reliable, Transacted
Web Services: Architecture and Composition." September, 2003.
http://www-306.ibm.com/software/solutions/webservices/pdf/
SecureReliableTransactedWSAction.pdf.

[WS-Atomic Transactions] Web Services AtomicTransactions Specification.
September, 2003. http://www.ibm.com/developerworks/webservices/
library/ws-atomtran.

[WS-Business Activity] Web Services Business Activity Specification. January, 2004. http://www.ibm.com/developerworks/webservices/library/ws-busact.

[WSCAF] Web Services Composite Application Framework. http://www.arjuna.com/standards/ws-caf/.

[WSCDL] Web Services Choreography Description Language. http://www.w3.org/TR/ws-cdl-10/.

[WS-Coordination] Web Services Coordination Specification. September, 2003. http://www.ibm.com/developerworks/webservices/library/ws-coor.

[WSDL 1.1] WSDL 1.1 Specification, http://www.w3.org/TR/2001/NOTE-wsdl-20010315.

[WSDL 2.0] WSDL 2.0 Last Call Specification. http://www.w3.org/TR/2004/WD-wsdl20-20040803/.

[WSDM] OASIS Web Services Distributed Management. http://www.oasis-open.org/committees/tc_home.php?wg_abbrev=wsdm.

[WS-Eventing] Web Services Eventing. http://xml.coverpages.org/WS-Eventing200408.pdf.

[WSFL] Web Services Flow Language (WSFL) 1.0. May, 2001. http://www-3.ibm.com/software/solutions/webservices/pdf/WSFL.pdf.

[WSI] WS-I: Web Services Interoperability Organization. http://www.ws-i.org/.

[WS-I BP 1.0] WS-I Basic Profile Version 1.0. http://www.ws-i.org/Profiles/BasicProfile-1.0.html.

[WS-Metadata Exchange] Web Services Metadata Exchange (WS-MetadataExchange). September, 2004. ftp://www6.software.ibm.com/software/developer/library/WS-MetadataExchange.pdf.

[WS-Policy Assertions] Web Services Policy Assertions Language (WS-Policy Assertions). Published online by IBM, BEA, Microsoft, and SAP. http://www-106.ibm.com/developerworks/library/ws-polas.

[WS-Policy Attachment] Web Services Policy Attachment (WS-PolicyAttachment). Published online by IBM, BEA, Microsoft, and SAP. http://www-106.ibm.com/developerworks/webservices/library/ws-polatt.

[WS-Policy Framework] Web Services Policy Framework (WS-Policy Framework). Published online by IBM, BEA, and Microsoft. http://www-106.ibm.com/developerworks/webservices/library/ws-polfram.

[WSREL] OASIS Web Services Reliability. http://xml.coverpages.org/
WS-Eventing200408.pdf.

[WS-ResourceProperties] Web Service Resource Properties.
http://www-106.ibm.com/developerworks/library/ws-resource/
ws-resourceproperties.pdf.

[WSRF] The Web Services Resource Framework.
http://www.globus.org/wsrf/.

[WSRP] OASIS Web Services for Remote Portlets. http://www.oasis-open.org/
committees/tc_home.php?wg_abbrev=wsrp.

[WS-Security] OASIS Standard. Web Services Security: SOAP Message
Security 1.0. March, 2004. http://www.oasis-open.org/committees/wss.

[XLANG] XLANG. Microsoft Corp., 2001.
http://www.gotdotnet.com/team/xml wsspecs/xlang-c/default.htm.

[XML] Extensible Markup Specification (XML) 1.0 (Third Edition).
http://www.w3.org/TR/2004/REC-xml-20040204/.

[XML-Encryption] W3C Recommendation. XML Encryption Syntax and
Processing. December, 2002. http://www.w3.org/TR/xmlenc-core/.

[XML Infoset] XML Information Set (Second Edition). http://www.w3.org/
TR/2004/REC-xml-infoset-20040204/.

[XML Namespaces] Namespaces in XML. http://www.w3.org/TR/1999/
REC-xml-names-19990114/.

[XML Signature] W3C recommendation. XML-Signature Syntax and
Processing. February, 2002. http://www.w3.org/TR/xmldsig-core/.

[XML Schema] XML Schema Part 0: Primer. http://www.w3.org/TR/2001/
REC-xmlschema-0-20010502/.

[XOP] XML-Binary Optimized Packaging. http://www.w3c.org/TR/2004/
CR-xop10-20040826/.

[XPath] XML Path Language (XPath) Version 1.0. http://www.w3.org/
TR/1999/REC-xpath-19991116.

[XQuery] XQuery 1.0: An XML Query Language. W3C working draft.
http://www.w3.org/TR/2004/WD-xquery-20040723/.

[XSL] Extensible Stylesheet Language (XSL) Version 1.0. http://www.w3.org/
TR/2001/REC-xsl-20011015/.

Index

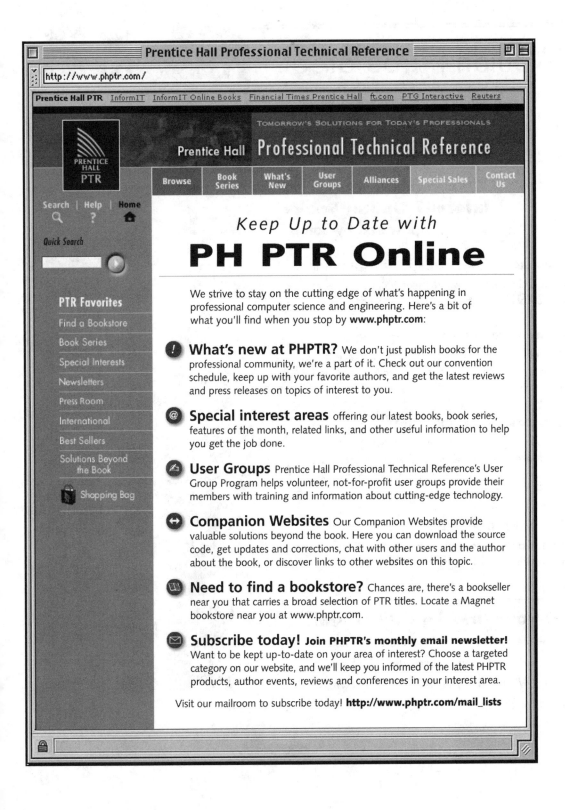